# *Family, Marriage, and the Struggle of the Sexes*



*EDITED BY*

HANS PETER DREITZEL

*Recent Sociology No. 4*



The Macmillan Company, New York, New York
Collier-Macmillan Limited, London

The Macmillan Company
866 Third Avenue, New York, N.Y. 10022
Collier-Macmillan Canada Ltd., Toronto, Ontario

Library of Congress Catalog Card Number: 72-77649

FIRST MACMILLAN PAPERBACKS EDITION 1972

Printed in the United States of America

Permission to reprint the following is gratefully acknowledged:

"Some Hypotheses about the Family" by Marion J. Levy, Jr. Published in *Journal of Comparative Family Studies*, 1970.

"The Role of the Sexual Constellation" by Ingjald Nissen. Published in *Acta Sociologica*, Vol. 14, No. 1–2 (1971).

"A Conflict Theory of Sexual Stratification" by Randall Collins. Published in *Social Problems*, Vol. 19, No. 1 (1971), pp. 3–21, The Society for the Study of Social Problems, Notre Dame, Ind.

"Love, Marriage, and the Division of Labor" by Martha Baum. Published in *Sociological Inquiry*, Vol. 41 (1971).

"The Passing of the Dominant Husband-Father" by Ersel E. LeMasters. Published in *Impact of Science on Society*, Vol. 21, No. 1 (1971) © UNESCO.

"Who Has the Power? The Marital Struggle" by Dair Gillespie. Published in *Journal of Marriage and the Family*, August 1971, pp. 445–458.

"Sex Roles and Social Change" by Harriet Holter. Published in *Acta Sociologica*, Vol. 14, No. 1–2 (1971).

"Consumption Society, Sex Roles, and Sexual Behavior" by Joachim Israel and Rosmari Eliasson. Published in *Acta Sociologica*, Vol. 14, No. 1–2 (1971).

"The Women's Liberation Movement: Its Origins, Structures, and Ideas" by Jo Freeman. Copyright 1971 by Jo Freeman. Reprinted by permission.

"Sex Politics: Class Politics" by Branka Magaš. Published in *New Left Review*, Vol. 66 (1971).

"On Body Politics" by John O'Neill. Copyright 1972 by Hans Peter Dreitzel.

"Child-Rearing Practices in the Communal Family" by Bennett M. Berger, Bruce M. Hackett, and R. Mervyn Millar. Progress Report on Communal Child Rearing by Department of Sociology, University of California, Davis, Cal., 1971. This study was supported by Grant #MN–16579–03 from the National Institute of Mental Health, Department of Health, Education, and Welfare.

"Family Life in the Kibbutz of Israel: Utopia Gained or Paradise Lost?" by Benjamin Schlesinger. Published in *International Journal of Comparative Sociology*, Vol. 11, No. 4 (1970), pp. 252–272.

"Is Monogamy Outdated?" by Rustum and Della Roy. This article first appeared in *The Humanist* March/April 1970, and is reprinted by permission.

# Contents

*Introduction: Family, Marriage, and the Struggle of the Sexes* 5

I.
FAMILY AND THE SEXUAL CONSTELLATION

1. Marion J. Levy, Jr.
Some Hypotheses about the Family 23
2. Ingjald Nissen
The Role of the Sexual Constellation 42
3. Randall Collins
A Conflict Theory of Sexual Stratification 53

II.
MARRIAGE AND THE PRISONS OF LOVE

4. Martha Baum
Love, Marriage, and the Division of Labor 83
5. Ersel E. LeMasters
The Passing of the Dominant Husband-Father 107
6. Dair L. Gillespie
Who Has the Power? The Marital Struggle 121

III.
GENDER DIFFERENTIATION AND THE AMBIGUITIES OF SEXUAL IDENTIFICATION

7. Harriet Holter
Sex Roles and Social Change 153

8. Joachim Israel and Rosmari Eliasson
Consumption Society, Sex Roles, and
Sexual Behavior 173

IV.
LIBERATION AND THE POLITICS OF THE BODY

9. Jo Freeman
The Women's Liberation Movement: Its Origins,
Structures, and Ideas 201
10. Branka Magaš
Sex Politics: Class Politics 217
11. John O'Neill
On Body Politics 251

V.
COMMUNAL LIVING AND THE OBSOLESCENCE OF THE NUCLEAR FAMILY

12. Bennett M. Berger, Bruce M. Hackett, and
R. Mervyn Millar
Child-Rearing Practices in the Communal Family 271
13. Benjamin Schlesinger
Family Life in the Kibbutz of Israel:
Utopia Gained or Paradise Lost? 301
14. Rustum and Della Roy
Is Monogamy Outdated? 332

# Introduction: Family, Marriage, and the Struggle of the Sexes[1]

HANS PETER DREITZEL

A GROWING TIDE of popular and scholarly literature concerns itself with changes in sex-role behavior and its impact on family life. Discussions of the "sexual revolution," the increasing permissiveness of sexual norms, and the family crisis are abundant. Since the protest movements of the late sixties these concerns have been nourished by the public's increased awareness of a number of facts and phenomena. The disaffection of the younger generation with their parents' idea of a good family life may not be an altogether new development. However, the strength of the women's liberation movement, the growing acceptance of homosexuals' struggle for recognition, and a new attitude toward general public discussion and presentation of sexuality cannot be dismissed as a passing fad. While these developments may reflect only the disenchantment of some minorities with the traditional Protestant ethic, the unprecedented rate of divorce in America seems to indicate that the structure of the nuclear family is shaken by its own inherent problems. The opinions of the partisans in this struggle over the redefinition of sex roles and sexual standards are diverse, confusing, and frequently salted by bitter polemics.

Given this situation it might be useful to distinguish between facts and myths and to consider what social scientists have to say. The present collection of essays, the fourth volume of *Recent Sociology*, is directed to the question of whether, in view of the new trend in sex-role differentiation and of the new climate in the struggle between the sexes, marriage and family have become obsolete. It must be admitted that social scientists have produced nothing comparable in strength and imagination to the partisan literature of the Germaine Greers, the Kate Milletts, or the Norman Mailers. While every bookshop in the country has its women's lib corner, sociologists have been remarkably quiet. All over the country parents are discussing the drug problems of their children, and women's liberation groups are blossoming in small towns. Yet the majority of family sociology textbooks still hold that the middle-class family is the bulwark of traditional values and virtues. To be sure, there are the problems of premarital sex, of sexual adjustment and marital conflict, but these can be overcome by psychological counseling and, at the worst, a few visits to the psychiatrist. Basically the family is regarded as a well-functioning unit, adequately providing a basis for child care, emotional protection, and sexual security. Recently this view has been challenged by a few sociological studies, some of which are included here. Most of the articles presented in this volume are based on empirical research; the emphasis of the collection is on a new perspective and a fresh outlook within the framework of scholarly thought and empirical inquiry.

The charge that the family has lost many of its functions is not a new one. It has long been recognized that since the industrial revolution kinship relations have become less and less important as a basis of social status. The change from the traditional large family system to the modern nuclear family was obviously determined by changes in the sphere of production. The basic characteristic of the traditional family was that of a production unit which was, in the case of farmers, to a large extent self-sustaining. All family members above a certain age would be engaged in farming or home manufacturing in or near the household. In the early stages of industrialization, men, women, and children were forced to sell their labor on an open market. With an increasing degree of mechanization and the intensification of work productivity, qualitative changes in the type of labor necessitated more and more skilled and semiskilled workers. Accordingly the family came to be seen as a base for the reproduction of the labor force. Minimum socialization, recreation, and emotional stabilization became its major tasks. With the new need for a more highly qualified labor force, child labor was gradually abolished and women were protected against the more brutal forms of exploitation. With the loss of the basic production function and with the father being forced to work outside the home, the family was left with the residual functions of reproduction and the care of the children, the old, the unmarried, and the sick. These became the main tasks of the married women. The housewife—mother, teacher, nurse, housekeeper, hostess, and mistress—was born. Since she was unrelated to the production process she was without a status outside the home.

Meanwhile, a further erosion in the functions of the family has taken place. To some degree socialization of the children has been taken over by public agencies; the job market was opened to unmarried women; childbirth has become the province of hospitals. Birth and death, once central events in the life cycle of the family, no longer take place in the family's own home. The development of scientific medicine has further deprived the family of one of its main functions. The growing population of the aged can no longer be taken care of by the family alone. New birth-control devices and the high value placed on economic achievements have led to a decline in the average number of children per family. What is left is the two-generation nuclear family which basically serves as a consumption unit. (This is not to say that the "extended family" was in fact larger than modern families. Recent studies by a group of Cambridge, England, social historians have cast doubt on this widely held notion of the traditional family.)

It is interesting that the family as a household unit has rarely been studied. Economically, the average household, in spite of the technological development of household machinery, is still an underdeveloped and neglected area. It can be characterized as a one-man, i.e., one-woman, enterprise based on semimechanized handwork. It is said that the work of a housewife never ends. Studies have shown that a housewife with two or three children may work as much as a hundred hours per week. Of course, this is highly class specific. A surburban middle-class housewife will have much less work. For this freedom she has to pay the high price of loneliness, of being tied to her home, and of being unprotected against continuous exposure to her children and to the mass media.

Whatever the work load of women, the fact remains that they receive neither ideal nor material compensation for it. Housework is socially necessary yet it is unproductive work in an economic sense and is unpaid. A man receives a salary for his work, but it does not include payment for the necessary reproductive functions his wife fulfills. Here the inequality of the distribution of costs and profits typical of a capitalist economy prevails. The surplus value of the husband's work is privately appropriated while the costs for his labor force are placed on his unpaid wife. Insofar as this is true, marriage is an institution of exploitation. Protagonists of women's liberation and the "open marriage"[2] have demanded that husbands share household duties with their wives. However, the fact remains that only husbands in privileged positions have the chance to overcome their traditional prejudice toward housework. The overwhelming majority of men are simply too exhausted physically and emotionally from the rat race to offer more than token help to their wives. This situation is legally sanctioned by the marriage laws of most Western countries, which provide that management of the household is the duty of the wife and that she is only to take an outside job if this does not jeopardize the satisfactory fulfillment of such duties.

It is not difficult to see why women should be dissatisfied with their lot. In addition to economic exploitation they often feel emotionally deprived. This seems paradoxical, since aside from the organization of consumption their main functions are to provide for emotional stability and sexual security. However, the typical situation is apparently one where the husband feels alienated and emotionally undernourished in his work and comes home to a wife who has her own "little" problems and is equally desirous of a companion with whom to share her needs and difficulties. The husband expects her to appear as his beautiful mistress for his leisure time, but his wife's work is not finished as long as the children are not irrevocably in bed. Moreover, she wishes to be acknowledged as a housewife and not simply as a complement to her husband's needs. This structural setting provides for frustration on both sides, with the result that both begin to be tempted by outside relationships. The tragedy of marriage under strictly monogamous norms has already been exposed by such authors of the nineteenth century as Strindberg, Ibsen, Butler, and Tolstoi. Yet in marriage an element of free choice still prevails which is absent in all other relationships within the family network. For most couples, children are an enormous burden, even though this is rarely admitted. As Barrington Moore, Jr., in one of the more honest appraisals of family life, has remarked:

> Popular consciousness is at least dimly aware of the barbaric nature of the duty of family affection and the pain it produces, as shown by the familiar remark, "You can choose your friends, but you can't choose your relatives." Even if partly concealed by ethical imperatives with the weight of age-old traditions, the strain is nevertheless real and visible. Children are often a burden to their parents. One absolutely un-bohemian couple I know agreed in the privacy of their own home that if people ever talked to each other openly about the sufferings brought on by raising a family today, the birth rate would drop to zero. But this couple is in no sense "abnormal." Furthermore, a revealing remark like this made to a friend is worth more as evidence than reams of scientific questionnaires subjected to elaborate statistical analyses. Again, how many couples harassed by the problems of getting started in life have not wished that their parents could be quietly and cheaply taken care of in some institution of the aged. Such facts are readily accessible to anyone who listens to the conversations in his own home and among the neighbors.[3]

However, the problem is not simply one of personal preferences. The effectiveness of the family as a child-rearing agency has been structurally reduced by the fact that it no longer serves as a production unit. The father has lost his unquestioned authority not only toward his wife but also toward his children (see below, Ersel E. LeMasters, pp. 107–118). Simply because he works outside the home in some office or factory, invisible to the children and often engaged in highly abstract activities, he no longer serves as an intelligible role model for his children. Work as the source of legitimation for his authority has become obscured, with the result that the children have shifted their orientation to peers and the mass media. In modern families the father role is not an enviable one. Confronted with the emotional frustration of his wife and the disregard of his children, husband and father still has to keep fit for the next working day. It is also because of their sheer exhaustion that so many couples spend their evenings in front of the television set.

The plight of the family in modern society is a difficult if not miserable one. The question then arises: Why do most people marry at all? The marriage rate has increased steadily over the past decades and at the age of fifty there are very few individuals left who are not married or who have not experienced marriage at one point during their life. At the same time the average age of first marriage has dropped significantly. Between 1890 and 1954 the proportion of persons fourteen years and older who were single dropped from 36.7 percent to 28.4 percent. Yet this increase in the married population provides no unequivocal support for a view which sees marriage and the family as a fundamentally healthy institution. These facts must be considered together with the rise in the divorce rate of fivefold for women and ninefold for men during the same period.[4] Presently about 40 percent of all marriages end in divorce, and it is estimated that marriages entered into in the late 1960s have no more than a 50 percent chance of remaining at least nominally intact (see below, Rustum and Della Roy, pp. 332–350).

The only conclusion to be drawn from these figures is that people look for something in marriage which, in fact, only a minority finds there. This much-desired goal is not simply romantic love (which can be adverse to a good marriage) but, rather, companionship and an attempt to overcome the alienation present in "rational" social relationships in the place of work and leisure (see below, Martha Baum, pp. 83–102). Paradoxically, the need for emotional security both drives people to marriage and may later lead to divorce. As long as women are condemned to be housekeepers and nurses for their children and husbands, both partners are unlikely to attain the emotional security they seek. Real companionship can exist only where the tasks of life are mastered together, that is, where productive and reproductive functions are actually shared and not channeled into two different and often mutually exclusive roles.

The motivation to marry as quickly as possible is apparently to a large extent determined by a lack of meaningful relationships outside the intimacy of the family. For a woman, marriage seems to provide an economically and emotionally secure niche where she can raise her children. For a man marriage means sexual security and in spite of the decline of his dominant father role is still the only relationship where he actually has or perceives he has power (see below, Dair L. Gillespie, pp. 121–147). As a rule, both are disappointed in their expectations but won't admit it. The result is often a neurotic symbiosis based on false expectations and pseudo-satisfactions. Thus couples never become aware of their real situation. When one partner fails to satisfy the other's affective needs (because he or she alone cannot serve as a safety valve for the alienating experience of housewife or wage earner), the other typically begins to look for outside relationships which will fulfill him. Characteristically people who remarry after divorce tend to marry a person with a personality very similar to that of their first mate. Consequently the next stage of the cycle soon shows the same flaws.

It is often said that the younger generation is less apt to fall into this kind of vicious circle because it displays a more permissive attitude to sexual behavior. Research findings do not unanimously support this assumption. The so-called sexual revolution demonstrates more than anything else the horrible inflation of words like "revolution." What really has happened is not so much a genuine change of behavior as changes in attitudes and norms (see below, Joachim Israel and Rosmari Eliasson, pp. 173–195). Comparison of Kinsey's data with more recent data does not show any substantial increase in sexual contacts. Apparently sexual promiscuity of the younger generation is more a myth created by the mass media than a reality. While the rigid taboo against premarital sex is gradually disappearing, there is a strong tendency to stick to one partner at a time and to establish long-term relationships, including marriage, as early as possible.

Among the multiplicity of factors involved in the complete picture of what is called the "sexual revolution"[5] three points need to be emphasized:

1. The role of women as an industrial reserve army, either as unpaid housekeepers or an underpaid labor force on the job market, is no longer accepted without question. Paradoxically the relative proportion of women with a college degree holding jobs was slightly higher during the 1920s and 1930s. The increasing marriage rate and the "feminine mystique" prevailing during the postwar years, accompanied by a baby boom, has kept many highly trained women at home; and in their later years they would not or could not obtain jobs. Meanwhile, the new women's liberation movement presses for equality in the labor market as well as in marriage (see below, Jo Freeman, pp. 201–216). While it is highly unlikely that full equality for women in the labor market will be achieved soon, it may well be that the movement will eventually attain more equality in marriage. In fact, one possible result may be that the gradual increase in the marriage rate will stop or reverse, since the more radical factions of the women's liberation movement are often averse to marriage. However, as Branka Magaš has argued (see below, pp. 217–245), sexual politics is part of class politics. Women will achieve a better position in society only if (*a*) the task of socialization of small children is no longer left to isolated housewives, and (*b*) the unemployment problem is no longer solved at the expense of women's potential labor-force participation. The question of women's labor is directly linked with women's marital situation. Day-care centers for children and part-time jobs for both husband and wife must be abundant if the goal of companionship in all spheres of life is to be realized. One major impediment to such liberation has been overcome with the invention of oral contraceptives which have alleviated the continuous fear of pregnancy, a strong factor in women's dependency on men. The future impact of oral contraceptives on our sex lives cannot be overestimated, especially if the biological revolution (which might be the only *real* revolution

in the end) continues to produce new techniques for artificial insemination, provides male contraceptives, and provides the possibility of determining the sex of one's children.

2. A second point concerns the general change of attitudes toward sexuality. There is reason to believe that this change affects the public realm more than the private bedroom. In recent years the public presentation and discussion of sexuality has become a familiar phenomenon. On the other hand, psychiatrists are not known to have reported a decrease of sexual neuroses in their patients. In fact, a sociological observer might be drawn to the conclusion that the former double standard has been reversed to an opposite double standard, where everything is possible in word and picture, while the actual behavior remains restrained. The "sexual revolution" is the advent of a new voyeurism. Here, too, the medium is the message. The enormous success of such sterile magazines as *Playboy* and *Penthouse* cannot be explained by the needs of shattered male egos alone since it is eventually accompanied by a similar exposure of the male body which is not meant for the "gay liberation movement." Sexual intercourse, long described in great detail in literature, can now be inspected in well-reviewed movie pictures and even on the stage. Law agencies fight a losing battle against all kinds of pornography and it seems to be only a matter of time until television programs will be opened to free sex. This new voyeurism is the logical result of the ever growing impact of visual communication, culminating in the television culture. Whether this visual liberation is to be accompanied or followed by a similar liberation of actual behavior is not yet clear. As long as the present "relations of production" with their division of sex roles prevail it seems more likely that the changes in the attitude toward sexuality will remain a form of repressive desublimation.[6]

3. A third factor involved in the present change is the narrowing differences in life-style and identification between the sexes. Current fashion—long-haired men in colorful dress and trousered women wearing boots and leatherware—may be an indication of what the future holds. The trend toward unisex is but an expression of a more general depolarization of the sexes. Many have deplored the libidiniza-

tion, while some have already warned against a desexualization, of American life.[7] Unfortunately these tendencies are not incompatible. On the contrary, once it is admitted that much of what is termed the "sexual revolution" is voyeurism on a public scale, the consequence may be a de-eroticization of our real life. This is already visible in many areas of everyday life which once had erotic connotations. Clothes are one example; prepackaged, colorless food is another. Our streamlined, beige-colored, deodorized, air-conditioned, neuter environment does not easily lend itself to erotic attachments which would penetrate beyond the pink façade of *Playboy* pictures. Thus the inherent dialectics of all emancipation processes may well lead, in the case of the "sexual revolution," to a neuter and desexualized society. Within the past ten years a new generation with a different and somewhat blurred sexual identity has emerged. Young people now significantly more often identify themselves with personality traits traditionally claimed for the opposite sex. This may, of course, also indicate a new openness for the other side of one's personality, which may broaden one's understanding of the other sex. One relevant observation is the new awareness of the sensuous (more than just the sexual) dimension of human life emerging from the counter-culture. The potential of what John O'Neill has called "body politics" is directed against *all* forms of alienation in interaction (see below, pp. 251–265). Closer observation of the counter-culture leads to the conclusion that a stronger emphasis on all our senses may help to overcome the average American's obsession with sex. However, the realization of this potentiality will depend on whether the present role differentiation between the sexes rather than the difference of sexual identity becomes less rigid; in other words, whether the division of labor according to gender can be overcome.

While gender differentiation usually contributes to the maintenance of the social order, changes in sex-role differentiation are not determinants but resultants of social change in other areas, especially within the economic sphere (see below, Harriet Holter, pp. 153–171). It seems today that economic needs demand a quasi-egalitarianism to which individuals are already trying to adjust subconsciously. Women have gained access to schools and universities, and their employment opportunities, though far from equal, are greatly improved. As Randall Collins in his conflict theory of sexual stratification points out (see below, pp. 53–76), since women have their own income, they are in a better bargaining position economically as well as in the sexual market. In turn, among the young this has provoked a new conception of male sexual attractiveness. This may explain why the role ideals of the sexes seem to approximate each other. The "sexual revolution" may turn out to be no more than a new phase in the struggle of the sexes, the women's liberation movement being a more recent expression.

This struggle is further intensified by psychological factors. From a psychoanalytic point of view, Ingjald Nissen claims that men's striving to control women is caused by the fact that they are sexually weaker than women in the second half of their life (see below, pp. 42–50). It may be that women maintain that older men are still sexually attractive *because* men are sexually weaker and women need to keep them interested. The reverse may also be true; men's emphasis on the youth and beauty in women may function to protect them against the potential sexual aggressiveness of women during the later years. This "sexual constellation" helps to maintain a sexual stratification system which is reified in the institution of monogamous marriage.

There appear to be strong forces at work to keep the battle of the sexes confined to the walls of monogamy. The sexual market has become more open, but marriage is still the stronghold of male domination, indirectly but effectively supported by the economic relations of production. Even though economic conditions and sexual constellations determine to a large degree the relative bargaining power of the sexes, thus relegating notions of a "sexual revolution" to the realm of myth, the struggle of the sexes is not in a deadlock. Perhaps more than ever it holds a strong potential for liberation and emancipation of both sexes.

What are the alternatives open to us in view of the miserable state of family, of marriage, and of current sex-role definitions? In a highly interesting volume titled *The Family in Search of a Future*, Herbert Otto has published the answers of fifteen experts to this question.[8] While some authors simply extrapolate current tendencies, others look for entirely new solutions. All the authors agree that the present situation is insufferable and that legal impediments to experimental change should be abolished immediately. One group of authors argue that we have already entered the age of serial polygamy. Therefore, divorce should be made easier so that it will no longer be a humiliating experience but, rather, rebirth in the context of a new relationship. Yet, since most people tend to choose a new partner similar to the one they have just divorced, such rebirth is not likely to occur.

Not unlike the view that serial polygamy should become "progressive monogamy" is the notion of institutionalizing "student marriages" in order to test the relationship before permission is granted to make the marriage permanent and have children. A family celebration of the loss of virginity is suggested as one of a number of rites of passage to emphasize the meaning of each new step in one's sexual life. These ideas follow the present trend toward the legitimation of more than one long-lasting relationship during a lifetime. Two members of Maryland's House of Delegates have already introduced a bill which would allow three-year contract marriages with the option to renew.

While these authors try to emphasize the positive aspects of the present situation, others take refuge in professional aids. "Marriage inventors" are suggested for the promotion of new ways for men and women to cohabitate and raise their children and to help with an alteration of situational roles in marriage oriented to the goal of a "serial polygamy to the same person." Another author proposes the institution of a "third parent," a male figure educated and trained to socialize male children in place of the absent father. The problems of the present family system are correctly diagnosed but the remedies seem extremely weak.

More radical yet is a third group of authors who suggest a legalization of polygamy, polyandry, or various forms of tribal family structure. Polygamy and polyandry are apt to meet with a variety of emotional and legal difficulties. While the polygamy of the Mormons in America shows that it is not altogether unfeasible, their experience is also not an encouraging one. Some type of communal family, however, is a serious alternative, since it satisfies certain needs fulfilled in monogamy while avoiding some of monogamy's shortcomings. The reports by Bennett Berger and Benjamin Schlesinger on communal families (see below, pp. 271–300, and pp. 301–326) indicate that a communal family structure has at least three advantages over the nuclear family type: (*a*) communal property is more economic, especially in the use of household machinery and transport facilities; (*b*) the polarization between alienated formal social relations and intimate family relations disappears in favor of more affective direct relations between a larger group of adults; and (*c*) the children are raised communally, that is, they have more than one or two adult references and live in direct contact with any number of other children of different age groups. On the other side, the parents are not overburdened by continual exposure to their own brood. These advantages need to be studied in more detail. Unfortunately the Israeli kibbutz is the only communal family type which has been thoroughly examined by social scientists.[9] To my knowledge the research carried out by Bennett Berger and his associates is the only sociological study presently in process which focuses on communal living in America or Europe. This study concentrates on rural communes founded by various types of dropouts.

Yet, given the high degree of urbanization in industrialized countries, the urban family commune seems to be the most promising alternative to the nuclear family. Although an unknown number of such communes exists in various Western countries, especially in Scandinavia, Germany, and the United States, this phenomenon has yet to be discovered by empirical sociology. (One of the reasons that urban communes have not been studied must be seen in the methodological difficulties of participant observation.) Most of these communes seem to be rather short-lived, because urban communes are confronted with particular problems. First, there is the architecture of the available apartments. It does not overstate the case to say that the structure of the nuclear family is literally cemented by the architectural design of modern apartment buildings. Second, there is a general scarcity of apartments in the big cities in all industrialized countries. It is extremely difficult to find suitable and adjoining apartments for a communal family setting. Third, there is the problem of regional mobility, which may split the family. Many jobs and professions require people to change location in order to meet the demands of their corporation or career. And these are only the external difficulties.

Internally members have to overcome much of what they have internalized from their own families. Apparently there are a number of preconditions for a successful communal family, some not dissimiliar to those for a normal successful marriage and others different. There must be an unusual degree of openness and candidness, which is not easy to achieve for those who have learned to keep their intimate problems a secret. There must be a serious attempt to give up attitudes of economic or sexual competitiveness, i.e., the emphasis on private property has to be devalued. On the other hand, there are also certain "bourgeois" virtues which must be maintained. Many urban communes failed because they tried to "liberate" themselves from certain achievements of the early bourgeoisie. Apparently communes, unless they are religiously motivated, cannot succeed without a relatively strict "incest taboo" among the new clan. The famous nineteenth-century Oneida commune in upstate New York, which survived thirty years of internal promiscuity, was such an exception. Normally, an exogamous attitude is necessary to establish secure social relationships within a family. Finally, a "backstage" (E. Goffman) for privacy is an absolute necessity for modern, urban man.

In view of these difficulties, the proposal of Frederick Stoller (in *The Family in Search of a Future*) to establish *intimate contacts between several families* seems to me the most fruitful:

An alternative structure is an intimate network of families in which three or four families come together on a regular basis to explore their living arrangements, to exchange intimacies, to provide services for one another, and to develop new and more realistic and more exciting systems of values and attitudes.

This would provide for more nonalienated, affective relationships than just the one between the spouses. Such an arrangement would have the advantage of being highly flexible in responding to different needs and changing constraints. It would help to overcome the most serious deficiency of modern family life, the hiatus between intimate family ties burdened with the duty of affection and formal everyday relationships devoid of all meaningful affection and relevant content. This should be supplemented by the institutionalization of structured communal socialization of children and, if localities permit, a communal arrangement for the use of household machinery, shopping, and transportation facilities. This could be worked out even in cases where families live in different apartments and do not share everything. In such an open arrangement there is no reason why polygamous and polyandrous relationships should not develop if this can be tolerated by the members of the family network. In cases of severe emotional disturbance of the network, a professional counselor or therapist could and should be called in. It is interesting to note that in many cases therapy and encounter groups are already functioning as surrogates for the larger family network. Sometimes individual ties to such groups may prove to be stronger than either marriage bonds or career motivations. Yet therapy groups have a limited effect if they are not tied closely to everyday family problems. Professional help would not be necessary in a larger family network once members began to focus on their personal problems in an open atmosphere and in a framework of pragmatic arrangements. When the erotic undercurrents are dealt with openly and candidly there is a probability that sexuality will decline in importance.

The question of child care seems more important. Suggestions for alternative family structures which disregard the existence of children and the aged are futile. The basic question is whether public agencies will gradually take over more of the socialization tasks, as a long-range tendency in all industrialized countries seems to indicate, or whether this problem will be left, as seems to be the trend for the near future, to the parents. The question of socialization procedures will be examined in detail in the next, the fifth, volume of *Recent Sociology.* The studies in the present volume focus on crises in sexual and emotional relationships among adults, and range from Marion Levy's firm statements about what we know of the family network to the open question of Rustum and Della Roy, "Is Monogamy Outdated?" It is my hope that this collection of essays will not only lead to a fresh look at problems of sex-role differentiation but will also serve as incitement to continue the fight for liberation with as many experiments in family relations as are feasible. The family remains a basic structural element of this society. Any change in the family system will not only help to produce unalienated relations among us but also will tend to result in a qualitative change in the social system at large.

NOTES

1. I gratefully acknowledge the help of John Reed, my teaching assistant during the 1972 spring term at Cornell University, with the manuscript of this Introduction.
2. See George O'Neill and Nena O'Neill, *The Open Marriage* (New York, 1972).
3. See Barrington Moore, Jr., *Political Power and Social Theory* (Cambridge, Mass., 1958), "Thoughts on the Future of the Family," p. 164.
4. *Ibid.*, p. 170.
5. As an interesting appraisal of this development, see Lester A. Kirkendall and Robert N. Whitehurst (eds.), *The New Sexual Revolution* (New York, 1971).
6. For an elaboration of the concept of repressive desublimation, see Reimut Reiche, *Sexuality and Class Struggle* (New York, 1971).
7. See Charles Winick, *The New People: Desexualization in American Life* (New York, 1968).
8. Herbert Otto (ed.), *The Family in Search of a Future* (New York, 1971).
9. See, for instance, Bruno Bettelheim, *The Children of the Dream* (New York, 1969).

# I

# Family and the Sexual Constellation

*This first chapter is designed to outline a theoretical framework in which changes in family life and sex-role differentiation can be interpreted. Even though family life is often agonizing, the idea of doing without some form of the family system seems futile. In an article modestly titled "Some Hypotheses about the Family" so eminent a scholar as Professor Marion J. Levy, Jr., from Princeton University, flatly states, "I believe the family to be a requisite of human life if not for every single human, and I hold it to be the single most critical organizational context for any and every society." Her compilation of what social scientists presently know about the functions of this organizational unit clearly indicates the hiatus between the family system of traditional societies and that of modern industrialized societies. Her article was first published in 1970 in the first issue of the* Journal of Comparative Family Studies.

*Professor Levy applies a structural-functionalist point of view, while Ingjald Nissen, who is one of the few Scandinavians to have specialized in psychoanalysis during the 1930s, takes a look at what he calls the "sexual constellation" from a psychological perspective. Ingjald Nissen, who has written several books on psychoanalytic problems, demonstrates that certain important findings of Alfred C. Kinsey's investigations can throw new light on the problem of equality for women and on the relations of women to war. The main thesis of his article, reprinted from* Acta Sociologica, *Vol. 14, 1971, is that man's suppression of women results from an attempt to solve the major problem of his being bound to a lasting sexual union, during the last half of which he is sexually the weaker. This leads to a number of interesting insights which should warn us against enthusiasm for a women's liberation cause that does not take into account the biological constellation between the sexes and the resulting deeply rooted psychological problems.*

*This constellation has found very different expression in the course of history. Randall Collins, an Assistant Professor of Sociology at the University of California, San Diego, develops a historical theory of sexual stratification which helps to illumine the changing role of women in society. His article, which first appeared in* Social Problems *in 1971, is a major contribution to the sociological study of the struggle of the sexes. Based on the perspectives of Freud and Weber, it attempts to explain historical changes in sex roles resulting from variations in the social organization of violence and economic markets. These determine the resources available for men and women in the struggle for control, and they condition prevailing ideologies about sexuality. Randall Collins emphasizes the economic system as the most important single determinant of sex-role differentiation.*

# 1

# Some Hypotheses about the Family

MARION J. LEVY, JR.

## *Introduction*

EVEN THE ATTEMPT to be scientific about the family has a maudlin ring about it. For the old, today, the family doesn't seem to be what it once meant to them. For the middle-aged, it is frequently the focus of their most agonizing responsibilities. For the young, it is the most obvious and conveniently identified source of their difficulties, since virtually without exception they know their origins to be rooted there. Down through the years no organization has been the focus for greater moralizing or musing. Most people throughout time have had the feeling that, if there is any uniformity about "human nature," that uniformity somehow centers overwhelmingly on family questions.

In the scientific realm, however, we seem to have taken leave of our senses in the handling of this whole field. We seem to have been preoccupied either with family pathology and family therapy on the one hand or with the enormous variety of family customs on the other. And finally today most seem to agree that we are firmly settled on a course such that the family has already diminished to a position of slight importance in social structure, that only a lack of inventiveness and good will toward one's fellows keeps this unit from being an anachronism altogether. I hold otherwise. I believe the family to be a requisite of human life if not for every single human, and I hold it to be the single most critical organizational context for any and every society—if such a statement can have any meaning in situations where high levels of interdependence are the essence of the game.

We do not know with any certainty a single solitary fact about how the human family came into being. I do firmly believe that, if we ever have a good explanation of that, it will be one understandable in evolutionary terms—that it will prove to be a further development for the representatives of this species of patterns characteristic of closely related species from which they evolved. I believe that, and I so hypothesize because I feel that not to do so is to be mired forever in the kind of dividing line that holds in essence that man is different from the animals in that man has a "soul." If one substitutes the word "culture" for "soul," I hold that that too will be found to be different in kind from its predecessors only if one goes to the level of very specific detail rather than general considerations, much in the same sense that that can be held to be true of the human finger.

I am not expert about, or even a student of, familial forms in other mammals, but if certain human patterns associated with the family do not have the kind of biological bases that we are not at all loath to assume when other species are under consideration, the kind of mutational change which must have taken place with regard to the human species would require a kind of curious probability at which the mind boggles. For example, however malleable the reaction may be, if there is no biological basis for protective and nurturant behavior by a mother toward a newborn infant of the human species—if that had to wait on a specific cognitive cultural breakthrough with the attendant acceptance of social engineering—I cannot imagine any of the species to have survived. We do not seem to find it difficult to regard certain displays in other mammals, and many other living species as well, as indicative of a desire for food or water, nor do we have any difficulty in reconciling ourselves to a continuity between those displays and similar desires on the part of human beings, however modified in their expression. I do not see why we should feel differently—certainly not those of us who claim to be concerned with science—about familial-type displays.

We fought so hard against naïve forms of biological determinism in the early part of the twentieth century that most of us still go to the opposite extreme of feeling autonomically that biological factors have nothing to do with case. Those of us who regard ourselves as having an ounce of social conscience are further reinforced in this because we happen to live in a period in which some of the nastier forms of human inhumanity to humans are based on pseudo-scientific assertions about actual or alleged biological distinctions. Nevertheless, such a rejection of the biological relevance of human prehistory and of what she/he is today for how she/he behaves is in one direction romantic theology and in the other ignorance.

It is possible to state a set of hypotheses about the family in any and all societies. It is also possible to point to some of the distinctions which inhere in the distinction between those societies characterized by high levels of modernization and the vast majority of all societies in the history of the world—those which are or were not highly modernized. In what follows I have tried to state some of those generalizations. If any substantial proportion of them hold true at all, the basis for my belief that family phenomena constitute the single most strategic lead into an understanding of general social questions, even in a society like our own in which the family sphere is so much more tightly curtailed than it has been in many, will be established.

## *Some Hypotheses about Any and All Societies*

### *Hypothesis 1*

There are no societies that are not characterized by family structures.[1]

### *Hypothesis 2*

The initial placement of the overwhelming majority of all individuals is in terms of some presumed family connection.

*Hypothesis 3*

The overwhelming majority of all children are reared from birth to some point well past infancy largely if not overwhelmingly in a family context.

*Hypothesis 3:1*

In the vast majority of all societies, for the vast majority of all children, the rearing in a family context has continued up to adulthood.

*Hypothesis 4*

Initial learning on which all other learning is based—the learning characteristic of the steepest part of the learning curve for every individual—takes place for the vast majority of all individuals in a family context. The family is the context in terms of which practically everybody learns to walk, to talk, to control bodily functions, to interact with other people, to differentiate the sexes, to respond to allocations of power and responsibility, goods and services, and so forth.

*Hypothesis 5*

Nepotism as a criterion for the selection of individuals has never been absent from any society, and for most societies family membership has been the most important criterion for selection ideally and/or actually for the vast majority of the people for the majority of the time.

*Hypothesis 6*

Initial learning for human beings always takes place in terms of considerations of age, generation, and sex. All other forms of role differentiation are learned initially in these terms rather than vice versa.

*Hypothesis 6:1*

Many if not most of the distinctions on the basis of age and generation in terms of which initial learning takes place are common to all the human beings of that society. For example, all go through a period which can be described as infancy; each is somebody's child, and presumably will someday have an older-generation role relative to someone else.

*Hypothesis 6:2*

Role differentiation on the basis of sex is the first specialized role differentiation learned by all individuals in all societies. All individuals learn that in some sense common to their setting they are either males or females and will not be the other. This specialization has some features common to all human beings and of course for the males and females respectively of any given society. At the present state of our biological knowledge, these differentiations are never confined solely to those factors that are biologically explicable. Some of them are, however, common to all known societies. For example, if we can believe our modern anthropologists, there are no truly matriarchal societies—and there never have been any. Ideally speaking family heads are always males even in matrilineal settings.

*Hypothesis 7*

Despite variations in the ideal patterns the vast majority of all human beings have been reared in a family context that involved or involves a total of five or fewer members. The probability was and is overwhelming that those five members will include representatives of no more than two generations, of one marital spouse pair, and will contain representatives of each sex.

*Hypothesis 7:1*

Even where three- or four-generation families are the ideal, the vast majority of grandparents do not long survive the birth of the first grandchild.

*Hypothesis 7:2*

When grandparents in general survive the birth of their grandchildren by several years, three- or four-generation families cease to be the ideal if they were previously that.

*Hypothesis 8*

Wherever the care of the aged is, ideally speaking, supposed to be carried out on a family basis, very few individuals will survive long enough to experience senility. (In all relatively modernized contexts, care of the aged is carried out on nonfamily bases. Either the individuals concerned provide for themselves or they are taken care of in other organizational contexts—usually public governmentally organized ones.)

*Hypothesis 9*

Ideally and/or actually what happens to an individual in terms of his family affects the way he behaves in every other organizational context in every known society. Such a statement cannot be made of any other organizational context unless one speaks as close to the completely descriptive level as possible, at which point, in interdependent systems, everything is, I suppose, as relevant to everything else as anything is. The statement given above holds true of the family at extremely general levels. For example, all learning with regard to allocations of power and responsibility which are of course relevant to any organizational context is based on initial learning in this regard that takes place in terms of the family. The influence goes far beyond this, however. In many cases what happens to one in terms of one's family is ideally supposed to affect the way one behaves in other contexts, and even when it is not supposed to do so, it is overwhelmingly likely to do so. In all known societies family particularism is the most general and influential form of particularism.

*Hypothesis 10*

In all family systems—even when they are matrilineal—ideally speaking the family head is male.

*Hypothesis 11*

The sex ratio of family members is roughly 1:1.

*Hypothesis 12*

In all known societies general sexual intercourse as between father-daughter, brother-sister, and mother-son is tabooed. Frequency of actual violations probably decreases in the order named, with mother-son incest being much the rarest of the three for all peoples.

*Hypothesis 12:1*

The incest taboo is never confined solely to these three type relationships.

## *Some Hypotheses about Families in Relatively Nonmodernized Societies*

*Hypothesis 1*

Even when family considerations do not, ideally speaking, take precedence over other considerations, the vast majority of all individuals in fact orient most of their behavior most of the time to family considerations.

*Hypothesis 2*

The vast majority of all individuals in fact operate in a family context the vast majority of the time.

*Hypothesis 3*

Not only initial placement and learning but the vast majority of all learning of all individuals for adult roles takes place in a family context.

*Hypothesis 3:1*

Most of this learning is from older members of one's own family, especially one's mother or father.

*Hypothesis 4*

The last unit of decentralization of control in all relatively nonmodernized societies is the family unit.

*Hypothesis 4:1*

Ideally speaking, the head of that unit is always a male, though not necessarily the father.

*Hypothesis 5*

Very few grandparents long survive the birth of the first grandchild and therefore are not ordinarily members of family units even when they would be if they survived long enough.

*Hypothesis 6*

Despite high fertility rates, rarely do more than two siblings per marital spouse pair survive to maturity.

*Hypothesis 6:1*

Since the sex ratio is roughly 1:1, problems with primogeniture are not what they might otherwise be.

*Hypothesis 6:2*

Wherever primogeniture exists, there is always in some context a cadet problem, since all possible successors to the position must be reared so that they could succeed to the position. If more than one survives when that succession takes place, there is a cadet problem.

*Hypothesis 7*

In all known societies up to the age of say three, four, or five, all infants and children regardless of sex remain largely under the direct supervision and minute-to-minute care of the female side of the family. In all relatively nonmodernized contexts, at roughly age five the boys come under the direct domination and supervision of the male side of the family, usually their father and older brothers, if any. The females continue under female supervision. This differentiation is carried out even if the children do roughly the same things. It continues until adulthood.

*Hypothesis 7:1*

In relatively nonmodernized societies full sexual identification precedes maturity by roughly a decade. Most of the patterns with which one is expected to be familiar as an adult are thus learned on a sexually differentiated basis.

*Hypothesis 8*

In relatively nonmodernized social contexts the overwhelming majority of individuals operate in terms of a restricted number of organizational contexts, most of which are not highly specialized. Of these the family is much the most important. It is the unit in terms of which the overwhelming amount of allocation of goods and services, allocation of power and responsibility, religiously oriented and recreationally oriented activity takes place.

*Hypothesis 8:1*

The family is never regarded as overwhelmingly specialized with regard to any one of these aspects of behavior.

*Hypothesis 9*

In relatively nonmodernized contexts family solidarities take precedence over any other solidarities in the vast majority of all cases, ideally as well as actually.

## *Some Hypotheses about Families in Any Relatively Modernized Society*

Those hypotheses which are alleged above to hold for any society, of course, continue to hold with regard to relatively modernized societies. In general the changes in family structure characteristic of relatively modernized societies fall under two headings. (1) Changes in the structure of the family itself. The main factors in this connection have to do with the changes involved in shifting to a multilineal conjugal family unit based overwhelmingly on husband-wife solidarity. This, I suspect, has never been the main basis of solidarity for any other type of marital arrangement save ones in which nuclear families are the ideal and no children have yet arrived. In all relatively modernized societies such a family becomes the ideal if not the actual structure, regardless of whether children have been born. (2) The second type of change, however, is on the whole more important. This is a type of change that has to do primarily with regard to the place of family structure in general social structure. There is a sense, of course, in which either of these two changes can be looked at from the point of view of the other. After all, a switch from an extended family to a multilineal conjugal family ideal can be viewed as a change of the position of the family in general social structure. Correspondingly a situation in which ordinarily education for adult roles is not conducted in terms of family units can be looked at from the point of view of a change in the family structure as such. I think it is more fruitful in what is to come to differentiate these two types of changes as I have just done here, however.

## *Some Hypotheses about Changes in Family Structure as Such*

### *Hypothesis 1*

Whatever has previously been the case, the ideal family structure of all relatively modernized societies is a multilineal conjugal family unit.

#### *Hypothesis 1:1*

It is overwhelmingly probable that the actual pattern will coincide closely with the ideal one in this respect.

*Hypothesis* 1:1:1

There may be some lag in the case of latecomers to modernization, but the trend is always in this direction.

*Hypothesis* 2

The solidarity that takes precedence over other solidarities in family structure switches to the husband-wife solidarity both ideally and actually.

*Hypothesis* 2:1

It should be kept in mind that it was overwhelmingly probable that the main solidarity for all relatively nonmodernized societies accented some intergenerational male solidarity such as father-son or uncle-nephew. This is no longer ever the case after societies become relatively modernized. The higher the level of modernization the greater the switch to husband-wife solidarity.

*Hypothesis* 3

The choice of spouse is overwhelmingly likely to be made by the parties to the marriage themselves and is likely to be based on romantic love—certainly on the personal preferences of the parties concerned.

*Hypothesis* 4

The family structures are likely to remain patriarchal although the ideal patterns of equality may be expressed.

*Hypothesis* 4:1

Egalitarianism as an ideal pattern in relatively modernized societies is overwhelmingly likely to be a utopian pattern.

*Hypothesis* 5

Ideally and actually the family will be neolocal.

*Hypothesis 6*

The family (families) of procreation and the family (families) of orientation of each individual will be different.

*Hypothesis 7*

The solidarity of children with parents is expected to be greater than that of children with their siblings.

*Hypothesis 8*

The solidarity of children with parents is, ideally speaking, not biased in favor of either the male or the female parent for either male or female children.

*Hypothesis 8:1*

Actually the solidarity of children of either sex is likely to be greater with the mother than with the father.

*Hypothesis 9*

Ideally speaking, the father is the family head, or egalitarianism is stressed. Actually the mother is the effective acting family head as far as the children are concerned most of the time.

*Hypothesis 10*

The solidarity between each parent and each child is expected to be roughly the same. Actually it is established on the basis of personal preferences and not by some such ordered ideal structure as primogeniture.

*Hypothesis 10:1*

Actually both father and mother are likely to give preference to male children.

*Hypothesis 11*

Ideally speaking, as far as sex-role differentiation is concerned, treatment of children is egalitarian insofar as possible.

*Hypothesis 11:1*

Actually such egalitarianism is never approximated. Sex-role differentiation always exceeds what is presently explicable biologically.

*Hypothesis 12*

In relatively modernized contexts, as in all other contexts, the vast majority of initial learning for infants on which all other learning is based takes place in a family context that is not likely to involve more than five people, with the sex ratio roughly 1:1, and with at the most two generations being represented, the older being the parents of the children concerned. Unlike relatively nonmodernized contexts, the maintenance of these numbers in relatively modernized contexts is a function of the fact that the parents limit fertility rather than a function of high mortality rates in general and of high infant mortality rates in particular.

*Hypothesis 13*

There is no expectation, ideally speaking, that the children will follow the same adult roles as their parents, and insofar as they do, it is not expected that they shall learn how to do this from their parents or older members of their own families.

## *Some Hypotheses about the Place of Families in General Social Structure*

*Hypothesis 1*

Neither ideally nor actually speaking does family solidarity take preference over all other nonfamily solidarities.

*Hypothesis 2*

Starting at quite early ages the overwhelming majority of all individuals do not operate in family-oriented contexts most of their time.

*Hypothesis 2:1*

Those individuals who spend the largest amount of time in family-oriented contexts fall into two categories: (1) infants or very young children and (2) mothers with infants or very young children.

*Hypothesis 3*

Where there are alternatives to care and supervision of the children by family members, that care is relatively rarely done in terms of related kinship organizations. It is much more likely to be done in terms of school units, day nurseries, and so forth, which are essentially nonkinship organizations.

*Hypothesis 4*

The family is rarely the organization in terms of which what are regarded as the productive economic roles are conducted.

*Hypothesis 4:1*

The economic aspects of the family are regarded as being overwhelmingly concerned with consumption. Ordinarily such activities as child rearing, food preparation, housekeeping, and the like are not viewed as productive activities but are, rather, viewed as aspects of consumption.

*Hypothesis 5*

The family is not the final unit of political decentralization. Ideally speaking, in relatively modernized contexts, the state has a monopoly on the legitimate use of force, and even intrafamily uses of force may be called to account by representatives of the state.

*Hypothesis 6*

Intrusion of family considerations into any area regarded as important outside the family area itself is regarded, ideally speaking, as improper. Ideally speaking, nepotism is regarded as a sin.

*Hypothesis 6:1*

Actually there is, of course, a great deal of nepotism. Parents, particularly those "better placed" in social structure, make considerable efforts to secure special advantages for their children.

*Hypothesis 7*

Not only do most individuals not spend most of their time in family-oriented activities or in family contexts, but the other contexts in which they do spend the majority of their time are to a high degree specialized rather than general units such as the family, common neighborhood units, and so forth. These units are likely to be regarded as overwhelmingly concerned with economic considerations, political considerations, recreational considerations, educational considerations, and so forth. They obviously contain many other considerations, but they are regarded as specialized in this respect. In such specialized organizational contexts, individuals deal with one another primarily in one specialized respect, ideally speaking. The overwhelming predominance of these contexts is one of the things that have led to the oft-repeated statement that the family is losing all significance in relatively modernized contexts, but in such contexts the family assumes a new and special position in social structure. It becomes the only organizational context in which the individual is overwhelmingly likely to be considered as a "whole person." As the family "loses other functions," it becomes *the castle of the me.*

*Hypothesis 8*

The family remains the unit in all known relatively modernized societies in terms of which the majority of initial learning takes place. Greatly increased uses of day nurseries may change this substantially, but such usage has not characterized any very substantial proportion of the world's population or, I suspect, any substantial proportion of the population of any single country. Most children learn to walk, to talk, to eat, to sleep, to control bodily functions, and interact with other human beings in a family context.

*Hypothesis 9*

Mothers, or persons in a mother-type role, continue to have overwhelming responsibility for and supervision of children from birth to early childhood.

*Hypothesis 10*

The overwhelming majority of all fathers have occupational roles such that they cannot take their own children with them whether they wish to or not. Those occupational roles are conducted in contexts other than family contexts.

*Hypothesis 10:1*

Therefore, insofar as family supervision is concerned, it continues from birth to maturity largely in the hands of the mother or mother surrogate position in the family structure for both male and female children.

*Hypothesis 10:2*

In relatively modernized contexts full sexual identification and maturity tend to come together.

*Hypothesis 10:3*

In relatively modernized contexts coeducation of the young is generalized.

*Hypothesis 10:4*

When the person in the position of father or father-type position is home in the evenings and on weekends, that will of course make a considerable amount of difference especially as far as the male children are concerned, but the radical segregation of children by sexes between the ages of say five and fifteen for most training purposes for adult role is gone in family contexts and by specific ideals is likely to be gone in specialized educational contexts as well.

*Hypothesis 11*

The great competing organizational contexts for children as far as the family is concerned are likely to be educationally oriented contexts—primary- and secondary-type schools. These may or may not be overwhelmingly manned by females. If they are, supervision of young males by females is even more radically thorough than that implicit in the fact that most adult males have occupational roles that forbid them to be with their male children except during leisure periods.

*Hypothesis 12*

A new element is introduced into family structure by virtue of the fact that in general in relatively modernized contexts, and in the contexts of latecomers to the process of modernization, even though they have not yet become relatively modernized, it becomes necessary to educate children for an unknown future. This adds new dimensions. It does not affect the teaching of such factors as speech and locomotion, bodily control, and so on, but it increasingly affects most of the consciously oriented educational activities. As people acquire increasingly long-range futures within increased life expectancy, they have an increasingly short-range view of the future. In one sense, education from primary school grades upward out of family contexts takes some of the possible irrelevance of that education off the family context. This whole process is further reinforced by the fact that ordinarily children will not follow in the paths of their parents although daughters are more likely to approximate the adult roles of their mothers than are sons. Thus even if the futures of the children were known they probably would not receive their training from older members of their own families or close approximations thereto. This undermines the strength of family solidarities as adulthood approaches.

*Hypothesis 13*

The family context remains overwhelmingly particularistic, but even in family contexts there is likely to be an increased emphasis on predominantly universalistic criteria.

*Hypothesis 13:1*

To some extent the intrusion of predominantly universalistic criteria into kinship contexts may undermine warmth, security, and so forth. But in the absence of such preparation children would probably be totally unprepared for the radical increase in predominantly universalistic criteria they will meet as soon as they begin to operate at relatively early ages in nonkinship contexts.

*Hypothesis 13:2*

No economically practical method of teaching has so far been discovered that makes it possible for the school systems of relatively modernized societies to be conducted, ideally speaking, on a predominantly particularistic basis.

*Hypothesis 13:2:1*

If this were feasible economically, it is probably true that many of the things that have to be taught could not generally be inculcated on such a basis.

*Hypothesis 13:2:1:1*

This would seem to follow at least in part from another hypothesis to the following effect: in all relatively modernized contexts the amount of specialized knowledge accelerates exponentially, and that acceleration requires a continuous increase in the basic knowledge generally shared by all the members of the society. For example, the generalization of computer technology requires as a minimum a radical increase in arithmetic and algebraic sophistication on the part of the school population at large. There are no effective predominantly particularistic criteria for whether a sufficient number of the young have learned to follow and use a program on the computer.

*Hypothesis 14*

Although many of the details of sex-role differentiation in kinship terms would appear to be a function of tradition or prejudice rather than implicit in the human condition (unless the former two be considered implicit in the human condition), in no relatively modernized context has sex-role differentiation in the family context been reduced to the mere minimum implied in the physiological differences that bear on sexual intercourse and child bearing as such.

*Summary Statement*

With these many stones lying about, someone must be able to build a cathedral; surely a more substantial structure than any we presently possess can be built of them. Even in the most highly modernized of our societies the family continues to be universal and critical. We may not be entirely what we are reared to be or the result of those with whom we live in the castle of the me, but I doubt that we can understand anything that we are without resting it critically on these.

NOTES

1. The definitions of terms such as "society" and "family" are to be found in M. J. Levy's *Modernization and the Structure of Societies* (Princeton, N.J., 1966), unless otherwise specified.

# 2

# The Role of the Sexual Constellation[1]

INGJALD NISSEN

When I here use the expression the "sexual constellation," I am thinking of the fact that mankind is divided into two different groups: men and women. The effect this division has on the formation of the structure of human society is of a more fundamental nature than the effect the different impulses in human beings have on the creation of that structure.

In the last twenty years a new light has, through the investigations Alfred C. Kinsey has undertaken, fallen upon the phenomenon I here call the sexual constellation.

A main point in the traditional view has been the idea that in different periods of life, male and female individuals of about the same age have about the same need for sexual activity. It has been supposed that they suit each other in this respect. All our thinking about the relation between man and woman, all our institutions, all organizational and administrative formation of society, our whole moral system, have as a matter of course been built upon this supposition. As regards sexuality, our leading moral idea has come to be the point of view that sexual relations are only to take place between individuals of about the same age.

The new moment brought to light by Kinsey is that this parallelism in sexual life in human males and females simply does not exist. The sexual activity of men and women develops at a different tempo, in different phases. In the male, the activity is already great in his early youth, it reaches its highest point before he is twenty-five years, and it sinks during the rest of his life continually. In the female, sexual activity develops slowly, reaches its highest point when she is near thirty years and stays nearly constant for the rest of her life.

This difference between the sexual development in man and in woman leads to the phenomenon that a disproportion may arise as regards the sexual strength of two individuals of the same age living in a lasting relation. In general, it may be said that in the first half of life, the man is the sexually stronger, in the last half of life the woman is the sexually stronger. There are of course many factors which act in the direction of an adaptation (the state of health, conditions in work, love itself). But in a lasting relation the difference will practically always make itself felt at some period of life.

It has been objected to this interpretation of Kinsey's material that his figures show that the sexual activity of man in the last half of life sinks to near the level of woman's activity, but never under hers. From this it has been concluded that it is not correct to say that man in the last half of life is the sexually weaker. To this it may be replied that Kinsey has not restricted himself to talking only of sexual *activity* (defined as he has done it). He has also drawn the concepts of sexual *capacity* and sexual *ability* into his reasoning. And when this is done, one may well say that *in a lasting relation* the man in the last half of life will as a rule be the sexually weaker. This is in fact Kinsey's standpoint (see *Sexual Behavior in the Human Female*, p. 353).

This difference in the sexual situation of man and woman in different periods of life has had a fundamental effect. It has led to the result that it has become nearly impossible to solve two great problems, namely, the question of equality for woman and the question of eliminating war.

As regards the problem of equality for woman, there are today two factors which dominate the picture. The first is that until now there has not been found a convincing explanation as to *why* we have the suppression of woman. The second is that the work for the liberation of woman, after its initial great success, has come to a nearly total halt.

The fact that sexual activity in the female is relatively restrained in the period of life when sexual activity in the man is strongest, that is, in early youth, leads, in connection with the idea that sexual relations are only to take place between individuals of about the same age, to the result that the young men come to be a relatively isolated group in society. At the same time when all other groups have a social and legal place for their sexuality, the group of younger men is the only one that does not have such a place.

This has the consequence that a deep complex of bitterness is created in the young man. This complex is in the first part of life hidden behind the amazing experience the meeting with woman represents. But it has a latent existence in the man and it makes itself felt throughout life in a continually increasing degree. In the older man it as a rule becomes manifest. It takes the form of a stabilized conviction of the correctness of the view that women, who ignored him in the best time of his life, are beings who lack something as regards the deeper knowledge about life, beings who cannot reach the same degree of maturity as he himself can and who never can have full equality.

The fact that the man in the last part of life becomes the sexually weaker leads him to try to find means to secure the happiness of the sexual relation. He seeks to be the partner who determines the point of time for and the length of sexual activity. He seeks on the whole to be the one who administers the sexual life for both partners in the relation. In order to do this, he must seek to be the leading one even in other fields of life. He therefore becomes a being who strives for individual, social, and political power. With this striving the suppression of women is introduced.

When in the man his complex of bitterness, stemming from his youth, and the leadership forced upon him in later life act together, a situation is created which makes it virtually impossible for him to give woman equality.

In this way the society where the older men were the leading and ruling group was established.

The old men have sought to conserve their society by such arrangements as killing the first son, bringing women into such a condition that they were worn out at the age of thirty, and securing their power by the invention of the institution we call the men's club.

The different forms of the men's club were originally organizations intended to take care of the common interests of the men. In many cases they were simply clubs promoting the assembling of men for leisure. Often a sum had to be paid to secure membership. In other cases, they were police organizations and were more directly engaged in domination of the whole group.

The old men's society may be called the original form of the men's society.

The reaction of the female to the development of the men's society was that she has agreed to live in it on the condition that she has two fundamental needs satisfied: first, that she gets sexual life at the moment in her life when it suits her best, that is, when she is nearing thirty years, and second, that she is satisfied as to that which in our world of expectations and despair is the secret and most tempting dream: the quest for freedom from responsibility and guilt.

As regards woman, her two fundamental needs can best be satisfied through the system of monogamy. Woman has therefore demanded monogamy.

And the man has given her what she demands. He has agreed to live in a society where he first has a social and legal sexual life long after his best years are over, and where he later has to live in the situation of the sexually weaker. And he has given woman freedom from responsibility and guilt, he has accepted the role of the being who is responsible for all and guilty in all respects.

That form of the men's society, which has adopted monogamy, we may call the general form of the men's society.

Woman has in eagerness received the gift. She has accepted that form of sexual order, which for her represents a maximum of suitability and security. She has continually worked in the direction of making it still more adapted to her needs by demanding increased isolation of the younger men and harder binding of the elder men in their situation of the sexually weaker. She has entered the paradise of freedom from responsibility and guilt, and has here developed the philosophy that when she has satisfied the thousand prescripts for everyday life, she is independent of social and political duties.

Following the development toward this state of things, woman has cooperated with the group consisting of the strong men. In this way, we got a form of the men's society which may be called the strong men's society. It is characterized by the phenomena that the strong men make the ruling group and that sexual life is regulated according to the structure of absolute monogamy. It may be said to represent the men's society in its most accomplished form.

It has in opposition to this view been said that the fact that women willingly marry weak men shows that it is incorrect. But this fact does not refute the view, for there is no contradiction in stating that women willingly marry weak men and at the same time cooperate with strong men as regards the formation of society.

Insofar as the men's society—especially in the form of the strong men's society—is a structure adapted to the needs and wishes of woman, it may more adequately be denoted the women's society.

The cause of the stagnation in the movement for the liberation of women today is then that woman at the same time wants to have both monogamy and equality. This is to demand the impossible. Woman must choose between these two things.

Let us hope that she chooses equality.

The work which has been done to determine the causes of war suggests that the economic, political, and cultural factors may well be the *releasing* causes of the actual individual wars. To this extent, it may be important that we study human conflicts and the ways to evade them and solve them. But beneath and independent of the conflicts there evidently is *an underlying tendency to war*, a constant disposition for war which exists in mankind as a universal phenomenon. One is led to the supposition that this tendency has something to do with the sexual forces in the human being. But the connection is not simple and direct. It is indirect and complicated.[2]

Even here, Kinsey's investigations bring new light to the problem.

As already said, the fact that the sexual activity in woman is at its lowest point in the period when it is at its highest point in the man has, together with the idea that sexual relations are only to take place between individuals of about the same age, led to the traditional situation in which the young men have come to be a group in society which in sexual respects was isolated.

Seen in the light of the fact that the young men make the group in society which has the greatest fund of physical and mental forces concentrated in the shortest period, it is evident that the isolation in which this group lives must have great social and political consequences.

The isolation led to the result that the group was beset with an extremely high degree of suggestibility combined with a labile disposition for action in some direction.[3] Society therefore was met with the problem of holding the young men under discipline.

It is probable that the adult women, if they had been able to give the young men a sexual life of the character the young men are in need of, could have eliminated or at least reduced the problem of adaptation the situation of the young men presented. But women were not and still are not able to do this. They may well give the young men relations which are lasting and characterized by faithfulness, that is, something in the direction of "marriages." But by this they bind the young man in a form which presupposes the experience, mental assurance, and social position of the adult man. This is the opposite of what the young man is in need of. His sexual craving is deeply connected with his quest for knowledge. He is in need of relations for shorter periods with different women, relations which give him insight into the complicated world of expectations, the mechanism of the feeling of guilt, the functioning of the human soul, relations where the complete sexual union plays a secondary role and where the partial impulses to some degree may be satisfied, that is, relations where the erotic moment is the dominating factor. But adult woman points to the moral rule that sexual relations are only to take place between individuals of about the same age, and declines to take upon herself the task.[4]

The social and cultural development has therefore taken the most unfortunate direction. This attitude in woman has led to the result that the adult men have taken over the task of bringing the young men under discipline.

The most natural way to do this was by taking the young men up in the men's clubs.

This led to an unforeseen and essential change in the nature of the clubs. When the young men, with their immense fund of unused sexual forces, were taken up in these clubs, they were changed to institutions with a sexual foundation. The adult men were not able to hold all the new forces under control without creating a bond of sexual character between the men. This took place by the process that the homosexual partial impulse, which belongs to the nature of what we call normal man, was activated. In order that the partial impulse could be used in this way, it had to be activated to such a degree that the men were bound together, but not to such a degree that it became conscious. The means to this was the cult of masculinity. In this way, the men were bound together in an organization which has been called the secret male society.

The secret male society existed in nearly all primitive societies and had an important place in most of the great civilized states in Asia, Africa and other parts of the world.

The organization resided in primitive society as a rule in the so-called men's house. This was in most cases a great building in a central place in the group's territory. It was adorned with sexual symbols, above all the symbol expressing male sexuality in its retained and conserved form, the so-called phallus. According to this, the secret male society was an ascetic organization. Women were not allowed to enter the men's house. In many societies the women who acquired knowledge about the secret of the men's house were killed. It was, with respect to its practical policy, built upon the ideas of comradeship and leadership. It was, with regard to its structure, a mechanism which is most suited for conducting wars.

Today among the higher civilized peoples, the secret male society exists in the form of a *tendency*, that is, in organizations expressing the *spirit* of the secret male society. The more general of these are the ordinary military organizations. The more special of them are found in Nazism and Fascism.[5]

The costs of disciplining the young men through the creation of concrete secret male societies and institutions representing their spirit have been high. The readiness for war created by these social forms has led to the disposition for starting wars which has been the attitude in all peoples.

The sexual freedom we have aquired in recent years has not in principle changed the situation. This is because of the persisting idea that sexual relations are only to take place between individuals of about the same age. The arrangement places the young men in dependence on just that group which is most reserved toward sexual relations.

The fact that the secret male society and its derivatives are the condition for the existence of war leads us to the idea that, in order to eliminate war, we must get rid of the secret male society.

This is theoretically correct. But we stand here before great practical difficulties.

The administrative officials among all peoples have, probably instinctively or unconsciously, seen that in order to stop foreign secret male societies from entering their territory, it is necessary to activate the spirit of the secret male society among their own people. It will therefore be no easy task to bring administering authorities to work for the elimination of the secret male society in general.

The male individuals all over the world feel, perhaps instinctively and unconsciously, that information about the character of the secret male society means an unveiling of something in the constitution of the human male. And one cannot consciously take part in what is felt as a bringing to light hidden forces in oneself.

The women in general know, perhaps intuitively, that the secret male society in principle and from the very beginning was created to give them protection with respect to sex. They are therefore convinced that it has a function essential for their very existence. And what is felt as having such a function one cannot willingly combat.[6]

The direct attempt at removing the secret male society has therefore few chances of success. We must try the indirect approach.

It is evident that monogamy is a factor which increases the isolation of the young men and so increases the need for the secret male society. According to this, one can by abolishing the prescription about monogamy *to some degree* reduce the isolation of the young men and in this way *reduce* the need for the secret male society.

It may be admitted that this is not a very great step forward. But it is the step we can safely take today. And as it is at least a step in the direction away from war, it ought to be taken.[7]

The elimination of the prescription about monogamy must be accompanied by certain reforms regarding the economic situation of women in general and the economic foundation of the position of the children.[8]

As regards the opinion of women concerning their own relation to war, it must be said to be amazing. Their standpoint is that war is caused by forces in the man alone, that there is nothing in the constitution or action of woman which leads in the direction of war, and that there is no reason for her to feel responsible for it or guilty in connection with it. I have in my analysis tried to show that woman is involved in the mechanism leading to war and that she therefore has responsibility and can be expected to feel guilty.

If we are to have the slightest hope of eliminating war, woman must see that it is the secret male society which is the central factor in the complex of factors which lead to war. In order to do this, she must learn to see the difference between the men's society and the secret male society. Only when she does this will it be possible for her to see that she herself has contributed to calling the secret male society into being and that she continually contributes to keeping it in existence.

NOTES

1. Dr. philos. A. C. Ewing has, without taking any responsibility for the reasoning in this paper, corrected my English and established adequacy between what I intended to say and what actually is said. As regards the books here used, I will mention: Hans Blüher, *Die Rolle der Erotik in der männlichen Gesellschaft* (Jena: Eugen Diederichs, B. 1, 1924, B 2, 1927); Erik Grönseth, *Familie, seksualitet og samfunn* (Oslo: Pax, 1966); Harriet Holter, *Sex Roles and Social Structure* (Oslo, Bergen, Tromsö: Universitetsforlaget, 1970); Alfred C. Kinsey, Wardell B. Pomeroy, Clyde Martin, *Sexual Behavior in the*

*Human Male* (Philadelphia and London: W. B. Saunders, 1948); Alfred C. Kinsey, Wardell B. Pomeroy, Clyde Martin, Paul H. Gebhard, *Sexual Behavior in the Human Female* (Philadelphia and London: W. B. Saunders, 1953); Sofie Lazarsfeld, *Wie die Frau den Mann erlebt* (Leipzig and Wien: Verlag für Sexualwissenschaft. Schneider, 1931); Ingjald Nissen, *Menneskelige oppgaver og utveier.* Ledende ideer i mitt forfatterskap (Oslo: Aschehoug, 1966); Ingjald Nissen, *Absolute Monogamy, the Attitude of Woman, and War* (Oslo: Aschehoug, 1961); Heinrich Schurtz, *Altersklassen und Männerbünde* (Berlin: Georg Reimer, 1902); Lionel Tiger, *Men in Groups* (New York: Random House, 1969); Thorkil Vanggaard, *Phallos* (Kobenhavn: Gyldendal, 1969).

2. It will, according to this view, be seen that I reject practically all the traditional simple explanations of why we have war. Especially misleading are the ideas that it is a fighting impulse in man which is directly the cause of war and that sexual frustration as such leads to war.
3. I will stress the moment of suggestibility. The old idea that suppression of sexuality in young men leads to aggressiveness is after all unrealistic. In perhaps the majority of the young men, sexual frustration leads to passivity. The only generally acceptable point of view is therefore the more formal one that sexual frustration leads to increased suggestibility.
4. This is meant as a description, not as a suggestion of solution. In one of my books I say: "Now it may be laid down as an absolute principle that no human being can be expected to perform sexual acts which do not spring from his individual impulses and personal longings. The sexual integrity of the individual must in any case be guarded. Therefore no reform can be accepted which presupposes that woman can perform such acts. The fact therefore is that the limits of the effectiveness of any sexual reform undertaken in order to counteract war are given by the structure of sexuality in woman" (*Absolute Monogamy, the Attitude of Woman, and War*, p. 61).
5. It is in my opinion a dangerous political mistake to try to characterize Nazism and Fascism by saying that they are movements using violence as part of their regular program. In doing this one has only stressed a factor which these movements have in common with many other movements. This line leads to the point of view that Communism and the ordinary police organizations are forms of Nazism and Fascism. But while Nazism and Fascism are based upon the secret male society, Communism and the police organizations are phenomena which are completely free from this tendency.
6. It is a disturbing phenomenon that sociologists, to the degree they have done it, have overlooked or ignored the deep need in women for having men integrated into the secret male society. It is evident that if such a fundamental fact as this need is not

observed and registered, sociology cannot be of effective use in politics.

7. My view that monogamy ought to be eliminated as an actual social form does not imply that I advocate polygamy. As my point of view is that the isolation of the young men is a contributing factor to war, it may be argued that polygamy in the form of polygyny to an especially high degree leads to war.
8. As regards woman, I think the following disposition must be taken: every woman shall because of her greater share in the reproduction, conservation, and general care of life have a yearly sum from the state. The reasons for this may be summed up in the following points: (*a*) The disposition is the only one which represents a solution of woman's problem of having to choose between work in the home and work outside of the home. (*b*) It is an arrangement which gives a better foundation for the family life than the system of monogamy with an individual provider can give. (*c*) As a consequence of the fact that the sexual life cycles in the two sexes are different, it has been necessary that one of the sexes should take over the task of adaptation. In most societies, the task has fallen upon woman. To make the work of adaptation effective, woman should have the means to do it.

In general it may be said that woman should have the compensation independent of whether she has children or not, independent of whether she works in the home or outside it, independent of whether she has a lasting sexual relation or lives alone.

The transition to the new order can take place by gradually reducing the age at which woman gets the compensation.

As regards children, the leading idea ought to be that no child should be dependent on an individual provider with respect to all sides of its existence. Therefore the expenses of its living should be borne by the strongest organization of society, that is, the state.

# 3

# A Conflict Theory of Sexual Stratification[1]

RANDALL COLLINS

IN RECENT YEARS we have been sharply reminded that there is a system of stratification by sex. This essay presents a sociological theory of sexual stratification, constructed from the perspectives of Freud and Weber. Freud's work has been interpreted as a general theory of individual psychological functioning. Sociological and historical perspectives have been introduced primarily in criticism of Freud's psychology, especially to argue that sexual repression and its related family constellations are not universal, but only characteristics of Victorian Europe. But what may be a limitation on a psychological theory can prove fruitful in historical sociology. Freud's major discoveries—the biologically universal drives of sexuality and aggression, and the historically specific repression of these drives through an idealized moralism—thus become the keys to unlock the history of sexual stratification.

Weber provides a sociological perspective in which to interpret these insights. He presents a conflict model of stratification: that persons struggle for as much dominance as their resources permit; that changes in resources lead to changes in the structure of domination; and that ideals are used as weapons in these struggles, both to unify status communities and to justify power interests. From a combination of these perspectives we may derive a theory to explain both the general fact of sexual stratification and the conditions for variations in it throughout human history.

## *Sexual Discrimination in Employment*

Employment discrimination on the basis of sex is widespread. Women are concentrated in the lowest-ranking positions of the work force.

Table 1 shows that for the United States in 1960, in white-collar employment women are concentrated in clerical and sales positions, making up 67.6 percent and 36.4 percent of those categories, respectively. In terms of female participation in the labor force, they are overrepresented in these categories by ratios of 1:97 and 1:06 respectively. Of women in sales, 84.3 percent are low-ranking sales clerks (compared to 41.0 percent of male salesman) rather than in the more responsible sales positions of manufacturing, wholesale trade, insurance, and real estate. Women make up 14.5 percent of managers, officials, and proprietors, and 4.8 percent of farm owners and farm managers; these figures are 0:42 and 0:14 of the proportions expected on the basis of total numbers.

Women comprise a mildly disproportionate section of the professional and technical positions (ratio 1:11 of expected); within this category, however, they are concentrated in the traditional female jobs of teaching, nursing, and librarianship, which include 68.4 percent of all female professionals. The higher ranking the profession, the lower the proportion of women: women make up 85.8 percent of elementary school teachers, 47.0 percent of high school teachers, and 18.0 percent of college professors. The high-ranking professions of lawyers and judges are 3.3 percent female; physicians are 6.5 percent female.

In the manual-labor force, women occupy the lowest ranks except for positions of heavy physical labor in farm and industry. Thus women are 3.0 percent of the craftsmen and foreman (jobs requiring the least physical strength) but 28.1 percent of the machine operators, 52.4 percent of the service workers, and 95.9 percent of the household servants. Within the service category, women are concentrated in personal services; for example, they make up 80.9 percent of the waiters and counter workers. The duties of the female glamour occupation, airlines stewardess, consists of these

*Table 1*
WOMEN IN THE U.S. LABOR FORCE, 1960

| Occupation | Total Labor Force (thousands) | Percent Female | Ratio Observed/Expected |
|---|---|---|---|
| Professional, Technical, and Kindred | 7,336 | 38.0 | 1:11 |
| Elementary Teachers | 1,010 | 85.8 | 2:50 |
| Secondary Teachers | 521 | 47.0 | 1:37 |
| College and University Teachers (1963) | 138 | 18.0 | 0:52 |
| Lawyers and Judges | 213 | 3.3 | 0:10 |
| Physicians | 230 | 6.5 | 0:19 |
| Farmers and Farm Managers | 2,526 | 4.8 | 0:14 |
| Managers, Officials, and Proprietors | 5,489 | 14.5 | 0:42 |
| Clerical | 9,617 | 67.6 | 1:97 |
| Sales | 4,801 | 36.4 | 1:06 |
| Retail | 2,725 | 54.0 | 1:57 |
| Other | 2,076 | 13.2 | 0:38 |
| Craftsmen, Foremen, and Kindred | 9,241 | 3.0 | 0:09 |
| Operatives and Kindred | 12,846 | 28.1 | 0:82 |
| Private Household Workers | 1,760 | 95.9 | 2:80 |
| Service Except Private Household | 5,765 | 52.4 | 1:59 |
| Waiters, Bartenders and Counter Workers | 1,133 | 80.9 | 2:36 |
| Farm Laborers and Foremen | 1,560 | 17.3 | 0:50 |
| Laborers Except Farm and Mine | 3,530 | 3.5 | 0:10 |
| *Total Labor Force* | 65,026 | 34.3 | |

Source: *Statistical Abstract of the United States, 1966*, Table 328. Teaching Faculty in *Universities and 4-Year Colleges*, Spring, 1963 (U.S. Office of Education), Appendix C, Table 1.

traditional female services; nurses perform many of these same tasks within a medical setting.

## *Explanations of Job Discrimination*

Two common explanations of the low occupational rank of women are (*a*) lack of training, and (*b*) low commitment to jobs due to marriage and child-rearing. The first explanation is contrary to the facts. A comparison of the educational attainment of workers with the skill requirements of their jobs indicates that women are currently overtrained for their present jobs (Berg, 1970: 38–60). The second explanation is a self-fulfilling prophecy. If women are given opportunities only for menial jobs, they might well view home and children as preferable employment. To argue that someone must take care of the house and children does not settle the point: it is conceivable that men could take over or share these tasks, or that less emphasis could be placed on having a house and children. If women are given the opportunity for satisfying careers, they appear to pursue them no less consistently than men: the percentage of law-degree holders who are in practice is similar among women and among men, and figures for male and female doctors also are similar (Smigel, 1964: 46–47; Epstein, 1970: 73).

A more plausible explanation is that women are the subordinate class in a system of sexual stratification. That is, there is a system of stratification by sex which is different from familiar forms of stratification by economic, political, or status group position, although it interacts with these other stratification systems. The principle of this system is that women take orders from men but do not give orders to them; hence only men can give orders to other men, and women can give orders only to other women. This principle is modified primarily when sexual stratification interacts with economic or other stratification (for example, when upper-class women give orders to male servants).

Table 2 shows that women managers are found almost exclusively in organizations hiring many women: apparel manufacturing, retail trade, hotels, laundries, schools, hospitals, and companies with huge clerical pools to be supervised, such as big banking, insurance, transportation, and utilities. In most organizations, women constitute a hermetically sealed promotional hierarchy of clerical workers and their immediate supervisors, usually regarded as so legitimate as to be taken for granted. Employers questioned about opportunities for promotion in their organizations generally view career opportunities for clerical workers as fully open, even though the top of this career channel is not higher-management positions. One personnel manager in a 1967 San Francisco area survey stated: "We never hire people for jobs who can't be upgraded. All of our file clerks are trained to become secretaries" (Collins, 1969: 234).

In the professions women are concentrated in specialties

*Table 2*

PERCENT OF ORGANIZATION WITH VARIOUS PERCENTAGES OF WOMEN MANAGERS, BY INDUSTRIAL SECTOR: SAN FRANCISCO-OAKLAND-SAN JOSE METROPOLITAN AREAS, 1967

| Industrial Sector | 0% | 0–4.9% | 5.0%–14.9% | 15.0% or more | T(%) | N |
|---|---|---|---|---|---|---|
| Construction | 87 | | 13 | | 100 | 23 |
| Food | 62 | 23 | 15 | | 100 | 26 |
| Apparel Manufacturing | | | 100 | | 100 | 2 |
| Printing, Paper, Chemicals, Metals, Machinery, Transportation Equipment, Other Manufacturing | 80 | 9 | 8 | 4 | 101 | 80 |
| Transportation and Utilities | 46 | 25 | 14 | 14 | 99 | 28 |
| General Merchandise Trade | 14 | | 14 | 71 | 99 | 7 |
| Apparel Trade | 33 | | | 67 | 100 | 3 |
| Eating and Drinking Places | 50 | | 25 | 25 | 100 | 4 |
| Other Trade | 73 | 9 | 9 | 9 | 100 | 22 |
| Finance | 40 | 20 | 30 | 10 | 100 | 20 |
| Hotels | | | 50 | 50 | 100 | 2 |
| Laundries | 33 | | | 67 | 100 | 3 |
| Business Services | 38 | 25 | 25 | 13 | 101 | 8 |
| Educational Services | 33 | | 22 | 44 | 99 | 9 |
| Medical Services | | | 20 | 80 | 100 | 10 |
| Other Services | 83 | | 17 | | 100 | 6 |
| Government | 18 | 46 | 36 | | 100 | 11 |
| *All Organizations* | 60 | 12 | 15 | 12 | 99 | 266 |

Source: Randall Collins, *Education and Employment* (Ph.D. dissertation, University of California at Berkeley, 1969, pp. 236–237).

where they deal principally with children or other women, rarely with men of high status (Epstein, 1970: 163–164). The highest-ranking women's job is likely to be president of a women's college or Mother Superior of an order of nuns. Similarly, women can be given high status as actresses or singers, but not as movie directors or symphony conductors, because they do not give orders to anyone.

Women's subordinate position at work may be viewed as a continuation of their subordinate position in the home. Although twentieth-century American society has changed a good deal from the traditional husbandly dictatorship, the female role in the home continues to center around that of domestic servant. The married woman has primary responsibility for cooking, dishwashing, laundering, housecleaning, and child care—occupational roles that are classified as low-prestige service positions when listed in the labor force. The modern American male is more likely to help voluntarily with some of these tasks than his ancestors or his non-Western counterparts (Goode, 1963: 66–70), but the responsibility for these tasks still rests generally with the woman, even if she has an outside job. The basic pattern is male dominance in practical activities both at home and at work, although there is some weakening of this pattern in some highly modern societies.

## *Basic Propositions*

What is the basis of this form of stratification? We may begin with two propositions: (1) that human beings have strong sexual and aggressive drives; and (2) that males are physically dominant over females, since they are generally bigger, and females are further made physically vulnerable by bearing and caring for children.[2] The combination of these propositions means that men will generally be the sexual aggressors, and women will be sexual prizes for men.

Evidence for this is widespread. Rape is defined as a crime only as committed by males, and cases of sexual assault by women are virtually unknown (Kanowitz, 1969: 18); men are the sexual aggressors in free-courtship systems; men are much more motivated by sexual interests as a reason for marriage, whereas women emphasize romantic love, intimacy, and affection more highly than men (Burgess and Wallin, 1953: 669; Burgess *et al.*, 1963: 368); exclusively male culture has a heavy component of sexual jokes, bragging of sexual conquests, pin-ups, and pornography, which have little or no equivalent among women (Polsky, 1967: 197); prostitution occurs almost exclusively among women, and male prostitutes are sex objects for male homosexuals, not for women (Kanowitz, 1969: 15–18);[3] men are much more likely to masturbate, experience sexual arousal earlier in life, and are generally more active sexually than women (Kinsey and Gebhard, 1953: 422–427). Men act as the sexual aggressors in modern society, as in virtually all other societies.

It is not necessary to assume a lesser sexual drive on the part of the human female to explain this pattern. There is reason to believe that female sexual drives are comparable to those of males (Ford and Beach, 1953), and that women are simply more deeply and pervasively repressed sexually than men. The sources of varying restraints on female sexuality will be discussed below, but the basic explanation can be derived from man's physical dominance. Human beings have relatively strong sexual preoccupations compared to most other animals, but even so, no one person is sexually arousable all the time. Since members of the bigger sex can force themselves on the smaller sex, the former can satisfy their sexual drives at will, whereas the latter have sex forced upon them at times they may not want it. Unattractive males can force themselves on attractive females, but unattractive females can rarely do the converse. Males thus become the sexual aggressors, and females generally adopt a defensive posture. The element of coercion is thus potentially present in every sexual encounter, and this shapes the fundamental features of the woman's role. As we shall see, sexual repression is a basic female tactic in this situation of struggle among unequals in physical strength.

### *Basic Pattern: Male Sexual Property*

The basic feature of sexual stratification is the institution of sexual property: the relatively permanent claim to exclusive sexual rights over a particular person. With male dominance, the principal form of sexual property is male ownership of females; bilateral sexual property is a modern variant which arises with an independent bargaining position of women.

Levi-Strauss (1949) has made the most sweeping use of the notion of sexual property, to explain the basic structure of kinship systems. Men taking permanent sexual possession of particular women constitutes the biological family; children are part of the family because they belong to the woman and hence to the owner of the woman. Within the family, we may note, the incest taboos reflect the facts of sexual property; indeed, they are the negative side of sexual property rights. The most serious kind of incest is mother-son incest, for this is a violation of the father's primary sexual property by his most immediate rival. Sibling incest violates the father's rights to dispose of the sexual property of his daughters as he sees fit. The father-daughter incest prohibition is hardest to explain in this fashion, although rules of sexual exchange can perhaps account for it.[4]

As Levi-Strauss argues, if sons cannot get women in their own families, they must get them elsewhere, and that means from those men who have women to spare—the fathers, brothers, or husbands who can give away their daughters, sisters, or wives. Levi-Strauss applies Marcel Mauss's model of gift-exchange systems to marriage customs: they are sets of rules which guarantee that if a man gives away some of his women, he can get others back from other families. In this way develop kinship networks properly speaking, as opposed to the biological family. Beneath variations in rules of descent, household locality, and marriage choice, kinship systems can be seen as based on sexual property and its related rules of sexual prohibition and exchange.

In modern societies, the pattern is overlaid with a complex set of moral injunctions backed up by church and state, but beneath the ideological surface similar forces operate. Marriage is fundamentally a socially enforced contract of sexual property, as indicated by the facts that marriage is usually not legal until sexually consummated, sexual assault within a marriage is not legally a rape, and the major traditional ground for divorce has been sexual infidelity (Kanowitz, 1969). That the basis of sexual property rights is male violence is still demonstrated by the generally acknowledged dispensation of fathers and brothers to kill rapists of their daughters and sisters.

Variations on this theme may be found historically. At the precultural level, primates are typically organized polygamously, with the strongest male surrounding himself with a retinue of females and driving the smaller and weaker males away. This pattern is also found in some human societies, where political and social power enables dominant men to get more than their share of women.

Once women have been acquired for sexual purposes, they may also be used as menial servants. In primitive societies, women are generally the agricultural and handcrafts workers, while men are the armed fighters and hunters.

One may say generally that sexual stratification is the sole basis of social stratification in societies with a very low technological level. In a situation of social instability, women are often regarded as booty in war,[5] and it is likely that the institution of slavery began with women and was later extended to men (Thompson, 1960: 196–198).

## *Variations in Sexual Stratification*

Male sexual property in women is the basic pattern of sexual stratification. Variations result from two factors: forms of social organization affecting the use of force, and those affecting the market positions of men and women. These two factors operate interdependently. Where force operates freely, the distribution of power among males determines the nature of sexual stratification quite straightforwardly, and women have no bargaining power of their own. In such a context, any market of sexual exchange operates only as part of the system of bargaining among heads of families and is based on family resources, not on the personal resources of individual men and women. A market for personal sexual qualities and other personal resources can emerge only where the private use of force is limited by the state. Thus the emergence of a personal sexual market, like that of an economic market, depends fundamentally on the emergence of a particular form of the organization of power. Hence, social structures determining the distribution of force and those producing individual resources for use on a sexual market must be treated together, as interrelated structural complexes.

Figure 1 presents in summary form hypotheses about the effects of four main types of social structure on sexual stratification. It states the male and female resources made available in each situation, the resulting system of sexual roles, and the dominant sexual ideology. *Low-technology tribal society* is that in which the degree of economic productivity allows little stratification. *Fortified households in stratified society* refers to the typical preindustrial organization based on independent households; it corresponds to Weber's patriarchal and patrimonial forms of organization. *Private households in market economy* refers to the typical domestic organization in a society dominated by the bureaucratic state, where the work place is separated from the home. *Advanced market economy* refers to the development of the preceding type into a society of a high level of affluence and widespread nonmanual employment. The four types of social structure are ideal types; combinations of these yield intermediate forms of stratification, combining elements from adjacent systems of sexual stratification.

### 1. *Low-Technology Tribal Society*

Societies in which the technology produces little or no economic surplus beyond that necessary to keep each producer alive have little economic, political, or status stratification (Lenski, 1966: 94–141). Accordingly, sexual stratification can exist only in a mild form. Superior male force can be used to enforce sexual property rights (marriage, incest taboos), but women cannot be forced to do a disproportionate amount of the work, since all members of society must work to survive. Insofar as work is divided and leisure is possible, women appear to work longer and at the more menial tasks. Since there is little surplus and little economic and political stratification, which intermarriages occur makes little difference to affected families; where the economic system does not permit substantial brideprices or dowries and no families are powerful enough to be highly preferred for political alliances, there is little reason for daughters to be strongly controlled, since they are not used as property in a bargaining system. Thus it is in low-technology tribal societies that most known norms favoring premarital sexual permissiveness are found.[6] The greater the economic surplus in such societies, the greater the tendency for male control over daughters to be asserted (Zelditch, 1964: 687), and for women to do a larger proportion of the menial labor.

### 2. *Fortified Households in Stratified Society*

In most historical preindustrial societies, the basic social unit is the fortified household (Weber, 1968: 356–384, 1006–1069). The use of force is not monopolized by the state:

*Figure 1*

TYPES OF SOCIAL STRUCTURE, SEXUAL STRATIFICATION, AND DOMINANT IDEOLOGIES

| Social Structure | Male and Female Resources | Sexual Roles | Dominant Ideology |
|---|---|---|---|
| 1. Low-Technology Tribal Society | Male: personal force, personal attractiveness<br>Female: personal attractiveness | Limited male sexual property; limited female exploitation | Incest taboos |
| 2. Fortified Households in Stratified Society | Male: organized force; control of property<br>Female: upper-class women head lineage during interregnum of male line | Strongly enforced male sexual property; high female exploitation; women as exchange property in family alliances | Male honor in controlling female chastity |
| 3. Private Households in Market Economy (protected by centralized state) | Male: control of income and property<br>Female: personal attractiveness; domestic service; emotional support | Sexual market of individual bargaining; bilateral sexual property in marriage | Romantic love ideal in courtship; idealized marriage bond |
| 4. Advanced Market Economy | Male: income and property; personal attractiveness; emotional support<br>Female: income and property; personal attractiveness; emotional support | Multidimensional sexual market of individual bargaining | Multiple ideologies |

economic and political organization usually coincides with the family community. Thus the owner of a farm, workshop, business, or political office not only makes his place of work or his official seat in his home; his own family helps in his work, as do family servants. All work subordinates are treated as servants (of higher or lower level) and are supported from the household economy. The family occurs in an intact form only around the heads of such establishments; servants generally do not have an active family of their own so much as they are attached to their master's family. In the absence of police or other peace-keeping forces, the household is an armed unit; its head is also its military commander. Such households may vary considerably in size, wealth, and power, from the court of a king or great lord through the households of substantial merchants and financiers, knightly manors down to households of minor artisans and peasants. Stratified below the heads of even the smallest units, however, are the nonhouseholders—propertyless workman, laborers, and servants.

In this form of social organization, male sexual dominance is maximized. The concentration of force and of economic resources in the hands of household heads gives them virtually unopposable control. Where sharp inequality among households permits, an upper class may practice polygamy or concubinage, monopolizing more than their share of females. Correspondingly, men of the servant and laborer classes are sexually deprived, and may never be permitted to marry. Women are most exploited in such societies; they are likely to make up a considerable proportion of the slave class if there is one, as in ancient Greek and Roman society or in Arab society. Wives and daughters as well do most of the menial work, while men concentrate on military pursuits or leisure (Goode, 1963: 90, 141).

Male rights in sexual property are asserted most strongly in this type of society. Intra-household alliances carry much weight in a situation of general distrust and sporadic warfare; the giving of women in marriage is virtually the only gift-exchange system which can produce such ties regularly, and substantial dowries or brideprices usually add weight to the bargain. Women are thus important among the householding classes as exchange property, and hence are closely guarded so as not to lose their market value; the institutions of the harem, the veil, the duenna, and the chaperone are employed here.

On the ideological side, sexual property is regarded as a form of male honor. The honored man is he who is dominant over others, who protects and controls his own property, and who can conquer others' property. In highly warlike societies like that of the Bedouin Arabs, the result is an overriding concern for adultery and the institution of extreme controls over women. The ideal of female chastity (including premarital virginity) is an aspect of male property rights and is regarded as enforceable only by males; women are commonly regarded as sexually amoral, unclean, and lacking in honor, and hence are to be controlled by force.[7] The practice of clitoridectomy among the Bedouin in order to reduce women's sexual drives is an extreme reflection of this belief (Goode, 1963: 147, 211).

The ideological pattern is based on the fact that women are used as sexual objects for the men who properly own them; they are to act as sexual creatures, although within the confines of a male property system. Total asceticism by women is not allowed. Hence women have low status in the religious systems of societies of this type. In Brahmanism, Islam, Jainism, Confucianism, and the official Roman cults, women are usually regarded as incapable of detaching themselves from the mundane world, and high religious status is reserved for men.[8]

Women can achieve power of their own in this system only as adjuncts to dominant men. Thus the wife of a household head may derive some power over men servants in the household; in the case of a noblewoman, this can produce considerable deference. In the extreme case, a woman may exercise absolute authority as head of a household lineage during an interregnum in the male line. That this is an exceptional circumstance is proved by the fact that the general status of women does not improve during the reign of a queen; queens like Elizabeth I of England or Catherine the Great of Russia may combine a severe personal autocracy with the enforcement of traditional status of women in society.

In the lower ranks of fortified households, neither men nor women have much honor. Sexual permissiveness here is possible where opportunity permits, although women at the more attractive ages are likely to be monopolized (perhaps *sub rosa*) by their masters or masters' sons (Marcus, 1964: 77–160). In general, only the upper-class women will have the leisure and wealth to make themselves sexually attractive; there may also be some genetic selection for attractiveness among upper-class women, as dominant males may select attractive women from the lower orders as mates. What is left is a true sexual underground, with neither stable opportunities for marriage, ideological restraints in the form of notions of sexual honor, nor physical attractiveness and personal leisure. Sexual activity among the underclasses of traditional society must have had much of the elements of the grotesque. This circumstance may have helped the growth of Puritanism among the lower middle class during the breakdown of traditional society.

### 3. *Private Households in Market Economy*

The basic structure of home life changes with the rise of the centralized bureaucratic state claiming a monopoly on the legitimate use of violence. A complex of interrelated changes occur: the grand household declines with the diminution of private armaments (Stone, 1967: 96–134). The centralized state usually fosters expansion of commerce and industry, hence a proliferation of (*a*) small shops and crafts enterprises; and (*b*) large industrial establishments separated from the household. The bureaucratic agencies of the state provide further workplaces separate from the household (Weber, 1968: 375–381; 956–1003). The result is that households become smaller and more private, consisting more exclusively of a single family. With the expansion of a market economy, more persons can afford households of their own; a private family-oriented middle class appears (Aries, 1962: 365–404).

In this situation, sexual roles also change. The use of force by men to control women diminishes as household armaments disappear and the state monopolizes violence, especially with the setting up of a police force to which appeal can be made in violent domestic disputes. Men remain heads of household and control its property; they monopolize all desirable occupations in state and economy as well. Women become at least potentially free to negotiate their own sexual relationships, but since their main resource is their sexuality, the emerging free marriage market is organized around male trades of economic and status resources for possession of a woman. In petty bourgeois families lacking servants, women serve not only as sexual objects but as domestic labor as well. Where the crowded setting of a large household is replaced by the comparative solitude of a small one, the woman also can become an important source of companionship and emotional support. The woman's capacity to provide these things are her resources on the sexual market. In wealthier families, the woman's resources may also include her family's wealth and social status, although the general importance of interfamily alliances based on marriage diminishes as political and economic aid can be acquired from nonfamily organizations.

The ideology arising from this situation is that of romantic love, including a strong element of sexual repression. The most favorable female strategy, in a situation where men control the economic world, is to maximize her bargaining power by appearing both as attractive and as inaccessible as possible. Thus develops the ideal of femininity, in which sexuality is idealized and only indirectly hinted as an ultimate source of attraction, since sexuality must be reserved as a bargaining resource for the male wealth and income that can only be stably acquired through a marriage contract. An element of sexual repression is thus built into the situation in which men and women bargain with unequal goods.

In contrast to the male-supported female chastity norm of traditionalistic societies, the romantic sexual repression is upheld principally by the interests of women. A hierarchy of moral evaluation emerges among women, in which women who sell their favors for short-run rewards (prostitutes, "loose women") are dishonored; this moral code reflects female interests in confining sexuality to use as a bargaining resource only for marriage (cf. Riesman, 1956).

Within marriage itself, women can use their improved bargaining position to demand the extension of sexual property norms to the husband. Adultery becomes tabooed not only for women but for men. The strategy for the improvement of women's position both before and after marriage is the same: the idealization of sexuality, made possible by women's newly freed bargaining position and greater protection from violence. Sexual bargaining now takes place by idealized gestures and symbolization rather than through the frank negotiations of traditional parents or marriage brokers. The attractive (and the wealthy) woman, in particular, can demand much deference during courtship, including an outright ban on direct sexual advances and discussions. Sexuality is referred to only under its idealized aspect of spiritual devotion and aesthetic beauty, i.e. the romantic love ideal. Male sexual motives operate beneath the surface of polite manners, but they are forced out of official consciousness. It is in these social situations that sexuality becomes repressed in the sense that Freud observed it.

The romantic love ideal is thus a key weapon in the attempt of women to raise their subordinate position by taking advantage of a free-market structure. Used in courtship, it creates male deference; after marriage, it expresses and reinforces women's attempt to control the sexual aggressiveness of their husbands both toward themselves and toward other women. The idealized view of the marriage bond as a tie of mutual fidelity and devotion calls for absolute restriction of sexuality to marriage, thereby reinforcing the sexual bargaining power of the wife, since she is the only available sex object. Idealization further has the effect of reducing female subordination within marriage by sublimating aggressive male drives into mutual tenderness.

Goode (1959) has emphasized that this romantic love norm reflects increased needs for personal emotional support in a society of relatively isolated nuclear households. Both historical shifts from the large households of traditional society (Goode, 1963; Aries, 1962) and current shifts from the crowded, public living conditions of modern working-class life to a more affluent private home life (Rainwater, 1964) show an increase in the ideal and in mutual emotional support of spouses. This shift to greater interpersonal reliance is undoubtedly one source of the romantic love ideal; however, its classical features, notably the repression and idealization of sexuality, appear to derive only from the struggle over sexual domination. In this perspective, the needs of man for psychological support become important primarily as an additional bargaining point for women in attempting to improve their power position within the family. As the stratification theory predicts, woman are a good deal more attached to the romantic ideal than are men (Burgess *et al.*, 1963: 368).

The first approximation to the private-household market-economy structure appeared in the cities of the Roman empire, and it is here that the first major love ideal is found as well, contained within Christianity. Christianity had its origins among the small independent craftsmen, merchants, degraded landowners, and other petty bourgeois of this flourishing international economy (Weber, 1968: 481–484). Its major innovations were: (*a*) it established a community independent of family or ethnic ties; (*b*) it admitted women to full and equal membership. The first feature Christianity shares with the other great world religions: Buddhism, Islam, and (to a lesser degree) Confucianism; the latter feature was developed nowhere else to a similar degree. Indeed, the appeal to women was a key in Christianity's rapid spread and eventual success over its rivals (Weber, 1968: 488–490). The Christian community was united among its members by spiritual love and shared norms of asceticism; in a Durkheimian interpretation, the theological doctrine of mutual love between Christ and his followers reflects and sanctions this community bond. Christianity in this regard appears to be an adaptation of Oriental asceticism and spiritualism to an urban lower-middle-class community which could not escape into mystical contemplation in a tropical countryside.

The process by which Christianity arose cannot be reconstructed precisely. There was clearly an affinity of interests between the lower-middle-class women who were acquiring a sexual bargaining position during the shift from a society of armed households to the comparatively peaceful and highly commercial society of the Roman empire and the Christian priests attempting to spread an ascetic spiritual movement by acquiring new converts. A corollary of Christian church membership was the confining of sexuality to Christian marriage, with its idealized and desexualized view of the marriage bond. It is possible that the changed position of women in the Roman lower middle class had an important effect in shaping Christianity; it is also conceivable that the rise of the religion was important in raising women's status by giving them strong allies in the church. Probably influences operated in both directions.[9]

Until the modern industrial era, religious organizations have been virtually the only specialized culture-transmitting institution; hence all ideologies tended to take religious form, including the ideologies of sexual interest groups. The early Christian expression of the romantic love ideal has been obscured historically because of the decline of urban Rome and the reruralization of European society until approximately the fifteenth century A.D. The fortified household reappeared as the principal social structure; women's position reverted to traditional subordination. When private middle-class households do reemerge with the bureaucratic European state of the sixteenth and seventeenth centuries, the romantic love ideal, the idealized family ties, and the repression of male sexuality develop with it (Stone, 1967: 269–302; see also de Rougemont, 1956: 49–139). The Victorian ethic of extreme prudery and sentimental idealization does not originate in the nineteenth century; it is an ideal of middle-class families, and especially of middle-class women, found as far back as the early stages of emancipation of middle-class households from the great households of patrimonial society. Its original ideological form was Christian, although the rise of secular culture (through the mass reading market and public education) has given it other cultural bases. Where the private middle-class household spreads throughout the modernizing world, the romantic/puritanical love ideal seems likely to spread.

The romantic ideal has one major weakness as a strategy for improving the position of women. It is based on the relative inaccessibility of women as sexual objects; it is a strategy of "hard-to-get," of demanding idealized devotion (and firm economic contracts) in return for sexual access. This strategy maintains the cultural barrier between men and women; the very idealization of women, where it is most successful, keeps them confined in a fantasy world of aesthetic symbols, to be protected from the actualities of political conflict, economic activity, and aggressive sexual desire. Thus, male control of the economic world is reinforced because women with the greatest resources idealize themselves out of it; the all-male "backstage" (Goffman, 1959) culture of sexual jokes and discussions has served as a tangible social barrier against the employment of women in male-dominated occupations. Moreover, women must rely on men to protect their inaccessibility from sexual assault; the "helpless female" ideal, the woman as object to be protected, is simultaneously a way of exacting deference from men and of being trapped in a female role.[10]

### 4. *Advanced Market Economy*

A further shift in bargaining resources occurs with the attainment of a high level of affluence and the rise of widespread employment opportunities for women. Women become freed from parental homes to go to school and to work. This not only makes the sexual market freer, by reducing parental controls, but also gives women additional bargaining resources. To the extent that women have their own incomes, they are free to strike their bargains without economic compulsion; and their incomes may become a bargaining resource of their own.

As Table 1 (p. 55) shows, women's occupational position even in advanced industrial society does not match that of men. Hence the older sexual market in which female attractiveness tends to be traded for male economic prospects continues to operate (Elder, 1969; cf. also Waller, 1937). In the working class, however, a woman's earning capacity may be an important resource in establishing sexual relationships (although it may be balanced off by a freer use of male force; see Liebow, 1967: 137–160). In the educated middle class, women with qualifications for professional jobs can double a family income, and hence represent considerable bargaining power. In general, the higher the relative income of a wife compared to her husband, the greater her power within the family (Zelditch, 1964: 707); this circumstance, no doubt, gives a woman some bargaining power before marriage as well. Although women are far from economically equal with men, it is now possible for a number of different things to be bargained: income resources as well as sexual attractiveness, social status, personal compatibility, deference, and emotional support. The greater freedom of women from economic dependence on men means that sexual bargains can be less concerned with marriage; dating can go on as a form of short-run bargaining, in which both men and women trade on their own attractiveness or capacity to entertain in return for sexual favors and/or being entertained. Where women bring economic resources of their own, they may concentrate on bargaining for sexual attractiveness on the part of men. The result is the rise, especially in youth culture, of the ideal of male sexual attractiveness (Walster *et al.*, 1966). A pure market based on ranking in terms of sexuality, in the sense discussed by Zetterberg (1966), thus becomes more prominent for both men and women, but as only one of the many sexual markets in existence.

This is the situation in which the current ideology of women's liberation gains a following. As long as men controlled virtually all economic resources, women's primary strategy was to emphasize the feminine ideal, and with it to accept the compartmentalization of life which reinforced male economic dominance. Working-class women, who were in the least favorable position to use the feminine ideal, first cracked the job barrier on the manual level; lower-middle-class clerical workers provided a further opening, and the expansion of college attendance by middle-class girls (originally motivated primarily by status and husband-hunting considerations) has mobilized a large number of women with at least some work experience (usually clerical) and the capacity to articulate a new ideology, or at least to debunk previous ideologies of femininity.

## *Combined Patterns*

We have been dealing with ideal types. Historical reality is usually a mixture of forms and processes; we may characterize different historical situations (and the situations of different social classes in each period) by a particular weighting of resources in the struggle over sexual dominance.

Thus, force is still available as a male resource even in the modern middle class. A 1954–55 survey of girls at a midwestern college found that slightly more than half of them experienced sexual attacks, with the average number of reported experiences being six times in the year (Kirkpatrick and Kanin, 1957). (In another study, Kanin [1967] reported that 23 percent of a sample of midwestern male undergraduates admitted attempting rape on dates.) Paradoxically, the more serious the attack—attempted intercourse vs. petting below the waist vs. petting above the waist—the *less* likely was the girl to report it to the authorities or even to talk about it with her girl friends. The reason becomes clear when we find that the more severe assaults usually came from steady boy friends or fiancés. The closer to marriage, the more sex is expected.[11]

Thus a mild use of force is taken into account in the dating system; women generally allow themselves to be made subject to force only after a tentative bargain has been struck. The availability of male force simply adds another element to the bargaining situation, and generally requires women to take the role of the sexually pursued, and thus to attempt to enforce an ideal of some degree of sexual inaccessibility except under the idealized bond of romantic love.

As a general principle, the more male violence is available

in a sexual market, the more puritanical and sentimental the female ideology. Thus, working-class women are more puritanical than middle-class women (Rainwater, 1964), since male violence must be more continuously guarded against; it is among stably married working-class women that the distinction between respectable women and "loose" women is most strongly enunciated.

The casual use of force is most prevalent in societies organized around fortified households. As we have seen above, this type of social organization produces severe controls over female sexuality, but primarily as external restraints imposed by men. In the period of transition from the situation of patriarchal dominance to that of private households in a peaceful market economy, men's interests in controlling their women and women's interests in improving their position through an idealization of sexuality are likely to coincide in producing a maximal degree of puritanism. Idealization requires that women, although desired sexual objects on the courtship market, should be inaccessible to male assault; this allows women to exact deference and at least overt cooperation in idealizing themselves from prospective suitors. But in a situation where violence is still widespread, women must depend on men to protect them. Thus the initial effort at idealization leads women to reinforce patriarchal efforts at female sexual restraint; the improvement in women's power position comes only from extending this restraint to the men themselves—in effect, getting men to enforce sexual restraint on each other and hence on themselves.

The period of the greatest idealization and of sexual repression, then, is the transitional one in which the first great battle is fought by women to raise their status, using as resources both their new personal worth on a courtship market, and male ideologies and interests in female chastity surviving from traditional society. The heights of European sexual repressiveness, referred to popularly as Victorianism, were not confined to the nineteenth century; sexual puritanism developed as far back as the fifteenth century wherever the fortified household was giving way to the newer middle-class home. However, in the nineteenth century the number of families first undergoing the transition was great enough to make sexual puritanism into a dominant public ideology (cf. Marcus, 1964: 77–160). As the new family structure came to prevail and the relatively peaceful middle-class social order became taken for granted, extreme sexual restraint disappeared.

Freud's discoveries about sexual repression and idealization thus grew out of a particular historical era, as he treated the casualties of the first major battle in the struggle for woman's liberation. The pattern emerges in other places, however, whenever the same combination of conditions occurs. Families undergoing change from traditional rural settings to urban middle-class settings are likely to be the most puritanical, for the patriarchal organization tends to prevail in the countryside (especially in more backwoods or frontier areas), and hence the initial battle for woman's liberation is still being fought. Societies which attempt massive modernization, such as the Soviet Union or Communist China, thus generally undergo periods of sexual repressiveness during the transition.[12]

As the peaceful market system becomes fully established, the degree of sexual restraint relaxes, and the feminine ideal becomes more overtly sensual and less sentimentalized.[13] This does not foreshadow universal promiscuousness, however. Sexual attractiveness can still be used as a bargaining resource, although in a more complex market than previously; it remains a resource only to the extent that it is not simply given away. Hence we find only a mild increase in the rate of premarital intercourse in mid-twentieth-century America, a society in which the advanced market situation has been most nearly approached (Reiss, 1960: 228–234). Further shifts in sexual ideologies depend upon further equalization of the economic positions of women.[14] The cumulative advantage of males as a group monopolizing higher occupational positions would tend to reinforce existing emphases in the market of sexual relationships, and vice versa. Breakthroughs in one sphere of the struggle for sexual dominance thus would have repercussions in other spheres.

## *Conclusions*

The area of sexual relations may thus be fruitfully analyzed in terms taken from the conflict theory of stratification begun by Marx and Weber. Sexual stratification is analytically separable from stratification based on power, material property, or ideal status, in that it involves yet another good: sexual attractiveness itself. On a higher level of abstraction, the processes and arrangements of resources that determine variations in sexual subordination and in sexual ideals are similar to those emphasized by Weber in analyzing stratification as it is more conventionally defined. In general, variations in the distribution of the means of violence, and within the context set by this organization of violence, variations in market resources, determine both sexual behavior and sexual ideology. The prospects are good that the conflict theory of stratification may be extended to include a general theory of the forms of family structure and behavior.

NOTES

1. I am indebted to Joseph R. Gusfield and Stanford M. Lyman for critical comments on an earlier version of this paper.
2. Liebow (1967: 95–96) gives modern examples of how, in the relatively open sexual warfare of the urban black, lower-class men can exploit a woman's vulnerability through her children.
3. Gigolos are an exception. However, it appears that they cater exclusively to wealthy, elderly unmarried women (spinsters and widows), and the role occurs only in societies in which women are relatively emancipated from male control. Thus the stereotype of the wealthy American widow and the young man from Latin America or other relatively poor society.
4. Father-daughter incest is by far the most common form of incest, especially if the mother is dead or absent (Weinberg, 1955).
5. The *Iliad* gives a readily accessible example; the whole Trojan War is fought over possession of a woman, and Homer's poem begins with a quarrel between Achilles and Agamemnon over women captives.
6. This may be established from the data in Murdock (1949: 260–283), which deal almost exclusively with tribal societies and show widespread norms of sexual permissiveness; and in Goode (1963), which show strong restraints on sexual per-

missiveness in stratified agrarian societies, somewhat modified with industrialization.

7. The literature of medieval Arab culture shows an obsession with maintaining sexual property in the harems; the unabridged *Arabian Nights* consists largely of variations on the plot of men whose wives are unfaithful, usually with male slaves.
8. Christianity is a partial exception, for reasons discussed below. Buddhism in practice tends to give low status to women, although not in theory. Some of the heterodox Hindu and Buddhist-Taoist cults did explicitly include women as full members. See Weber (1968: 488–490).
9. In general, women's greater religious attachment and religious conservatism (in Christian countries at least) reflects the continuing alliance between the interests of priests in promoting spiritualism and asceticism, and women in protecting themselves against subordination to male sexual aggression. See Fichter (1952); Glock *et al.* (1967: 41–59).
10. Women's propensity to political conservatism (Lipset, 1960: 260) may be explained by their special reliance on the state to control private violence. "Law and order," for women, appears to have a special sexual meaning, as rhetoric about "crime in the streets" abundantly implies. The appearance of this conservatism, following the successful late-Victorian campaign for women's suffrage, is no anomaly, considering the nature of the battle for sexual liberation in that period. That the women's suffrage movement should overlap substantially with the temperance movement (Gusfield, 1963: 88–91) is in keeping with the conflict theory here presented; the prohibition of alcohol was an effort to eliminate a substance that made men uninhibited, as well as to destroy a masculine sanctuary, the saloon.
11. Conversely, rapes that are reported are almost always committed by strangers (Svalastoga, 1962). We can surmise that many successful rapes are never mentioned, because they are committed by boy friends.
12. Indeed, there may be an explicit alliance between radical politicians and women in bringing about a revolution both within the traditional male-dominated family and in the larger society; this has occurred most prominently in Communist China, and to a lesser degree in the Soviet Union.
13. The history of clothing styles could provide a further test of this hypothesis, as would changes in the sexual ideals depicted in literature.
14. Even in a situation of full economic equality, domestic domination would not necessarily disappear in all cases. Domestic service and personal subservience are goods that could be offered on the market, and less attractive or economically

productive persons could make an improved sexual bargain by offering them. Women are currently still household servants in conventional marriages because their economic disadvantage makes this part of the standard sexual contract. With greater economic equality, this might be part of the bargain by either sex in particular cases.

REFERENCES

Aries, Phillipe (1962). *Centuries of Childhood.* New York: Random House.

Berg, Ivar (1970). *Education and Jobs: The Great Training Robbery.* New York: Praeger.

Burgess, Ernest W., and Paul Wallin (1953). *Engagement and Marriage.* Philadelphia: Lippincott.

———, Harvey Locke, and Mary Thomas (1963). *The Family.* New York: American Book Company (3rd edn.).

Elder, Glenn H., Jr. (1969). "Appearance and Education in Marriage Mobility," *American Sociological Review,* 34: 519–533.

Epstein, Cynthia Fuchs (1970). *Woman's Place.* Berkeley: University of California Press.

Fichter, Joseph H. (1952). "The Profile of Catholic Religious Life," *American Journal of Sociology,* 58: 145–149.

Ford, Clelland S., and Frank A. Beach (1953). *Patterns of Sexual Behavior.* New York: Harper.

Glock, Charles Y., Benjamin B. Ringer, and Earl R. Babbie (1967). *To Comfort and to Challenge.* Berkeley: University of California Press.

Goffman, Erving (1959). *The Presentation of Self in Everyday Life.* New York: Doubleday.

Goode, William J. (1959). "The Theoretical Importance of Love," *American Sociological Review,* 24: 38–47.

——— (1963). *World Revolution and Family Patterns.* New York: Free Press.

Gusfield, Joseph R. (1963). *Symbolic Crusade.* Urbana: University of Illinois Press.

Kanin, Eugene (1967). "Reference Groups and Sex Conduct Norm Violation," *Sociological Quarterly,* 8: 495–504.

Kanowitz, Leo (1969). *Women and the Law.* Albuquerque: University of New Mexico Press.

Kinsey, Alfred C., and Paul H. Gebhard (1953). *Sexual Behavior in the Human Female.* Philadelphia: Saunders.

Kirkpatrick, Clifford, and Eugene Kanin (1957). "Male Sex Aggression on a University Campus," *American Sociological Review,* 22: 52–58.

Lenski, Gerhard (1966). *Power and Privilege.* New York: McGraw-Hill.

Levi-Strauss, Claude (1949). *Les Structures Elémentaires de la Parente.* Paris: Presses Universitaires de France.

Liebow, Elliot (1967). *Tally's Corner.* Boston: Little, Brown.

Lipset, Seymour Martin (1960). *Political Man.* New York: Doubleday.

Marcus, Steven (1964). *The Other Victorians.* New York: Basic Books.

Murdock, George Peter (1949). *Social Structure.* New York: Macmillan.

Polsky, Ned (1967). *Hustlers, Beats, and Others.* Chicago: Aldine.

Rainwater, Lee (1964). "Sexual Life and Interpersonal Intimacy: Class Patterns," *Journal of Marriage and the Family,* 26: 457–466.

Reiss, Ira L. (1960). *Premarital Sexual Standards in America.* New York: Free Press.

Riesman, David (1956). "Introduction," pp. v–xv, in John R. Seeley, R. Alexander Sim, and Elizabeth W. Loosley, *Crestwood Heights.* New York: Basic Books.

Rougemont, Denis de (1956). *Love in the Western World.* New York: Pantheon.

Stone, Lawrence (1967). *The Crisis of the Aristocracy, 1558–1641.* New York: Oxford University Press.

Svalastoga, Kaare (1962). "Rape and Social Structure," *Pacific Sociological Review,* 5: 48–53.

Thompson, E. A. (1960). "Slavery in Early Germany," pp. 191–203, in Moses I. Finley (ed.), *Slavery in Classical Antiquity.* Cambridge: W. Heffer and Sons.

Waller, Willard (1937). "The Rating and Dating Complex," *American Sociological Review,* 2: 727–734.

Walster, Elaine, Vera Aronson, Darcy Abrahams, and Leon Rotterman (1966). "Importance of Physical Attractiveness in Dating Behavior," *Journal of Personality and Social Psychology,* 4: 508–516.

Weber, Max (1968). *Economy and Society.* New York: Bedminster Press.

Weinberg, S. K. (1955). *Incest Behavior.* New York: Citadel Press.

Zelditch, Morris, Jr. (1964). "Family, Marriage, and Kinship," pp. 680–733, in R. E. L. Faris (ed.), *Handbook of Modern Sociology.* Chicago: Rand McNally.

Zetterberg, Hans L. (1966). "The Secret Ranking," *Journal of Marriage and the Family,* 27: 134–142.

# II

# *Marriage and the Prisons of Love*

*Wedlock is the fate of nearly 90 percent of the population. Consequently the struggle of the sexes is to a large extent identical with marital conflicts. Yet the marriage rate has been increasing continuously over the past decades. Martha Baum of the Ontario Institute for Studies in Education, in Toronto, reports in her article "Love, Marriage, and the Division of Labor" findings from a study of marriage motivation. A highly consistent image of marriage, as an institution in which to realize a comprehensive companionship with a partner of compatible temperament and similar life goals, emerged from her interviews with young engaged men and women, first published in* Sociological Inquiry, *Vol. 41, 1971. These findings have demonstrable implications for existing theoretical formulations about the dysfunctional aspects of the love marriage in contemporary American society. It is contended that "romantic idealization" during courtship leads to a high incidence of dissatisfaction and disruption. Findings from numerous studies are reviewed to present an alternative explanation for marital conflict in the context of the modern division of labor which (in view of the sharp role segregation by sex) integrates the spheres of work and the family but poorly.*

*This disjunction between work and family leads not only to the underprivileged position for women but also to an ambivalence of the husband's role. The once dominant child-frightening Victorian paterfamilias has turned into the embattled American husband-father of today. He is, as Ersel E.*

*LeMasters, a specialist in family sociology, has put it in his article "The Passing of the Dominant Husband-Father," "a family court jester . . . struggling to maintain his self-image in the face of an aggressive wife-mother and a powerful adolescent peer group." LeMasters, Professor of Sociology at the University of Wisconsin, Madison, explores factors which have contributed to the devaluation of the father role: the Great Depression, the increased frequency of divorce, women's drive for equality, and youth's challenge of father's authority and his values. His article was first published in 1971 by the UNESCO journal* Impact of Science on Society.

*Yet the embattled husband-father still holds the resources of power in the marital struggle, as Dair L. Gillespie shows in her essay on "Who Has the Power? The Marital Struggle." Her data point to the conclusion that differences in marital power are not due to individual resources or the personal competence of the partners but to the discrimination of women in the larger society. Dair Gillespie, who is writing a dissertation on this topic at the University of California, Berkeley, claims that husbands gain power in marriage as a class, not as individuals. Women are blocked as a class, not as individuals. Her article, which first appeared in 1971 in the* Journal of Marriage and the Family, *examines the sources of marital power (socialization, the marriage contract, income, occupational prestige, organizational participation, education, suburbanization, the family life cycle, physical coercion) and finds them to work for an unequal distribution of power in both black and white, white-collar and blue-collar families.*

# 4

# Love, Marriage, and the Division of Labor[1]

MARTHA BAUM

MANY SOCIAL SCIENTISTS in the United States have been concerned with the linkage of love[2] with marriage in modern society, particularly with respect to its functions, given contemporary social arrangements on the one hand, and its dysfunctions, given the high rate of marital disruption on the other. Although the institutionalization of love is viewed as serving both social system and personality needs, love is also defined as essentially romantic and therefore as seriously interfering with mate choice for companionship, which provides the cohesive core in modern marriage (Burgess, Locke, and Thomes, 1963; Luckey, 1960; Hobart, 1958; Christensen, 1958; Winch, Ktsanes, and Ktsanes, 1953).

Data from young engaged couples are presented in this paper to support two alternative hypotheses to the romantic-love theme. First, although American men and women do marry primarily for love, their conception of love is not basically romantic and therefore "irrational," as has been contended. Second, contemporary criteria for mate choice and marital goals are explicitly oriented toward the establishment of a comprehensive companionship on a number of dimensions. The results presented here substantiate studies which have found that marriages are made on the basis of general compatibility and contradict inferences which have been drawn from material on dating. Existing findings about marital satisfaction and dissolution are assimilated to propose an explanation for the failure of the companionate marriage in a framework of role segregation for spouses, in spheres with different value priorities and role obligations. On the evidence, it is this segregation which interferes with attempts to establish good communication and empathy between husband and wife.

## *Love and Marriage: Institutionalization and Functions in Contemporary Society*

Romantic love, as a concept in Western society, is generally thought to have originated in about the twelfth century (Biegel, 1951). Love, however, has existed historically and cross-culturally largely outside marriage until recent times (Goode, 1963; Benedict, 1946; Linton, 1936). In modern Western societies, love became institutionalized as the basis for marriage, especially in the middle class and most especially in the United States, through structural changes in society which led to the differentiation of the family from other social systems (Parsons and Bales, 1955; Gerth and Mills, 1953; van der Haag, 1964; Burgess, Locke, and Thomes, 1964). That the anonymity of modern urban life has led to a need for deep, stable personal attachments and that these are almost necessarily to be found mainly in the nuclear family, since other ties tend to be ephemeral in a highly mobile, rapidly changing, social world, seems to be a matter of fairly general agreement (Parsons, 1949; Schorr, 1962). From the point of view of society, love has to be institutionalized in order to maintain the family as the child-bearing and socializing unit in the context of a materialistic culture where individuals would have to be motivated to make economic sacrifices in order to fill family roles (Greenfield, 1969; Caplow, 1964). One means for tying love and marriage tightly together was a strong conviction on the part of the American middle class that sexual involvement is morally justifiable only in the context of a deep and lasting relationship, a relationship that culminates in or is expected to culminate in marriage (Greenfield, 1969: 351). Love as a basis for marriage, then, is very widely viewed as functional for the maintenance of social institutions (Waller and Hill, 1951; Burchinal, 1959), as well as for the psychological well-being of the individual (Foote, 1953; Kolb, 1950).

### *Dysfunctional Consequences of Love*

Yet the concentration of affective needs, expressed as love, in the family and most especially in the marital dyad is also seen as leading to a high incidence of marital disruption. This seeming paradox occurs because love is defined as highly romantic and therefore has been described as "institutionalized irrationality" in the context of an otherwise very rationally oriented culture (Greenfield, 1969: 361). The usually sober, pragmatic American is said to allow himself to give way to impossible idealization of the "only one," and this idealization leads inevitably to disillusion and disenchantment when combined with the everyday realities of married life (Hunt, 1959; Burgess and Locke, 1953). For romantic love to be preserved, some distance must be maintained between the lovers (van der Haag, 1964: 92–101). As Keats said of the lover frozen in pursuit of his lady on a Grecian urn: "Forever wilt thou love and she be fair." Perhaps the most important consideration is that the belief that "love conquers all" is thought to lead to mate choice regardless of considerations of compatibility in temperaments, tastes, and life aspirations (Groves, 1947; Waller, 1938). Marriages, then, are subject to stress and possible dissolution as the euphoria of love begins to wane and the actual, rather than the idealized, characteristics of the partner are revealed (Pineo, 1961).

A variant on the mutual-love theme is that men marry for romantic reasons and women for security (Mogey, 1969; Henry, 1966). This proposition evidently stems from the division of labor in the nuclear family where the husband is generally responsible for the economic (or instrumental) sphere and the wife for the socioemotional (or affective) sphere in the management of the household (Parsons, 1955; Zelditch, 1964). In order to provide the appropriate matrix for child-rearing in the nuclear family, the man offers security to the woman who, in turn, appeals to him on an emotional basis. The feminine appeal appears to be composed of a mixture of glamour or sex appeal and flattery (Bernard, 1968). In this version, then, the man becomes romantically disillusioned while the woman may complain about her husband's inadequacies as a provider.

### *Love as Companionship—An Alternate Hypothesis*

There are factors which cast doubt on the primacy of the "irrational romantic" component of love as a basis for marriage. For one thing it has been demonstrated that marriages are generally made between individuals within specific cultural categories, that is, from similar ethnic, racial, religious, educational, and socioeconomic backgrounds (Hollingshead, 1950; Katz and Hill, 1956). It has been pointed out that, through mechanisms of control operating through the family and the peer group, mate choice is actually reduced to a small field of eligibles (Goode, 1959; Mogey, 1969: 248–259). On the basis of these studies, the notion that free choice governed by blind attraction alone is the foundation for marriage becomes highly questionable. Further, it appears that control over mate choice is not completely unrecognized by those involved in the sense that people believe they marry solely on the grounds of personal choice without regard for other considerations; rather, individuals appear to eliminate as possible partners those with dissimilar backgrounds (Strauss, 1954; Bogardus, 1933). Marrying within cultural categories has been related to value consensus among partners (Schellenberg, 1960). In addition, Kerckhoff and Davis (1962) have shown, in a panel study of couples who were "engaged, going steady, or seriously involved," that not only were mate choices made from very similar backgrounds, but value consensus between partners tended to increase with the duration and feeling of permanence in the relationship. The Rapoports, particularly (Rapoport and Rapoport, 1965; Rapoport, 1964; Rapoport and Rapoport, 1964), in a unique depth study of a small number of young couples during engagement and the first year of marriage, have documented the deliberate care with which young people prepare for marriage and the number of life concerns which they discuss and attempt to resolve to mutual satisfaction before the marriage is consummated. These engaged men and women perceived themselves to be "in love" but appeared to see love in terms of being able to communicate with and understand one another, enjoying being together, and liking the same things. On the evidence, then, severe "reality shock" does not seem to be a very feasible explanation for marital dissatisfaction.

The belief that women marry primarily for economic security also does not seem to be supported by data which show that the overwhelming majority of both men and women say that what they desire most in marriage is love (Goldsen *et al.*, 1960). It would indeed be difficult to reconcile a desire for financial security with the early age of first marriages in the United States today: the median age for women is about twenty, for men, twenty-two (Burchinal, 1969: 499). The young husbands have not at this stage had much of an opportunity to prove themselves in the labor force. Rather it appears that very early marriage is possible because the women work and contribute to the support of the family in the early years at least (Myrdal and Klein, 1968).

Thus it appears possible that modern love has undergone a transformation and is a rather different phenomenon from that described by the Victorian poets or the troubadours of the Middle Ages. However, although the desire for love in marriage has been documented, there has been no systematic attempt to obtain definitions of love and relate them to marital goals and mate choice. It was for this purpose that the exploratory study to be reported on below was carried out in 1966, using as respondents young American men and women who were engaged and planning to be married within a short time.

## *Design, Method, and Sample*

For the purpose of investigating the problem outlined, it was necessary to gain information from the same respondents about several areas which are seen as crucial for the understanding of the love-marriage relationship. Questions had to be asked about the importance of love as a basis for marriage, the meaning of the term "love" in this context, the goals which are sought in marriage, and the desirable and undesirable characteristics of a marital partner. Once the main concerns of the study had been decided upon, a schematic outline of the possible goals to be sought in marriage was devised as guideline for the construction of the research instrument. The areas included dealt with aspects of the couple relationship per se, such as personal, philosophical (i.e., aspirations and life goals) and sexual compatibility. Other intracouple concerns identified were the management of the household division of labor and the desire for children. But we also wanted to explore relationships of the couple to other social spheres; therefore, orientations toward socioeconomic rewards, social life, recreation, community affairs, religion, and relations to other kin were included in the outline.

Given scarce resources, a questionnaire was developed for distribution to respondents. An attempt was made to compensate somewhat for the limitations of the questionnaire method of approach by deciding to arrange brief face-to-face talks with prospective respondents when the questionnaires were given out. In this way, it would be possible to make clear the purposes of the study and reinforce the instructions on the form, particularly those which very strongly urged that the questionnaire be filled out by the respondent alone without conferring with anyone else.

By taking a comprehensive approach, we hoped to find out not only about marital priorities but also about what factors were deemed unimportant or negatively valued in the approach to marriage. We also wanted to look at the patterning of responses with respect to certain life spheres, not only within the couple relationship but with other social groups and activities. For this purpose, it was decided to use both open-ended questions to obtain "free" responses and structured questions to ensure gathering systematic information about areas which might or might not be mentioned in the open material. Following a brief section on background characteristics, the body of the questionnaire contained five sections which respondents were instructed to fill out in order. The questionnaire began with open-ended questions on marital goals and mate choice. Three structured sections followed, each designed to approach from a somewhat different angle the concerns relevant for the study. In the final section, respondents were asked several questions on the importance of love in marriage and the meaning of the term "love" to them. These questions were placed last in order to avoid the possibility that love as a goal in marriage would be introduced artificially by the investigator.

Through the auspices of a large university in the Boston area,[3] it was possible to obtain a sample of engaged men[4] who would be asked to elicit the cooperation of their fiancées. The complex problems involved in obtaining engaged persons in any numbers as respondents, which in all likelihood account for the dearth of such samples in the literature, were solved here when the university agreed to attach to its registration forms a brief questionnaire concerning marital plans. From these questionnaires a sample of sixty-five men was drawn from those who announced themselves as engaged and planning to marry within one to nine months. Individuals who were formally engaged seemed most fruitful for our purposes, since it seemed desirable to be able to differentiate between men and women who were actually seriously considering marriage and relations between the sexes in the dating stage as they have been depicted in studies of dating. At the same time, it seemed essential to be able to estimate the degree of consensus between individuals who were planning to marry one another in order to relate the findings to the wealth of data on marital satisfaction obtained from couples after marriage.

The list of prospective respondents included sixty-five men and their fiancées. As far as possible, these men were contacted by phone and, if their consent was obtained, presented with questionnaires in person. The final response rate was just 50 percent: a total of sixty-five questionnaires (thirty-five from men, thirty from women) were returned. Most of the sample loss turned out to be attributable to those couples who were planning marriage within a very short time. Only about a third of the twenty-five men who planned to marry within three months after filling out the registration form completed the questionnaire, but nearly 75 percent of those whose marriage was not to take place for at least three months did so. Refusals, then, occurred largely on the basis of "time" problems for those whose marriage was imminent. This was even more true of the fiancées, only a fifth of whom completed the questionnaire if they were planning marriage within three months. All the respondents were white. About half were Protestant, and the remainder were about equally divided between Catholic and Jewish.

For the purposes of data analysis a coding key was devised for the entire questionnaire. In the case of the open-ended material, the categories were derived through content analysis. In order to categorize definitions of love, a sample of definitions of heterosexual love was extracted from the literature, and three coders (the investigator and two graduate students) separately classified the definitions and agreed that they fell into three analytically separable categories which can be outlined as follows:

*Companionate:* Love defined as companionship, understanding, sharing, reciprocity, the giving of mutual support and affection.

*Romantic:* Love defined as powerful attraction, discovery of the ideal or "only one," a phenomenon not subject to reason—unique, compelling, unpredictable.

*Altruistic:* Love defined as placing the other's happiness before one's own, learning to care for someone more than for oneself, directing one's efforts to the other's well-being, being prepared to sacrifice.

Although a dichotomy (companionate-romantic) would have been preferable for present purposes, the definitions classified as altruistic could not be forced into either of the other two. Definitions of love given by the respondents were then classified by the same three coders and an 88 percent agreement reached overall. An independent reliability check on every third questionnaire for all other items yielded an agreement of 87 percent.

## Results

The results from the questionnaire will be presented in tables or summary analyses. A summary of the findings as a whole will follow the completion of the presentation of the results. Statistical tests were made on all data with a few exceptions that will be mentioned as they appear. The tests were done with reference to whether response distributions on scaled items or among a set of response categories differed from what would be expected by chance. The Chi-Square Test was used, and, in every case where a cell involving ten or fewer responses was included, the Yates Correction for Continuity was employed.

Although there were too few cases for much manipulation of independent variables, it was essential for present purposes to make tests for sex differences on all variables used in statistical analysis. Chi-Square Tests with Yates Correction for Continuity were used for all items, first with the twenty-nine pairs[5] of individuals engaged to each other among the respondents, and then on the total sample of thirty females and thirty-five males. In no case were significant differences found, thus indicating a very high consensus in response across sex and of agreement by individuals planning to marry one another. This finding of no significant differences between the sexes is also important to emphasize because, although independence is claimed for the responses since all individuals filled out separate questionnaires,[6] it indicates that the significant differences in scalar distributions which will be reported would have been found even if responses for each sex were analyzed separately for each item, a procedure which would have made reporting the results far more cumbersome. Since the inclusion of the few "odd" cases did not appear to distort the results, it was decided to use all sixty-five cases available for the further analysis.

## *The Importance and Meaning of Love*

The questions on the importance and meaning of love will be discussed first (although they came last on the questionnaire), since it will be useful for interpreting the meaning of choices for love as they occur in other parts of the data. When asked how important love was to them personally as a basis for marriage, all respondents except two replied that it was very important; the remaining two said somewhat important.

In two subsequent questions, the respondents were asked first to give their own personal definitions of love and then to name the most important component of love as they saw it. As Table 1 shows, the definitions of love given overall

*Table 1*
DEFINITIONS OF LOVE

| | Engaged Men | Engaged Women | Total Sample |
|---|---|---|---|
| Companionate | 13 | 15 | 28 |
| Romantic | 8 | 3 | 11 |
| Altruistic | 7 | 7 | 14 |
| No Response* Unclassifiable | 7 | 5 | 12 |
| | 35 | 30 | 65 |

Tests of Significance:

Between sex: $\chi^2$ with Yates Correction for Continuity=1.42 (3 d.f.) N.S.;

Between categories (total sample): $\chi^2$=14.76 (3 d.f.) $p < .01$.

* Definitions of love were evidently difficult to give. This is the only question on which there were more than a very few missing cases. Several answers were placed in this category because they were unclassifiable, since they combined altruistic and companionate terms. The "no response" categories in Tables 1 and 2 could be treated in either of two ways: either as a separate or fourth category as presented above or by distributing "no responses" randomly among the other three categories. By mathematical computation, however, it was discovered that statistically the results would be almost exactly the same either way.

were significantly more companionate than romantic or altruistic (p=.01). Companionate definitions were even more overrepresented (p=.001) for "most important component" responses, and altruistic definitions particularly tended to diminish, as can be seen in Table 2. It might be inferred from this finding that altruism is fairly easily interchangeable with companionship in this context in the sense that it expresses the "input" side of the relationship, although in fact the same "output" is expected from the other. Love, then, is seen as the preferred basis for marriage, but it is not primarily "romantic love," at least as this has been defined in the social science literature.

*Table 2*
MOST IMPORTANT COMPONENT OF LOVE

| | Engaged Men | Engaged Women | Total Sample |
|---|---|---|---|
| Companionate | 20 | 20 | 40 |
| Romantic | 8 | 4 | 12 |
| Altruistic | 3 | 5 | 8 |
| No Response | 4 | 1 | 5 |
| | 35 | 30 | 65 |

Tests of Significance:
Between sex: $\chi^2$ with Yates Correction for Continuity=1.44 (3 d.f.) N.S.;
Between categories (total sample): $\chi^2$ with Yates Correction for Continuity=35.10 (3 d.f.) $p < .001$.

### *Marital Goals and Mate Choice*

The respondents were asked to write down, in order of importance to themselves, first the goals they wished to attain in marriage, and then, separately, what characteristics they would find most desirable and undesirable in a marital partner. For each section the following analysis is based on the first three items named. This summary is derived from content analysis, as described earlier, since the material is not appropriate for statistical treatment.

The respondents most frequently named "love" as the *most* important goal to be achieved in marriage, but less than half the sample ranked it first, and in fact only slightly over half the sample put down love as one of the first three goals. The great majority of the remaining responses referred to desired interpersonal relations between the marital pair; particularly stressed are companionship and compatibility, which, as has just been demonstrated, may be seen as interchangeable with love. The emphasis is very definitely on the couple relationship as an end in itself, with very few respondents seeing marriage as a means to other goals except for having children. Having children was included as one of the first three goals of marriage by about one-half of the respondents. A minority did mention economic security or just "security" as either the second or third goal.

Personal warmth—"a loving nature," "warm and giving"—was the most frequently named desirable characteristic in a marital partner. A mate who is companionable or compatible, including "a partner to share one's joys and problems," was the next most frequently mentioned. Characteristics denoting reliability and good nature were also named fairly often. There were very few references to physical attractiveness—good looks, sex appeal—or other characteristics that might be construed as "exciting" or romantic. Some mention was made of domestic qualities, such as being "a good homemaker" or "good husband and father," signifying a concern for role compatibility, although this was clearly subordinate to the personal relationship. It is interesting to note that ill-temper, that is, "a bad disposition" or "difficult to live with," was by far the most frequently named undesirable characteristic. Finally, almost a third of the respondents listed as undesirable characteristics such things as "different social background" or "different education."

### *Structured Questions: Marital Goals and Mate Choice*

The findings from the three structured sections can be reported very briefly, particularly since they confirm consistently the open-ended data, although there is some additional information on what is unimportant. Formulation of the choices for each section was based on the schematic outline referred to earlier. First, respondents were asked to rate a list of fifteen goals on a seven-point scale from extremely important to extremely unimportant in marriage. Second, they were asked to check a list of fifteen possible disagreements or dissimilarities between individuals as to whether they personally would agree or disagree that people should *not* marry if such discrepancies existed. Third, 10 four- or five-line descriptions of hypothetical marriage partners were given, each potential partner portrayed as having the desire and willingness to pursue most strongly some particular goal in marriage. Respondents were asked to rank these "portraits" from one to ten in order of descending importance according to their own preferences in mate choice. All items were based on scales, and significance levels of .01 to .001 were reached for all the response distributions, indicating strong tendencies to cluster at certain scale points, with the exception of questions on leisure time. Responses to items on "sharing leisure time" or "sharing recreational tastes" appeared to be randomly distributed. Although considerations of space do not warrant full presentation of the structured section, the ten "portraits," together with their respective rankings by males and females, are shown in Table 3, to illustrate the kinds of choice items utilized with respect to the summary of the results on all structured items presented below.

*Table 3*

*Instructions.* Listed below are some of the things that a man/woman is said to be looking for in a wife/husband. Will you please look at all the items and rank them from 1 to 10 as to which you would consider the most to the least important in a wife/husband, that is you would give a "1" to the most important, a "2" to the next most important, and so on down to a "10" for the least important. Please try to rank all items. This is a difficult task but of major importance for the study. The qualities described are, of course, not mutually exclusive. They should only be considered as highly developed in the particular person.

| Descriptions for Men (N = 35) | Rank |
|---|---|
| A woman who wants a family of her own, who places high value on having children, and wishes to spend much of her time in their care and raising . . . . . . . . . . . . . . . . . . . . | 4 |
| A woman who seeks companionship, who places high value on being able to talk to her husband, to share ideas, interests and problems with him | 2 |
| A woman who enjoys an active social life, who places high value on being with people and having many friends, who enjoys going out and doing things . . . . . . . . . . . . . . . . . . . . | 7 |
| A woman who takes pleasure in having her own home, who places high value on making the home attractive and comfortable, enjoys keeping house and spending most of her time and talents there . . . . | 5 |
| A woman who believes in keeping up family relationships, who places high value on family ties beyond the couple relationship, enjoys being part of a larger circle of family activities and affairs . . . . . | 9 |
| A woman who believes strongly in love, who places high value on having a very close, intimate relation with her husband . . . . . . . | 1 |
| A woman who wants her husband to be successful in his work, who places high value on advancement in the occupational sphere and is willing to help her husband attain this in any way she can . . . | 6 |
| A woman who believes in being warm and understanding, who places high value on giving affection, appreciation, and support to her husband | 3 |
| A woman who takes her religion seriously, who places high value on living her life in the way that is called for by her faith . . . . | 8 |
| A woman who wants to be an active member of her community, who places high value on taking part in community affairs and in organizations such as school and civic groups, enjoys being useful in the community . . . . . . . . . . . . . . . . . . . . . . . . | 10 |

| Descriptions for Women (N = 30) | Rank |
|---|---|
| A man who wants a family of his own, who places high value on having children, and will devote much of his energies to their care and support | 4 |
| A man who seeks companionship, who places high value on being able to talk to his wife, to share ideas, interests, and problems with her . | 3 |
| A man who enjoys an active social life, who places high value on being with people and having many friends, who enjoys going out and doing things . . . . . . . . . . . . . . . . . . | 8 |
| A man who takes pleasure in having his own home, who places high value on making a home attractive and comfortable, enjoys working around the house and providing security for his home . . . . | 5 |
| A man who believes in keeping up family relationships, who places high value on family ties beyond the couple relationship, enjoys being part of a larger circle of family activities and affairs . . . . . . . . | 6 |
| A man who believes strongly in love, who places high value on having a very close, intimate relation with his wife . . . . . . . . . | 1 |
| A man who wants very much to be successful professionally, who places high value on advancement in the occupational sphere, and who is very much involved in his work . . . . . . . . . . . . . . | 9 |
| A man who believes in being warm and understanding, who places high value on giving affection, appreciation, and support to his wife . . | 2 |
| A man who takes his religion seriously, who places high value on living his life in the way that is called for by his faith . . . . . . . | 7 |
| A man who wants to be an active member of his community, who places high value on taking part in community affairs and in organizations such as school and civic groups, enjoys being useful in the community . | 10 |

An examination of the ways in which the distributions were skewed showed that the very highest valuations were placed on "love," "understanding," "warmth and affection," and "sharing thoughts and feelings," followed closely by sexual fulfillment and children, whether these items were formulated in terms of marital goals or desirable mate characteristics. Moderately high valuations were accorded items having to do with "having a home of your own," "a smoothly running home," "similar material or monetary aspirations," and "similar views about the importance of improving one's social position." Items tapping "occupational success for the husband," "similar tastes in friends," "similar religious faith," and "similar desire to participate in religious activities" had response clusters around the middle of the scale, indicating a neither important nor unimportant, or neutral, valuation. Very low valuation was always put on items connected with "enhancing material comfort," "having an active social life," "sharing tastes in the arts and literature," "making useful occupational connections," and "participating in wider family affairs," although two or three versions of such items occurred across the three sections.

As will be discussed below, the findings from all the structured sections strongly and consistently affirmed the results in the unstructured material. Although items were introduced in the structured sections, most particularly concerning relations of the couple to the outside, which did not come up at all in the responses to open-ended questions, these items turned out to be regarded as unimportant since they received consistently low valuation.

### *Summary of the Results and Comparison with Studies of Dating and Marriage*

The results reported here represent the findings from questionnaires completed by sixty-five young engaged men and women concerning their orientations toward love, marital goals, and mate choice. The choice of a marriage partner on the basis of compatibility and the fulfillment of affective needs was very strongly and consistently affirmed throughout the data. Companionship and sharing (mutual psychic support and communication about joys and problems) were the major marital goals. Although love was seen as a very important basis for marriage, definitions of love were not romantic, and indeed the high stress on couple harmony over so many areas of the interpersonal relationship seemed to be incompatible with "love at first sight." There were no significant sex differences, and, because of the nature of the sample, high agreement is also demonstrated between prospective marital partners.

Sexual fulfillment was certainly desired and the respondents wanted children, but these goals were not quite as much in the forefront of concerns. More secondarily, there is emphasis on intracouple harmony with respect to "life-style" goals, such as material aspirations, as well as on the practical handling of domestic affairs or role compatibility in the household. Explicit preferences for a partner who comes from the same social background are voiced by a significant minority but cannot be construed as important to the group as a whole. It could be argued, however, that the widely expressed desire for a mate who is "compatible" over dimensions from personal to philosophical to household management rather limits the field of choice to those who have been similarly socialized.

That marriage is not to be used as a means toward social advantage or obtaining access to new and valued social ties (beyond the partner) is clearly evident in the structured material. Although mate choice may indeed be "controlled" by internalized values which include preferences for marrying one of one's own kind, it would seem that marriage is nevertheless seen as a private affair contracted "for love" between the two persons concerned. Criteria for controlled mate choice as operating in other societies, i.e., the consideration of what one will gain in terms of status or economic advantage by marrying into another family, are considered irrelevant for these young people. Indeed, such criteria may even be regarded as immoral because they are viewed as "calculating" or "materialistic." Finally, the specific exclusion of external relationships as important for consideration in forming the marriage tie (e.g., family, friends, work connections) serves also to delimit the boundaries of the marital dyad as a specific social unit with its own unique interpersonal relationship and concerns. The dyad appears in the minds of the respondents to exist outside rather than as a part of a larger social nexus.

There is evidence from studies of dating that a certain amount of concealment or deceit is practiced by both sexes when participating in premarital relationships of this sort. Some deliberate "mystery" about the true nature of one's feelings may be maintained (Waller, 1936), and it appears to be part of the dating ritual to "gild" one's own image in order to mask any flaws and enhance one's value in the eyes of the opposite sex (Gitter, 1966). The female may also try to seem helpless and "dumb" in order to give the male a pleasant feeling of superiority (Komarovsky, 1945). Such postures and attitudes lend credence to the theory that love between the sexes is based on an illusion. Individuals marry strangers, who, on becoming familiar through daily intercourse, turn out to be much less attractive and interesting than they made themselves out to be.

This explanation for marital disharmony appears to fit well

with studies in which investigators have regularly found relationships between marital satisfaction and the presence of shared norms and statuses (Feldman, 1965; Ort, 1950). Similarity of background, giving rise to consensus in values, is highly correlated with marital happiness (Keeley, 1955; Buerkle, Anderson, and Badgley, 1961; Christensen, 1964). By far the most prominent interpersonal factor is "companionship," which seems to be directly related to the degree of communication between spouses (Feldman, 1965: 28; Burgess and Wallin, 1953; Locke, Sabagh, and Thomes, 1956). Husbands and wives are most satisfied when they can talk things over together freely, and this kind of interaction seems to be more important than anything else, including sexual adjustment (Brody, 1963; Levinger, 1965; Rollins, 1965). "Companionship," so defined, stems from similarity of background and consensus on values, goals, and tastes. If premarital relations between the sexes are based on mutual deception and marriages are contracted between strangers in an aura of "romantic idealization," high rates of marital disruption and dissolution are explained.

According to studies cited earlier on actual marriage patterns, however, this explanation is not tenable. The findings from the present study also substantiate the alternate view: these young engaged people, regardless of sex, want exactly those things from marriage and from their prospective spouses which have been found to be most likely to lead to marital satisfaction—companionship, communication, and consensus in those areas of life which most directly affect the couple relationship. The data base in this study is admittedly very limited; however, it seems reasonable to suggest that when numerous studies all show that married men and women consistently state that these are the things they want from marriage, that such wishes probably also existed prior to marriage. Present evidence suggests that these desires are explicit and shared, at least after the point of formal engagement has been reached. The obscurantist "games" of dating, devised to achieve popularity and protect the vulnerable self against possible rejection, are then relinquished once true commitment to marriage has been reached.

### *Marital Dissatisfaction and Role Segregation—An Alternate Explanation*

If it is accepted, however, that the basis of the contemporary love marriage is high psychological interdependency, and that people entering marriage recognize this and explicitly seek partners who can best supply their mutual needs, how can a very high rate of marital failure, as evidenced not only by divorce rates but by the recorded rates of dissatisfaction among couples who nevertheless remain together, be explained? If love is defined as comprehensive companionship, it would follow that involvement in separate life spheres which leads to reduction in communication and understanding between partners will be construed as a withdrawal of love, thus destroying the very legitimacy base of the institution of marriage. Yet extreme role segregation is actually required for married couples in terms of the division of labor in the nuclear family. Not only are men and women required to fill distinctly separate role obligations in areas of life physically separated from one another, but work and family roles are also governed by different sets of values (Parsons, 1953: 3–33). Indeed, studies of marital dissatisfaction have shown that it is precisely this uneven social involvement which leads to a breakdown in communication. Men are found to talk mainly about work, a theme which wives find boring and even incomprehensible in content (Komarovsky, 1962). Women, on the other hand, want to discuss home and family, personal feelings, and cultural topics, areas which evidently do not appeal much to men (Feldman, 1965: 14–16). Although the underlying norms of the companionate marriage feature an integrated interaction model, spouses in fact go their own separate ways, frequently with deep resentment, because neither understands the problems or the satisfactions of the other (Bernard, 1968: 234; Hobart and Klausner, 1959). Husbands and wives not only want to talk about different things, but they have distinctly different styles of communication which are related to the values which underlie their separate domains; thus men are embarrassed by the "expressive" communication which women enjoy (Bernard,

1968: 242). When communication between spouses is poor, sexual relations are also found to deteriorate (Jouard, 1964). Women are likely to feel even more deserted psychologically than men when marital discourse is low (Meyer, 1966). This is no doubt due to the more isolated position of the woman under contemporary social arrangements.

"Marrying for love," while it seems functional for the handling of personality needs, paradoxically conflicts with other values in the United States, primarily the achievement syndrome. In order to establish oneself in an occupation, a high degree of involvement is required, particularly in the early stages of the career. Even if the husband does not want to be a "success," however, he must strive to do as well as possible, for on him will fall most of the burden for providing for his wife and their children. Where the spheres of work and family are sharply demarcated, career involvement on the part of the husband almost necessarily puts limits on couple interaction which will be difficult to accept given the marital goals. The fact that children arrive fairly early in most American marriages only accentuates the problem, for they will be likely to appear just at the point when the husband is striving to establish himself and probably experiencing considerable anxiety. There is evidence to suggest that the arrival of children does interfere with marital communication and satisfaction (Blood and Wolfe, 1960; LeMasters, 1957). To the extent that each partner gets involved in spheres which drain off resources from the couple relationship, a strain is put on the marriage. Moreover, the role obligations and values attached to the separate spheres are too different to allow for empathy which would encourage sympathetic attention to the problems of the other. Simultaneous crises in "early career" and "early child-rearing" stages heighten the problem, since each partner desires more affective support from the other at precisely the time when it is least available. An "overload" of emotional tension is placed on the isolated marital dyad in a society where there are no other institutions to which such tension can be legitimately displaced.

In advancing a hypothesis which relates role segregation to marital dissastisfaction, it is interesting to note that in one long-term study of marriage, satisfaction was found to decrease during the child-rearing years and then to rise again when the children grew up (Feldman, 1965: 116–117). The periods of greatest satisfaction, then, are the pre- and post-child-rearing years, which also coincide with the periods in the life cycle in which the majority of married women in the United States are now participating in the labor force (Myrdal and Klein, 1968: 42). Thus it could be inferred that when role boundaries are crossed, couples can share more and are consequently more satisfied with their marriage. The wife's work participation also relieves other tensions, since she feels less isolated and the husband is relieved of some of the economic burden. Renewed happiness in the later years of marriage, then, may be directly related to the removal of obstacles which tend to confine men and women to highly separated and, to some extent, mutually incomprehensible roles.

A case has been made for an explanation of marital disorganization in terms of integration problems which have not been solved following the differentiation of work from the family, and which interfere with satisfactory management of psychological tensions by family interaction. Needless to say, one could connect this view of the division of labor in contemporary society and its consequences not only with feminine alienation generally but also with the rejection of "materialistic" or instrumental values by the young. In the latter case, socialization is being managed primarily by the "affectively oriented" mother in a context which also includes friction with the more "instrumentally oriented" father, whose direct influence on the young child is very limited.

NOTES

1. This research was carried out under the auspices of the Laboratory of Community Psychiatry, Harvard Medical School, Boston, Massachusetts.
2. The concern in this paper is with heterosexual love and not with love in any more generic sense.
3. Northeastern University.
4. There can be no claim that this group constitutes a representative sample, even of men in the particular university

utilized, since engaged men were relatively few in number and clustered mainly in the senior year. At the same time, the ages of the respondents were well grouped around the present median age for first marriages in the United States: the women were almost all between the ages of nineteen and twenty-two, the men between the ages of twenty and twenty-four. Also the percentage of young men in the population entering college in the United States today is very high, and very nearly all of the respondents of both sexes came from social backgrounds which would fall into that large segment of United States society which is roughly termed the middle class. One can then at least argue that they could not be termed a very "peculiar" or deviant group in relation to their peers, at least in this stratum.

5. There were twenty-nine "pairs" of individuals engaged to one another among the respondents, a total of fifty-eight. There were also seven "odd halves": one woman and six men whose respective fiancées did not fill out the questionnaire.
6. Independence is claimed, since although these were engaged couples, the filling out of the questionnaires was in no sense a collaborative effort. Each individual in the sample completed his own separate questionnaire, and we asked for and obtained verbal commitment from the respondents to avoid any consultation over their responses with any other persons, most particularly with their respective potential marital partners. The data therefore do not constitute a matched sample in the accepted statistical sense where nonindependence would be indicated. Neither is this panel research where correlational measures would have to be used if inferences were to be made about changes over time in responses of pairs of people who were in a particular continuous relationship with one another. Therefore the statistical techniques utilized for this paper were judged appropriate by the investigator and two methodologically sophisticated colleagues who were consulted in the matter.

REFERENCES

Benedict, R. (1946). *The Chrysanthemum and the Sword.* Boston: Houghton-Mifflin.

Bernard, J. (1968). *The Sex Game.* Englewood Cliffs, N.J.: Prentice Hall.

Biegel, H. G. (1951). "Romantic Love," *American Sociological Review*, 16: 326–334.

Bloode, R. O., and D. M. Wolfe (1960). *Husbands and Wives: The Dynamics of Family Living.* Glencoe: The Free Press.

Bogardus, E. S. (1933). "A Social Distance Scale," *Sociology and Social Research*, 17: 265–271.

Brody, S. A. (1959). "Husband-Wife Communication Patterns Related to Marital Adjustment," doctoral dissertation, University of Southern California.

Buerkle, J. V., T. R. Anderson, and R. F. Badgley (1961). "Altruism, Role Conflict, and Marital Adjustment," *Marriage and Family Living*, 23:20–30.

Burchinal, L. G. (1959). "Adolescent Role Deprivation and High School Age Marriage," *Marriage and Family Living*, 21: 378–384.

——— (1969). "Trends and Prospects for Young Marriages in the United States," pp. 477–499, in J. Ross Eshleman (ed.), *Perspectives in Marriage and the Family*. Boston: Allyn and Bacon.

Burgess, E. W., and H. J. Locke (1953). *The Family*. New York: American Book.

——— and P. Wallin (1953). *Engagement and Marriage*. Philadelphia: Lippincott.

———, H. J. Locke, and M. M. Thomes (1963). *The Family, from Institution to Companionship*. New York: American Book.

Caplow, T. (1964). *The Sociology of Work*. New York: McGraw-Hill.

Christensen, H. T. (1958). *Marriage Analysis: Foundations for Successful Family Life*. New York: Ronald Press.

——— (1964). "The Intrusion of Values," pp. 969–1006, in H. T. Christensen (ed.), *Handbook of Marriage and the Family*. Chicago: Rand McNally.

Feldman, H. (1965). *Development of the Husband-Wife Relationship*. Ithaca: Department of Child Development and the Family, Cornell University.

Foote, N. N. (1953). "Love," *Psychiatry*, 16: 245–251.

Gerth, H., and C. W. Mills (1953). *Character and Social Structure*. New York: Harcourt Brace.

Gitter, A. G. (1966). "Studies on Hypocrisy," paper presented at District of Columbia Sociological Society, Washington.

Goldsen, R. K., M. Rosenberg, R. M. Williams, Jr., and E. Suchman (1960). *What College Students Think*. New York: D. Van Nostrand.

Goode, W. J. (1959). "The Theoretical Importance of Love," *American Sociological Review*, 24: 38–47.

——— (1963). *World Revolutions and Family Patterns*. Glencoe: The Free Press.

Greenfield, S. M. (1969). "Love and Marriage in Modern America: A Functional Analysis," pp. 346–362, in J. Ross Eshleman (ed.), *Perspectives in Marriage and the Family*. Boston: Allyn and Bacon.

Groves G. H. (1947). *The Contemporary American Family*. Philadelphia: Lippincott.

Henry, J. (1966). "Forty-year-old Jitters in Married Urban Women," pp. 146–163, in S. M. Farber and R. H. L. Wilson (eds.), *The Challenge to Women*. New York: Basic Books.

Hobart, C. W. (1958). "Some Effects of Romanticism during

Courtship on Marriage Role Opinions," *Sociology and Social Research*, 42: 336–343.

——— and W. J. Klausner (1959). "Some International Correlates of Marital Role Disagreement and Marital Adjustment," *Marriage and Family Living*, 21: 256–263.

Hollingshead, A. B. (1950). "Cultural Factors in Mate Selection," *American Sociological Review*, 15: 619–627.

Hunt, M. M. (1959). *The Natural History of Love*. New York: A. A. Knopf.

Jouard, S. (1964). *The Transparent Self*. New York: D. Van Nostrand.

Karlsson, G. (1951). *Adaptability and Communication in Marriage*. Uppsala: Almqvist and Wiksells.

Katz, A. M., and R. Hill (1958). "Residential Propinquity and Mate Selection," *Marriage and Family Living*, 20: 27–33.

Keeley, S. J. (1955). "Value Convergence and Marital Relations," *Marriage and Family Living*, 17: 342–345.

Kerckhoff, A. C., and K. E. Davis (1962). "Value Consensus and Need Complementarity in Mate Selection," *American Sociological Review*, 27: 295–303.

Kolb, W. L. (1950). "Family Sociology, Marriage Education, and the Romantic Love Complex," *Social Forces*, 29: 65–72.

Komarovsky, M. (1946). "Cultural Contradictions and Sex Roles," *American Journal of Sociology*, 52: 188.

——— (1962). *Blue Collar Marriage*. New York: Random House.

LeMasters, E. E. (1957). "Parenthood as Crisis," *Marriage and Family Living*, 19: 352–355.

Levinger, G. (1965). "A Comparative Study of Marital Communication." Mimeo.

Linton, R. (1936). *The Study of Man*. New York: Appleton-Century-Crofts.

Locke, H. J. (1951). "Predicting Adjustment in Marriage: A Comparison of a Divorced and a Happily Married Group." New York: Holt.

———, G. Sabagh, and M. M. Thomes (1965). "Correlates of Primary Communication and Empathy." Research Studies of the State College of Washington, 24: 116–124.

Luckey, E. G. (1960). "Marital Satisfaction and Congruent Self-Spouse Concepts," *Social Forces*, 39: 153–157.

Meyer, J. E. (1966). "The Disclosure of Marital Problems, an Exploratory Study of Lower and Middle Class Wives." Institute of Welfare Research. New York: Community Service Society: 104–116.

Mogey, J. J. (1969). *The Family*, Chicago: Rand McNally.

Myrdal, A., and V. Klein (1968). *Women's Two Roles: Home and Work*. London: Routledge (rev. edn.).

Ort, R. S. (1950). "A Study of Role Conflicts as Related to Happiness in Marriage," *Journal of Abnormal and Social Psychology*, 45: 691–699.

Parsons, T. (1949). "The Social Structure of the Family," pp. 190–196, in R. N. Anshen (ed.), *The Family: Its Function and Destiny*. New York: Harper & Row.

——— (1955). "The American Family: Its Relations to Personality and to the Social Structure," pp. 3–33, in T. Parsons and R. F. Bales, *Family, Socialization and Interaction Process*. Glencoe: The Free Press.

——— and R. F. Bales (1955). *Family, Socialization and Interaction Process*. Glencoe: The Free Press.

Pineo, P. C. (1961). "Disenchantment in the Later Years of Marriage," *Marriage and Family Living*, 23: 3–11.

Rapoport, Rhona (1964). "The Transition from Engagement to Marriage," *Acta Sociologica*, 8: 36–55.

——— and Robert Rapoport (1964). "New Light on the Honeymoon," *Human Relations*, 17: 33–56.

——— (1965). "Work and Family in Contemporary Society," *American Sociological Review*, 5: 381–394.

Rollins, B. C. (1965). "Consensus of Husband and Wife on Companionship Values and Marital Satisfaction: Some Theoretical Implications," paper presented at Meetings of National Council on Family Relations.

Schellenberg, J. A. (1960). "Homogamy in Personal Values and the 'Field of Eligibles,'" *Social Forces*, 39: 157–162.

Schorr, A. L. (1962). "Family Policy in the United States," *International Social Science Journal*, UNESCO, Vol. XIV, No. 3.

Strauss, A. (1945). "The Ideal and Chosen Mate," *American Journal of Sociology*, 52: 204–208.

van der Haag, E. (1964). "Love or Marriage," pp. 92–101, in R. Coser (ed.), *The Family, Its Structure and Functions*. New York: St. Martin's Press.

Waller, W. (1936). "The Rating and Dating Complex," *American Sociological Review*, 2: 724–734.

——— (1938). *The Family: A Dynamic Interpretation*. New York: Cordon.

——— and R. Hill (1951). *The Family, A Dynamic Interpretation*. Homewood: Dryden Press.

Winch, R. F., T. Ktsanes, and V. Ktsanes (1953). "Empirical Elaboration of the Theory of Complementary Needs," *Journal of Abnormal and Social Psychology*, 51: 508–513.

Zelditch, M. (1964). "Cross Cultural Analysis of Family Structure," pp. 403–461, in H. T. Christensen (ed.), *Handbook of Marriage and the Family*. Chicago: Rand McNally.

# 5

# The Passing of the Dominant Husband-Father

ERSEL E. LE MASTERS

## *The Victorian Paterfamilias*

IF SIGMUND FREUD were alive today, viewing the family scene from his consulting room in Vienna, what would he make of the father in contemporary urban society? Freud saw the Victorian father as a stern, forbidding—almost frightening—figure, controlling his wife and children with a firm hand. This was expected of him because women were considered to be too emotional and too impractical to manage a family.

The procession of disturbed men and women who passed through Freud's office talked about their fathers—those shadowy figures in the background who frightened children and produced neuroses.

In family photographs from the Victorian era the husband-father is portrayed sitting down, with his wife standing dutifully at his side. Today, the scene is reversed: the wife has the comfortable seat while the husband-father stands, peeking over his wife's shoulder.

In the world of the nineteenth century, being a woman was dangerous—the hazards of constant pregnancy and frequent child-bearing were very real. Today, in the developed countries of the world, mothers are outliving fathers by several years.

The writer's father was a Victorian type—all of the money was earned and dispensed by him. Children filed their requests with the mother who relayed them to the father. The decision to grant or deny the request would eventually come back via the same route: "Your father says that he cannot buy you a pair of roller skates this month—but he will try to get them for you next month." (What would he say today in America with the "instant debt" credit card always available?) "Your father says you may have a new dress for graduation"—this was for my sister. "He will go with us Saturday afternoon to look for one."

In this system of communication a clever woman could affect many decisions by her manner of presentation. If she did not approve of a child's request she had only to present it in a negative (or lukewarm) fashion and the father would say, "No." A favorable presentation, on the other hand, would often bring approval.

Officially, however (on a formal level), the power in this Victorian family model resided in the husband-father. By means of sex appeal, or love, or cleverness, women could influence the exercise of this power, but the male figure remained dominant. (Incidentally, there is plenty of evidence that Mrs. Freud managed quite well in this system—partly because her husband was so busy writing books about family life and partly because Freud loved her so much.)

In this Victorian family model the "bad guy" was the father. "The Lord giveth and the Lord taketh away," the children used to say in the writer's family—which meant that, at best, the child's feelings toward the father were ambivalent.

The mother, in contrast, if she played her role skilfully, could emerge as the "good guy" in the soap opera of daily life in the Victorian era: "I was able to persuade your father that you needed some experience traveling and he says you may go with your friends on the camping trip."

"Thank you, Mother!"

## *The Current Scene*

All of the preceding sounds quaint and amusing today, at least in the United States. Virile (strong) men on television are either bachelors, widowers, or divorced, and the married men with children (fathers) are portrayed as being somewhat ridiculous, incompetent, and confused. Nobody could hate or fear the poor devils—a humane person could only pity them.

Psychiatrists and social-work clinicians report the typical family syndrome as a mother (and her children) whose husband (the father) will not assume enough responsibility. He drinks too much, he pursues other women, he stays away from home. . . .

Edgar Borgatta, a noted sociologist at the University of Wisconsin, recently remarked to the writer: "Any man who imagines himself lord and master of his house today should see a psychiatrist because he is having delusions."

Another person stated: "The man is no longer king in his castle; there has been a palace revolution and the father has emerged as the court jester."

If such a revolution has taken place, it would appear that the contemporary mother has emerged as the villain in the current family play. In several best sellers in the United States since the Second World War, mothers have been portrayed as emasculating their sons and traumatizing their daughters.[1] One writer even accused mothers of causing the psychiatric casualties experienced by American servicemen in the Second World War.[2]

Another observer has claimed that the contemporary American mother is the world's "first full-time mother," an ogre who devours her children, both male and female, because she has no other reason for existence.[3]

Thus, in the period from 1900 to about 1950—only half a century—the position and power of the father has been almost completely transformed in contemporary urban-industrial societies.[4] How did this happen? And what are some of its ramifications? The rest of this article will focus on these questions.

### *Did Fathers Abdicate?*

How did it happen that the father in contemporary society has become displaced as the dominant parent by the mother?

In his recent study of parents in the Soviet Union, Bronfenbrenner concludes that Soviet fathers do not play a crucial role in child rearing for the simple reason that they have not been home very much in recent decades—revolutions and wars have occupied most of their time.[5] In addition, millions of Soviet fathers were required to work away from their families for long periods of time. Thus, in the Soviet Union, it would seem that the father role was deemphasized because most fathers were likely to be missing from the home at any given time.

In the United States there is some evidence that the economic catastrophe of the 1930s (euphemistically called "the depression") had much to do with eroding the power and the glory of the American father. Studies by Cavan, Ranck, Komarovsky, and Angell have demonstrated that the father's position in the family deteriorated when he ceased to be the major breadwinner.[6]

It was not until the beginning of the Second World War that full employment returned to the United States, but this meant that millions of fathers moved from the ranks of the unemployed to the ranks of the armed forces. Thus an entire generation of children in the United States grew up in homes managed primarily by mothers.

One might hypothesize that the dominant father-parent system is dysfunctional in contemporary urban-industrial society. One study of fathers in Nigeria concluded that these men tended to adopt a Western father model as they assumed urban occupational roles—they became affectionate and permissive in their relationships with their children.[7]

A study of fathers in Turkey concluded that the traditional Turkish father, "stern, forbidding, remote, domineering, and autocratic," has become a liability for sons who must compete in the modern world.[8]

In three societies that seem to have flourished since the end of the Second World War—Japan, the Soviet Union, and the United States—the father model seems to be that of a warm, permissive parent who provides affection and encouragement for his children but exercises very little absolute authority.[9]

Based on the data at hand one has to conclude that the dominant-father model is neither practical nor functional in contemporary society and is tending to disappear.[10] Some fathers may mourn their lost glory but many others rejoice in their new relationship with their children.

## *The Divorced Father*

In a recent study of divorced men in the United States it was apparent that marital failure poses severe problems for men who wish to continue their parental role but do not want to go on living with the mother of their children.[11] This dilemma results from the peculiar nature of the father role: it has to be performed as a member of a marital team. Many of the men in the survey above felt that they were adequate fathers but were unable to function properly as a parent because they could not resolve their marital problems.

This "team" feature of the father role is not found in all male roles, the occupational role being a good example. A man can be an excellent surgeon, or a good carpenter, even though he is not successful as a husband.

The writer would hazard a guess that a majority of the American fathers who neglect their children do so because of marital failure.

This was not the situation in the Victorian family, because in that era fathers and mothers, even though they were unhappy in their marriages, were expected to go on living together "for the sake of our children." Today they will probably divorce, thus disrupting the parental team.

Mothers in most modern societies are not blocked out of their parental role by the failure of the marriage because they usually retain custody of the children. As a matter of fact, divorce or separation usually enhances their parental role, since the absence of the father puts the mother in a more central position in the lives of her children.

Marital failure creates other parent-role complexities for the divorced man. As he looks around for his second wife, the chances are that his new love partner will be a divorced woman with minor children. If his courtship progresses toward remarriage, the father will find himself involved with two sets of children: he will still be trying to serve as a father to his own offspring living with their mother, but inevitably he will begin to assume some foster parent functions with the children of the divorced woman he is courting.

If the new love affair culminates in marriage, the divorced man will eventually find himself in the role of step-parent, one of the most complex parental roles in modern society.[12] As he moves into the role of step-parent, the father will gradually withdraw as a parent of his own offspring and will be replaced there by his former wife's second husband. (The commonness of this situation is shown by the fact that about 80 percent of all divorced people in the United States remarry; actually, divorced women in their twenties or thirties have a better chance for marriage than single women in the same age group.)

In many cases the male will eventually adopt the children of his second wife, thus assuming the role of the adoptive father.

In some second marriages (to say nothing of third and fourth unions), the father role becomes incredibly complex. In one second marriage studied by the writer, both the wife and the husband had retained custody of the children from their first marriages, and then two children were born of the new marriage. This created, in effect, three different sets of children for the father to relate to: he was a stepfather to the children from his wife's first marriage; he was the biological father of the children from his own first marriage; then he and his new wife were the biological parents of the children born of their marriage.

Is it any wonder that father-child relationships can become confused in modern society?

One undergraduate female student at the University of Wisconsin made this statement to the writer: "Do you have to be buddy-buddy with your stepfather? Just because my mother loves this new man, do I have to love him also? I love my own father and I don't want two fathers—one is enough for me."

## *Fathers and Equality of the Sexes*

One source of stress for the contemporary father, it seems to us, results from the desire of modern women for equality with men. For centuries men have ruled most of the world, not only in public affairs but in the home as well, and now women are beginning to revolt against their status as second-class citizens. This is quite apparent in the United States, with an aggressive women's liberation movement which is trying to win for American women what an earlier struggle of the 1920s failed to achieve.[13] Some data—such as the enrolment in graduate schools—in fact indicate that women in the United States have actually lost ground to men in recent decades.

In a recent study of blue-collar men by the writer,[14] it was apparent that these males do not accept females as their equals any more than they accept blacks as their equals. They reveal deep-seated feelings of hostility and resentment toward the modern woman. Since parenthood in modern society requires the father and mother to work together as a team, such attitudes are not very helpful.

In a society such as that in the United States it may be that sexual prejudice and discrimination are deeper and more persistent than racism. Note that several large cities in 1970—Cleveland, Ohio; Gary, Indiana; and Newark, New Jersey—are headed by black men, but not one American metropolitan community has a woman mayor, white or black.

There is a trend toward a single standard of sexual morality in the United States along the lines of an earlier development in countries such as Sweden. American men have always been granted more sexual freedom than their sisters or their wives, and not all of them are happy about the new sexual freedom of women. The oral contraceptive has liberated millions of women from their fear of pregnancy, and now some of them are determined to find out whether sex is as wonderful as their boy friends have always claimed it was.

In a book about American men Brenton observes that some contemporary husbands are frightened and disturbed by this new sexuality of women—they are not sure they can satisfy their wives.[15] Brenton believes that the female orgasm has become a problem in some American marriages.

In a historical study, Ferguson documents the long history of male dominance in Western society: men controlled the gun, the ship, the explorations, the government, and the great corporations.[16] Women existed to please men, bear children, and help manage the domicile. How many modern men wish to change the arrangement? And how many modern women are willing to settle for the traditional roles assigned them?

In sociology it is a truism that changes in power distribution will always disrupt a group until a new level of accommodation is worked out.[17] It would appear that this will take some time, at least in the United States. And during this period, fathers will find it difficult to play their parental role because of the problems experienced in their role as husbands.

### *Fathers and the Youth Peer Group*

In societies such as that of the United States the adolescent peer group has become a potent force in recent decades.[18] This development has been another factor in reducing the power and authority of the contemporary father: not only does he have to cope with a new type of woman, but also with an aroused (and organized) youth generation that wishes to plan its own destiny.

Bronfenbrenner, in the study cited earlier, claims that the Soviets have been able to manage things so that the adolescent peer group supports adult values. This is certainly not the case in the United States. Colleges, universities, and high schools are experiencing repeated crises related to youth-adult conflicts. (Contradicting Bronfenbrenner, incidentally, in a dispatch dated 20 July 1970, the Associated Press reported sharp differences in values between Soviet youth and adults.)

Some fathers have responded to this youth challenge by adopting a "buddy" parent model, their strategy apparently being that "if you can't lick 'em, join 'em." In the opinion of this observer the "buddy" model has serious limitations in countries such as the United States in which parents are held responsible for children until the ages of eighteen to twenty-one.[19]

Thus we see the embattled father struggling to maintain his self-image in the face of an aggressive wife-mother and a powerful adolescent peer group. If he turns to television for relief, his ego (in the United States) will be additionally assaulted by programs in which women and children consistently outwit fathers, for advertisers slant their programs in favor of women because about 80 percent of family purchases are made by the wife-mother.

### *Fathers and Love*

Fathers in modern society suffer from a common syndrome: they are starved for love. One might say they exhibit chronic emotional malnutrition.

Living in vast, impersonal cities, and working in large depersonalized bureaucratic organizations, men need more than ever wives and children who love them. We have the impression that this need is often not satisfied.

The United States, to cite one example, has a divorce rate of about 25 percent; there is reason to believe that perhaps another one-fourth of the marriages are devoid of emotional significance. They are "shell" or "façade" marriages.[20] Although legally intact, these "holy deadlock" unions have long since been depleted of any love they once contained.

In these situations a father may turn to his children for love and affection. If he does, he is likely to be disappointed. Love is a one-way street between parents and children in the United States. Fathers (and mothers) are expected to exhibit unconditional love for their offspring, regardless of their behavior. This state of affairs has produced a folk expression: "Home is where you go when they won't take you anyplace else."

In contrast, the love of children for their parents is conditional. Parents have to prove over and over again that they are entitled to the respect and affection of their children. And in doing this they must compete with other parents who are trying to win the love of their children.

Kent Geiger, a student of the modern Soviet family, has pointed out that one of the problems of the nuclear family in the early days of the Soviet Union was this pattern of "conditional" love of children for their parents. Under Stalin, in the 1930s and the 1940s, "love for parents became an ethical absolute."[21] We wonder if Stalin simply ordered children to love their parents? This has been done by Christians for about 2,000 years ("Honor thy father and thy mother") with dubious results.

Thus, in essence, fathers in some contemporary societies become simply a means to some end, but not an end in themselves. The employer, the wife, and the children all want a part of his life. But who cares about him?

It may be that most fathers don't deserve any better fate, but being himself a father, this author would prefer to think otherwise.

## *Lower-Class Fathers*

In the United States there is ample evidence that fathers at the bottom of the social class system have very little chance, if any, to function as effective parents.[22] The act of procreation may be one of their few opportunities to demonstrate their masculinity.

To enable these men to become adequate fathers seems to involve more drastic social change than most Americans wish to contemplate.

These fathers suffer from at least three handicaps in trying to function as parents: (*a*) they are often not living with their wives and children—in the United States families are more likely to receive welfare benefits if the father deserts; (*b*) they cannot serve as an effective adult model for their children; and (*c*) they are unable to "launch" their sons and daughters into the competitive society.

At the present time, in the United States, the only "solution" to this problem appears to be various programs by which public and private agencies become, in effect, foster fathers to the children of these lower-class men.

Interestingly enough, the mothers in these low-income families seem to function reasonably well, considering their handicaps.[23]

Liebow, in the study cited earlier, concludes that these men at the bottom of the society would like to assume their parental role but lack the means to do so.

## *Fathers Ignored by Family Researchers*

It is an interesting fact, at least in the United States, that fathers are rarely interviewed when parents are studied. In several research reports surveyed by the writer, 2,295 mothers were questioned about their parental role—but not one father was interviewed. This omission is even more startling when it is remembered that the sampling design of these studies was given elaborate consideration by the researchers.

One can only conclude that students of the parent role either do not consider fathers worth studying or else they assume that mothers can report accurately what fathers think and do. Either assumption is open to considerable debate.

One study of upper-middle-class parents in Canada included fathers as well as mothers in the sample design and discovered substantial differences in child-rearing philosophy between fathers and mothers.[24]

It may well be that men and women are becoming more alike socially in modern society, but to interview only one sex in studying parents strikes this writer as being unscientific.

## *A Glimpse into the Future*

What will the fathers of tomorrow be like? Margaret Mead once argued that fatherhood, in its social aspects, was a cultural invention of man, that it had no biological base, as does motherhood.[25] With artificial insemination it would be quite possible to eliminate fathers as we now know them.

Some biologists have suggested that mothers could also be eliminated in the future by breeding-laboratories that would simulate the human uterus.

Fortunately (or unfortunately) these possibilities appear to be far in the future of man—if, indeed, he has any distant future.

More immediately, it seems to this writer, women are going to demand more equality with men, and if this transpires, the maternal role will have to be deemphasized. Does this mean that fathers will have to assume more responsibility for child rearing?

Our guess would be no, that outside agencies in the community, such as day-care centers, will be greatly expanded in urban-industrial societies. It may well be that the worship of the intense, nuclear family is coming to an end. The recent studies by Bronfenbrenner and Bettelheim, cited earlier, are receiving widespread attention in the United States. Both of them suggest that biological parents have limited capacity to produce the kind of young people needed for the world of tomorrow.

Historically the family has tended to be a conservative social institution. Parents, as a rule, attempt to internalize in the child values and norms that the parents absorbed when they were children.

Given the revolutionary mood of the human scene today, this emphasis on the past may be fatal, for it may not permit the evolution of social change that is deep enough or rapid enough.

In the study of the kibbutz child-rearing system in Israel by Bettelheim, cited earlier, he concluded that nonparental group care of children produced a new "type" of person in one generation: more durable emotionally, more mature, and more dedicated to the welfare of the community. If it should be decided that the world needs a new kind of human being, then it may well be that mothers as well as fathers will be deemphasized in the future.

If this happens, let us hope (*a*) that the new type of human being will be better than what we have now, and (*b*) that the displaced parents will use their new leisure to rediscover each other as human beings.

NOTES

1. These attacks on the American mother are reviewed in E. E. LeMasters, *Parents in Modern America* (Homewood, Ill.: Dorsey Press, 1970).
2. Edward A. Strecker, *Their Mothers' Sons* (Philadelphia: Lippincott, 1946).
3. Alice S. Rossi, "Equality between the Sexes," *Daedalus*, Spring, 1964.
4. For an extensive analysis of the literature on this social revolution, see Leonard Benson, *Fatherhood* (New York: Random House, 1968).

5. Urie Bronfenbrenner, *Two Worlds of Childhood: U.S. and U.S.S.R.* (New York: Russell Sage Foundation, 1970).
6. These studies are reviewed in E. E. LeMasters, *op. cit.*, chapter VII, "The American Mother."
7. Robert A. Le Vine *et al.*, "Modernization and Parent-Child Relationships," in Norman W. Bell and Ezra F. Vogel (eds.), *The Family* (rev. edn., New York: The Free Press, 1968).
8. Norman W. Bradburn, "When Is a Father a Liability to a Son?" in H. Kent Geiger (ed.), *Comparative Perspectives on Marriage and the Family* (Boston: Little, Brown, 1968).
9. See the studies of U. Bronfenbrenner, *op. cit.*, and E. E. LeMasters, *op. cit.* Another valuable source on American parents is by Daniel R. Miller and Guy E. Swanson, *The Changing American Parent* (New York: Wiley, 1958). On the Japanese father see Ezra F. Vogel and Suzanne H. Vogel, "Permissive Dependency in Japan," in H. K. Geiger, *op. cit.*
10. Bruno Bettelheim reaches this conclusion in his study of kibbutz fathers in Israel. See his *The Children of the Dream* (New York: Macmillan, 1969).
11. This is the subject of a research project at the School of Social Work, University of Wisconsin, Madison, Wisconsin; 125 men were interviewed but as yet the study is unpublished.
12. For an interesting analysis of this role, see Anne W. Simon, *Stepchild in the Family* (New York: Odyssey Press, 1964).
13. See William L. O'Neill, *Everyone Was Brave—The Rise and Fall of Feminism in America* (Chicago: Quadrangle Books, 1969).
14. E. E. LeMasters, *The Blue-Collar Aristocracy: A Study of Tavern Social Life* (in preparation).
15. Myron Brenton, *The American Male* (New York: Coward-McCann, 1966).
16. Charles W. Ferguson, *The Male Attitude* (Boston: Little, Brown, 1966).
17. This is also true at the subhuman level. See George Schaller, *The Mountain Gorilla* (Chicago: University of Chicago Press, 1963).
18. James S. Coleman, *The Adolescent Society* (New York: The Free Press, 1961).
19. For an analysis of this model, see E. E. LeMasters, *op. cit.*, chapter XII.
20. John Cuber and Peggy Haroff, *The Significant Americans*, (New York: Appleton-Century-Crofts, 1965).
21. H. Kent Geiger, "The Fate of the Family in Soviet Russia—1917–1944," in Norman W. Bell and Ezra F. Vogel (eds.), *The Family* (rev. edn., New York: The Free Press, 1968).
22. Elliott Liebow, *Tally's Corner* (Boston: Little, Brown, 1967). The men in this particular study happen to be black, but the circumstances apply to lower-class white men as well.

23. See Andrew Billingsley, *Black Families in White America* (Englewood Cliffs, N.J.: Prentice-Hall, 1968); also Alfred Kadushin, "One Parent Adoptions," *Social Service Review*, September, 1970.
24. John R. Seeley *et al.*, *Crestwood Heights* (New York: Basic Books, 1956).
25. Margaret Mead, *Male and Female* (New York: Morrow, 1949). Desmond Morris similarly argues that the father-child bond has always been the weak link in the human family. See *The Naked Ape* (New York: McGraw-Hill, 1967).

# 6

# Who Has the Power? The Marital Struggle

DAIR L. GILLESPIE

*Marriage is the destiny traditionally offered to women by society. It is still true that most women are married, or have been, or plan to be, or suffer from not being. The celibate [single] woman is to be explained and defined with reference to marriage whether she is frustrated, rebellious, or even indifferent in regard to that institution.*

*Simone de Beauvoir*

## *The Changing Power Structure*

MODERN THEORISTS OF THE FAMILY agree that the American family has evolved from a paternalistic to a much more democratic form. Before the Civil War married women had many duties, few rights. They were not permitted to control their property, even when it was theirs by inheritance or dower, or to make a will. To all intents and purposes they did not own property. The husband had the right to collect and use the wife's wages, to decide upon the education and religion of the children, and to punish his wife if she displeased him. The right to will children, even unborn, to other guardians was retained by the husband. In the case of divorce, when granted at all, the husband had the right to determine the control of the children. To a married woman, her husband was her superior, her companion, her master. In every sector of the social arena, women were in a subordinate position.

The church was one of the most potent forces for maintaining them in this position. Within the church (with the exception of the Quakers), women were segregated from men, were not allowed to sing, preach, or take public action.

There were no high schools for girls, and no college in the world admitted women.* Unpropertied males, slaves, and all women were not allowed into the political process at all.

Today, as the textbooks never tire of telling us, couples are more free to choose partners than formerly, they are able to separate more easily, the differences in age and experience between husband and wife are less marked than formerly, the husband recognizes more willingly the independence of his wife's demands, they may share housekeeping and diversions, and the wife may even work for pay outside the home. In fact, sociologists claim that the modern husband and wife are so nearly equal in power that marriage today can be termed "democratic," "equalitarian," or "egalitarian."

These changes in the form of marriage are generally attributed to the entrance of women into the economic structure and to the extension of an equalitarian ideology to cover women. This type of explanation is careful to emphasize socioeconomic conditions of the past and the "rise of women" in the American economy. However, socioeconomic conditions of the present are no longer examined, for it is assumed that women have won their rights in all social arenas, and if they haven't—well, ideology takes a while to filter down to the masses. New egalitarian ideals, they tell us, will bring about further socioeconomic changes and a better position for women.

In a major research project on the modern American family, Blood and Wolfe state:

> Under former historical circumstances, the husband's economic and social role almost automatically gave him preeminence. Under modern conditions, the roles of men and women have changed so much that husbands and wives are potential equals—with the balance of power tipped sometimes one way, sometimes the other. It is no longer possible to assume that just because a man is a man, he is the boss. Once upon a time, the function of culture was to rationalize the predominance of the male sex. Today the function of culture is to develop a philosophy of equal rights under which the saying goes, "May the best man win!"—and the best man is sometimes a woman. The role of culture has shifted

* Ed.'s Note: Mount Holyoke College, chartered in 1836 as Mount Holyoke Female Seminary, seems to be the exception which proves the rule.

from sanctioning a competent sex over an incompetent sex to sanctioning the competent marriage partner over the incompetent one, regardless of sex. (1960: 29–30)

There is good evidence, however, that the balance of power is tipped the same way it always was, and that the best man is very seldom a woman. I am arguing, then, against the *personal* resource theory which implies that the outcome of power distributions within individual families is due to differences in the competence of the husband or wife and am positing that, in fact, this is still a caste/class system rationalizing the preponderance of the male sex.

## The Measurement of Power

Before examining the causes of male dominance in marital power, I would like to examine first how Blood and Wolfe[1] conceive of power and how they measure it. Operationally, power is restricted to who makes the final decision in each of eight areas, ranging from those traditionally held entirely by the husband to those held entirely by the wife. These eight areas include: (1) what job the husband should take; (2) what car to get; (3) whether or not to buy life insurance; (4) where to go on vacation; (5) what house or apartment to take; (6) whether or not the wife should go to work or quit work; (7) what doctor to have when someone is sick; (8) how much money the family can afford to spend per week on food. These questions were asked because (*a*) they are all relatively important, (*b*) they are questions which nearly all couples have to face, and (*c*) they range from typically masculine to typically feminine decisions, but affect the family as a whole. (1960: 19–20)

This measurment of power leaves much to be desired. Constantia Safilios-Rothschild has made probably the most telling criticisms of such studies. She points out that all decisions are given equal weight even though not all decisions have "objectively" the same degree of importance for the entire life of the family. Which job the husband would take (with important consequences in terms of time spent away from home, location of job, salary level, amount of leisure available, etc.) and which doctor to call were considered decisions equally affecting the family and the balance of power within the family. Further, some decisions, such as "what food to buy," require daily or weekly enactment, while a decision such as "what car to buy" is made only every few years. In addition, some decisions are "important" and frequent, others frequent but not "important," others "important" and not frequent, and still others not important and not frequent. Thus, the familial power structure may not be solely determined by the number of areas of decisions that one can appropriate for himself/herself. She also mentioned the multidimensionality of some of the decision-making areas and suggested that it is possible that one spouse decides which make of car to buy while the other specifies the color. (1969: 297–298)

It seems, then, that the conception and measurement of power is already biased in that it does not expose certain kinds of power which automatically accrue to the husband by virtue of his job (time spent away from home, location of job, salary level, leisure time available, etc.), and second, that it takes no account of the differential importance of the eight decisions in the power structure of the marriage. Further, there is good evidence that even if we accepted Blood and Wolfe's measures as being true measures of power, the husband still controls most of the power decisions in the family (see Fig. 1). I must conclude, then, that the husband has much more power than he appears to have according to Blood and Wolfe's analysis.

Their discussion of "who decides" is even more convincing that there are power differentials which are being overlooked. For example, they explain:

That the husband should be more involved in his wife's job decisions than she with his is understandable. For one thing, her work is seldom her major preoccupation in life the way it is for a man. Even if she works just as many hours a week, she does not usually make the same life-long commitment to the world of work. Nor is her pay-check indispensable to the family finances (if only because it is smaller). In such ways the choice of whether to work or not is less vital to a woman than to a man.

In addition, the wife's decisions about working have repercussions on the husband. If his wife goes to work, he will have to

*Figure 1*
HUSBANDS' MEAN POWER IN FAMILY DECISION-MAKING AREAS

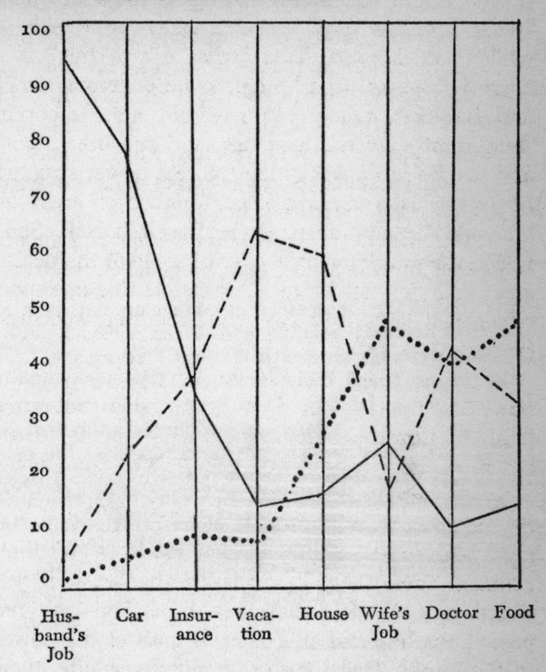


Husband's Mean Power (5 = total power; 0 = no power)

| | |
|---|---|
| Job | 4.86 |
| Car | 4.18 |
| Insurance | 3.50 |
| Vacation | 3.12 |
| House | 2.94 |
| Wife's Job | 2.69 |
| Doctor | 2.53 |
| Food | 2.26 |

— (husband prevails)
.... (wife prevails)
– – – (exactly the same)

help out more around the house. If he is a business executive, he may prefer to have her concentrate her energy on entertaining prospective clients at home. As a small businessman or independent professional, he may need her services in his own enterprise. On the other hand, regardless of his own occupation, he may want her to work in order to help him buy a house or a business, or pay for the children's education.

It may be, then, that the work role is so much the responsibility of the husband in marriage that even the wife's work is but an adjunct of his instrumental leadership, leaving this decision in his hands. (1960: 20–22)

In these *justifications* of the division of power, Blood and Wolfe use the device of examining why a husband would want more power in particular areas. The basic assumption is, of course, that he can have it if he wants it. I think a more pertinent question would be not who wants power, since there are always myriad reasons why anyone would want power, but why he is able to get it if he wants it. This question is not even broached.

William Goode in *World Revolution and Family Patterns* comments on this aspect of power and authority:

After evaluating the conflicting comments and data published by Shaffner, Rodnick, Schelski and Wruzbacher, Baumert comes to the conclusion which seems eminently reasonable, that claims of fundamental equalitarianism in the German family (or in any other European family) are not correct and that an unequivocally equalitarian family is rarely to be found. In the final analysis, only a few family relations are not determined by the male. It is not possible at present to state just how well such a statement could be applied to other countries. In reality, in all countries there are many women who manage to dominate the man, but it seems likely that in most countries, when the husband tries to dominate he can still do this. Even when the husband performs the household chores, his participation means that he gains power—the household becoming a further domain for the exercise of prerogatives for making decisions.

Perhaps the crucial qualitative difference is to be found in the extent to which, in one country or another, the male can still dominate *without* a definite effort to do so. (1963: 70)

In *The Family*, Goode calls this "negative authority—the right to prevent others from doing what they want." (1964: 75)

I must conclude, then, that the power structure is much more lopsided than Blood and Wolfe lead us to believe, and that it is the husband who holds this hidden power despite the fact that the family is supposed to be the wife's domain. Why does the husband have all this power? How does he obtain it? How does he maintain it?

It is assumed that most marriages begin with partners at a somewhat egalitarian level. All evidence points to homogamous marriages, i.e., that the woman's *husband* and *father* occupy similar positions in the socioeconomic structure. However, regardless of her background, "her future rank is mainly determined by the future job achievement of the man she marries, rather than by the class position of his family" (Goode, 1964: 87), or hers, needless to say. In discussing differentials in power which emerge in marriage, most social scientists use an individualistic perspective, as do Blood and Wolfe in *Husbands and Wives*. They remark:

> The balance of power is, after all, an interpersonal affair, and the wife's own characteristics cannot long be disregarded if we are to understand who makes the decisions. Whenever possible it is desirable to compare the wife and the husband on the same characteristics, for then the comparative resourcefulness and competence of the two partners can be discovered. Once we know which partner has more education, more organizational experience, a high status background, etc., we will know who tends to make the most decisions. (1960: 37)

The major error made by Blood and Wolfe (and others who use this perspective) is in assuming that this control of competence and resources occurs in individual couples by chance rather than being structurally predetermined (in a statistical sense) in favor of the male. To state it more clearly, I am arguing that it is still a caste/class system rationalizing the preponderance of males. The distribution of power is not an interpersonal affair, but a class affair.

Blood and Wolfe continue:

> Some husbands today are just as powerful as their grandfathers were—but they can no longer take for granted the authority held by older generations of men. No longer is the husband able to exercise power just because he is the "man of the house." Rather, he must prove his right to power, or win power by virtue of his own skills and accomplishments *in competition with his wife.* (1960: 29; italics added)

I am arguing that in the competition with his wife, the man has most of the advantages. If we assume that the marriage contract is a mutual mobility bet for gaining ascendency in power, personal autonomy, and self-realization, we will find that the opportunity for winning the bet is very slim for the woman. She is already at a disadvantage when she signs the contract. For further self-realization, for further gains in status and experience as compared with her husband, the cards are already stacked against her, for women are *structurally* deprived of equal opportunities to develop their capacities, resources, and competence in competition with males.

Since theorists of marriage have a quite notable tendency to disregard the psychological, legal, and social blocks put in the way of women as a class when they are discussing power differentials and their sources, I would like to examine some of these.

## Sources of Marital Power

### Socialization

Men and women are socialized differently. By the time women reach marriageable age, they have already been formed by the socialization process. They have been systematically trained to accept second best, not to strive, and to accept the "fact" that they are unworthy of more. Naomi Weisstein's "Kinde, Kuche, Kirche as Scientific Law" states this process clearly:

> How are women characterized in our culture, and in psychology? They are inconsistent, emotionally unstable, lacking in strong conscience or superego, weaker, "nurturant" rather than productive, "intuitive" rather than intelligent, and if they are at all "normal," suited to the home and family. In short, the list adds up to a typical minority group stereotype of inferiority; if they know their place, which is in the home, they are really quite loveable, happy, childlike, loving creatures. In a review of the intellectual differences between little boys and little girls, Eleanor Maccoby has shown that there are no intellectual differences until about high school, or if there are, girls are slightly ahead of boys. At high school, the achievement of women, now measured in terms of productivity and accomplishment, drops off even more rapidly. There are a number of other, non-intellectual tests which show sex differences; I chose the intellectual differences since it is seen clearly that women start becoming inferior. It is no use to talk about women being different but equal; all of the tests I can think of have a "good" outcome and a "bad" outcome. Women usually end up at the "bad" outcome. In light of social expectations about women, what is surprising is not that women end up where society expects they will; what is surprising is that little girls don't get

the message that they are supposed to be stupid until high school, and what is even more remarkable is that some women resist this message even after high shool, college, and graduate school. (1969: 7)

Thus, women begin at a psychological disadvantage when they sign the marriage contract, for they have different training and expectations than do men.

*Marriage: A Free Contract between Equals*

Sociologists universally fail to discuss legal differences in power when the marriage contract is signed.[2] Legally the husband has many more rights over his wife than she has over him. For instance, he can force her to have sexual intercourse with him against her will, an act which if committed against any other woman would constitute the crime of rape. By definition, a husband cannot be guilty of raping his own wife, for "the crime [of rape] is ordinarily that of forcing intercourse on someone other than the wife of the person accused." (Gallen 1967: 6) While a wife theoretically has similar sexual rights, this normally cannot occur against her husband's will.

Women may believe they are voluntarily providing household services, but the courts hold that the husband is legally entitled to his wife's services, and further, that she cannot be paid for her work. In *Your Marriage and the Law*, Pilpel and Zavin state:

As part of the rights of consortium, the husband is entitled to the services of his wife. If the wife works outside the home for strangers, she is usually entitled to her own earnings. But domestic services or assistances which she gives her husband are generally considered part of her wifely duties. The wife's services and society are so essential a part of what the law considers the husband is entitled to as part of the marriage that it will not recognize any agreement between spouses which provides that the husband is to pay for such services or society.

In a Texas case David promised his wife, Fannie, that he would give her $5000 if she would stay with him while he lived and continue taking care of the house and farm accounts, selling his butter and doing all the other tasks which she had done since their marriage. After David's death, Fannie sued his estate for the money which had been promised her. The court held that the contract was unenforceable since Fannie had agreed to do nothing which she was not already legally and morally bound to do as David's wife. (1967: 65)

The legal responsibilities of a wife are to live in the home established by her husband, to perform the domestic chores (cleaning, cooking, washing, etc.) necessary to help maintain that home, and to care for her husband and children. (Gallen 1967: 4) The husband, in return, is obligated to provide her with basic maintenance which includes "necessities" such as food, clothing, medical care, and a place to live, in accordance with his income. She has no legal right to any part of his cash income, nor any legal voice in spending it.[3] Were he to employ a live-in servant in place of a wife, he would have to pay the servant a salary, provide her with her own room (as opposed to "bed"), food, and the necessary equipment for doing her job. She would get at least one day a week off and probably would be required to do considerably less work than a wife and would not be required to provide sexual services.

Thus, being a wife is a full-time job for which one is not entitled to pay. (Chase Manhattan Bank estimates a woman's overall work week at 99.6 hours.) Furthermore, the wife is not entitled to freedom of movement. The husband has the right to decide where the family will live. If she refuses, he can charge her with desertion. This has been upheld by the courts even in cases where the wife could be required to change her citizenship. In states where desertion is grounds for divorce (forty-seven states plus the District of Columbia), the wife would be the "guilty party" and would therefore be entitled to no monetary settlement. (Gallen 1967: 6)[4]

### *A married woman's name*

Leo Kanowitz in *Women and the Law* found that the change in a woman's name upon marriage is not only consistent with social custom; it also appears to be generally required by law.

The probable effects of this unilateral name change upon the relations between the sexes, though subtle in character, are profound. In a very real sense, the loss of a woman's surname represents the destruction of an important part of her personality and its submersion in that of her husband. . . . This name change is consistent with the characterization of coverture as "the old common-law fiction that the husband and wife are one" . . . [which] has worked out in reality to mean that the one is the husband. (1969: 41)

### *The law of support*

The universal rule is that it is the primary obligation of the husband to provide financial support for the family. Kanowitz explored some of the legal ramifications of this general rule.

> The effects of the basic rule upon the marital relationship itself are complex. In common law marital property jurisdictions, the husband's legal obligation to support the family is not an unmixed blessing for the wife. That obligation has been cited, for example, as justifying his right to choose the family home. It has no doubt also played an important part in solidifying his legal role as head and master of the family. For in according the husband this position within the family, the law often seems to be applying on a grand scale the modest principle that "he who pays the piper calls the tune." However, even in the community property states, in which a wife's services in the home are theoretically viewed as being equal to or exceeding in monetary value the husband's earnings outside of the home, husbands have generally been given the rights to manage and control the community property, along with other superior rights and interests in it. (1969: 69)

Thus it is clear that husbands have access to legal advantages which wives do not have. True, the wife does gain legal protection against capricious action by the male, but in exchange, she becomes his vassal. He is the economic head of the joint household, and hence represents it in the view of society. She takes his name and belongs to his class. She follows where his work calls to determine their place of residence. Their lives are geared to the daily, weekly, annual rhythms of his life. She gives him her person and her private labor, but he wants more.

### *The "white man's burden"*

In today's "love match," the husband does not merely require an obedient and efficient worker, he wants something more. He wants his wife to love him, that is, to freely choose over and over again to be subjected to the control of the other, to make his welfare the center of her being.[5] Because the housewife is expected to be keeper of the castle, she has little life of her own other than the management and maintenance of the house, grounds, and family affairs in her areas of control. To fit the master plan of the other becomes her life's work. She becomes the family-servicer. For the working-class wife, her husband's activities affect the daily routines in setting the hour for breakfast, supper, and bedtime. If a husband does not work the standard eight-hour day (from 9:00 to 5:00), she may have to fix her big meal at 2:00 in the afternoon instead of at noon or in the early evening. If the husband has an extra job in the evening or on the weekends, this enlarges the amount of home and yard responsibilities she must undertake. If he drives the car to work, she finds herself isolated in her own immediate neighborhood while he's gone. Her daily life is centered upon the tasks of homemaking, child-rearing, and husband-servicing. She fixes breakfast, washes clothes, dresses children, cleans the house, does the dishes, makes lunch, irons the clothes, makes supper, makes light snacks, makes the beds, dusts, mops, mends old clothes, washes the windows, scrubs the kitchen, works out in the yard, shops for the groceries, and sews on new clothes or curtains. She describes her life as "dull, just dull." (Rainwater, Coleman, and Handel, 1968: chapter 2)

The middle-class housewife, too, is a child-rearer and husband-tender. She fixes their meals, sews their clothes frequently, and makes sure they get to school and work on time. She, however, experiences more variety in her life because she has more personal, avocational, and outside interests than does the working-class wife. But she, too, is a husband- and family-servicer. She must be understanding and helpful when he has problems at work and must do a good job of representing him socially to work associates, the boss, and clients when that is necessary. Her life, too, revolves around the other. (Rainwater *et al.*, 1968: 95) For the middle-class wife, even the formation and maintenance of friendships are dominated by the husband. (Babchuk and Bates, 1963: 377–384)

This "obligation" and supreme justification to make the

other's welfare the center of her being is the crux of what husbands term their "oppression," as Simone de Beauvoir has so clearly observed:

> . . . Her very devotion seems annoying, importunate; it is transformed for the husband into a tyranny from which he tries to escape; and yet he it is who imposes it upon his wife as her supreme, her unique justification. In marrying her, he obliges her to give herself entirely to him; but he does not assume the corresponding obligation, which is to accept the gift and all its consequences.
>
> It is the duplicity of the husband that dooms his wife to a misfortune of which he complains that he is himself the victim. Just as he wants her to be at once warm and cool in bed, he requires her to be wholly his and yet no burden; he wishes her to establish him a fixed place on earth and to leave him free; to assume the monotonous daily round and not to bore him; to be always at hand and never importunate; he wants to have her all to himself and not to belong to her, to live as one of a couple and to remain alone. Her life through, she measures the extent of that betrayal. (1964: 452)

Throughout their lives together, she attempts to wrest back from him some measure of her independence. Surely it is not entirely an accident that divorce rates are highest at the early phase of the marriage cycle and drop with the birth of children, when women are most dependent upon the husband economically and emotionally.

### *Economic Sources of Power*

It is clear that an economic base of power is important in marriage, for the higher the husband on the social scale, the greater his decision-making in the family. Using three indices of success in the community, Blood and Wolfe found that all three affected power differentials in the family: (1) The higher the husband's occupational prestige, the greater his voice in marital decisions. (2) Income was an even more sensitive indicator of power than his occupation. The higher the husband's income, the greater his power. (3) The higher the husband's status (based on occupation, income, education, and ethnic background), the more power he had to make decisions.

The major break in power fell between white-collar occupations and blue-collar occupations, the white-collar husbands having much more power than blue-collar husbands. The increment to power by income was steady. By social status, there is a curvilinear relationship to power. The low blue-collar workers had more power than the high blue-collar workers, and the power for the husband increased again at the low white-collar level and the high white-collar level. White-collar workers, then, are generally more powerful than blue-collar workers, but in the blue-collar marriages, the low blue-collar worker has more power than the high blue-collar husband. I will discuss some of the possible causes of this in the section on education.

These material bases of power were operant despite the fact that middle-class husbands espouse a more egalitarian ideology than do working-class husbands. William Goode comments on this tension between the ideal and the real distribution of power.

> Since at present this philosophy [of equalitarianism in the family] is most strongly held among the better educated segments of the population, and among women more than among men, two interesting tensions may be seen: Lower-class men concede fewer rights *ideologically* than their women in fact *obtain*, and the more educated men are more likely to concede *more* rights ideologically than they in fact grant. (1963: 21)

He then supplies us with an excellent example of how ideology may be modified to justify the current distribution of power:

> One partial resolution of the latter tension is to be found in the frequent assertion from families of professional men that they should not make demands which would interfere with his *work*: He takes preference as a professional, not as a family head or as a male; nevertheless, the precedence is his. By contrast, lower-class men demand deference as *men*, as heads of families.

Marital power, then, is a function of income more than philosophy. It seems clear that the authority of the male is used as a justification of power where it is useful (working class), and new justifications arise when needed. Professional men demand deference because of their work. This enables them to accept the doctrine of equality without having to live it.

Blood and Wolfe claim that this superior power of high-status husbands is not due to coercion, but to the convenient recognition by both partners that the husband is the one eminently qualified to make the decisions in the family. This argument is reminiscent of arguments in labor relations. The labor contract is assumed to be freely entered into by both partners. The power conferred on the one party by difference in class position—the real economic position of both—is not taken into account. That economic relations compel the worker to surrender even the last semblance of equal rights is of no concern. Coercion (however subtle) based on economic power is still coercion, whether it involves wife-beating or not.

As further evidence that individual competence and resourcefulness (regardless of sex) are not the real issues, we must examine Blood and Wolfe's discussion of the *deviant* case—wife dominance. In these cases, they claim that the wives who have superior power acquire it not because they have access to pragmatic sources of power or because they are more competent than their husbands (heaven forbid!), but by default.

> We will find throughout this study dissatisfaction associated with wife-dominance. This is not, however, simply a reflection of the breaking of social rules. Rather, the circumstances which lead to the wife's dominance involve corresponding inadequacies on the husband's part. An inadequate husband is by definition unable to make a satisfactory marriage partner. So the dominant wife is not exultant over her "victory" but exercises power regretfully by default of her "no good" or incapacitated husband. (1960: 45)

For Blood and Wolfe, wives can never gain dominance legitimately; it falls in their unhappy laps and is accepted only unwillingly and with much bitterness.

Despite the superior power gained by the husband because of his economic position, there are conditions under which wives do erode that power to some extent. Not surprisingly, the wife's participation in the work force is an important variable. Women who work have more power vis-à-vis their husbands than do nonworking wives, regardless of race or class. The number of years the wife has worked also affects the balance of power—the longer she has worked, the more power she is able to obtain. This, to some extent, explains why blue-collar wives have more power than white-collar wives (in comparison to their husbands), since their participation in the work force is much higher than for the wives of high-status, high-income husbands. (Blood and Wolfe, 1960: 40–41) In addition, their proportional contribution to the family income is greater and their wifely services less easily replaceable.

### *Organizational Participation*

Participation in formal organizations, too, is a factor which affects marital decision-making as shown by Blood and Wolfe's data. Women with much more organizational participation than their husbands alter the balance of power in the wife's direction. In those cases where the participation is equal or in which the husband is superior (by far the most frequent), the balance of power increases in the husband's direction. (1960: 39)

### *Education*

Education is also influential in the distribution of power. The more education the husband has, the greater his power. Highly educated white-collar husbands continue to gain power if they exceed their wives' education (and chances are good that they do, in fact, exceed), and they lose it if they fall short of the wife. The same trend holds within the low white-collar and high blue-collar groups, but not with the low blue-collar families. Low blue-collar husbands have more power even when their wives have superior educations. (Blood and Wolfe, 1960: 28, 38)

In working-class families, the less-educated and unskilled husbands have more power than do those husbands with higher incomes. Mirra Komarovsky in *Blue Collar Marriage* attempted to explain some of the causes of this power anomaly. First, patriarchal attitudes are more prevalent among the less educated and hence a source of power in some families. High school graduates, because of a social milieu which does not sanction patriarchal authority (though it does sanction male privilege), tend to lose power. Second, among the less educated, the husband is more likely to excel in personal resources for the exercise of influence, and this margin of male superiority narrows among the high school graduates. Among the less educated, the husband has wider contacts in the community than his wife. He represents the world to his family, and he is the family's "secretary of state." In contrast, a few of the more educated wives enjoy wider contacts and higher status outside the home than their husbands. Third, the education of the spouses was found to affect their degrees of power because of mating patterns. The effect of educational inequality appears to explain the lower power of the skilled workers in comparison with the semiskilled. The skilled worker is more likely than the semiskilled worker to marry a high school graduate. By virtue of their relatively high earnings, skilled workers may be able to marry better-educated women, but by marrying "upward" they lose the degree of power enjoyed by the semiskilled over their less-educated wives. (1967: 226–229)

### *Physical Coercion*

Komarovsky is one of the few sociologists who has mentioned physical coercion as a source of power in the family. In her discussion of the low blue-collar family, she found that the use of physical violence was a source of masculine power. However, not only the use of physical violence, but its *threat* can be an effective form of control. She reports that one woman said of her husband: "He is a big man and terribly strong. One time when he got sore at me, he pulled off the bannister and he ripped up three steps." With the evidence of this damage in view, this woman realized, as she put it, what her husband could do to her if he should decide to strike her. (1967: 227)

Lynn O'Connor has suggested that threats of violence (in gestures of dominance) are not limited to any particular class, but are a universal source of male power and control. After discussing dominance gestures in primates, she states:

> Although there have been no systematic studies of the gestures of dominance and submission in human groups, the most casual observation will show their crucial role in the day to day mechanics of oppression. An example should clarify.
>
> A husband and wife are at a party. The wife says something that the husband does not want her to say (perhaps it reveals something about him that might threaten his ranking with other men). He quickly tightens the muscles around his jaw and gives her a rapid but intense direct stare. Outsiders don't notice the interaction, though they may have a vaguely uncomfortable feeling that they are intruding on something private. The wife, who is acutely sensitive to the gestures of the man on whom she is dependent, immediately stops the conversation, lowers or turns her head slightly, averts her eyes, or gives off some other gestures of submission which communicate acquiescence to her husband and reduce his aggression. Peace is restored; the wife has been put in her place. If the wife does not respond with submission, she can expect to be punished. When gestures of dominance fail, the dominant animal usually resorts to violence. We all know stories about husbands beating up their wives after the party when they have reached the privacy of their home. Many of us have experienced at least a few blows from husbands or lovers when we refuse to submit to them. It is difficult to assess the frequency of physical attacks within so-called love relationships, because women rarely tell even one another when they have taken place. By developing a complicated ethic of loyalty (described above in terms of privacy), men have protected themselves from such reports leaking out and becoming public information. Having already been punished for stepping out of role, the woman is more than a little reluctant to tell anyone of the punishment because it would mean violating the loyalty code, which is an even worse infraction of the rules and most likely would result in further and perhaps more severe punishment. (1970: 9)

That violence or threat of violence may be more widespread than is currently admitted is also suggested by complaints made by wives in divorce. Goode in *Women in Divorce* found that almost one-third (32 percent) of the wives reported "authority-cruelty" as the reason for divorce. Authority problems are defined as being disagreements concerning the permissible degree of dominance over a wife and include cruelty, beating, jealousy, and "wanted to have own way." (1956: 120, 123) Since Goode did not code cruelty or beating separately, we have no definite evidence as to the frequency of such behavior, but there is evidence that problems with male dominance are widespread in the population. Goode comments:

> . . . In different strata and groups, the husband may be permitted different control techniques. For example, the middle-class male will very likely be censured more if he uses force to control his wife than if he uses techniques of nagging, jealousy, or sulking. On the other hand, there is a strong reservoir of attitude on the part of the American male generally, that he has a *right* to tell his wife what to do. This attitude is given more overt expression, and is more frequently backed by force, in the lower strata. It is not so much that beating and cruelty are viewed as an obvious male right in marriage, but only that this is one of the techniques used from time to time, and with little or no subsequent guilt, for keeping control of the wife. . . . In our society, the husband who successfully asserts his dominance does enjoy some approval and even a modicum of envy from other males. Male dominance is to some extent actually approved. (1956: 122)

A more recent article, "Middle-Class Violence," indicates further that physical coercion is an overlooked variable of some importance. One-fifth of all Americans approve of a husband's slapping his wife on appropriate occasions. What is even more startling is that this approval increases with education and income. Of those with eight or less years of schooling, 16 percent approve of the husband's slapping his wife, but of those with a college education, 25 percent approve of wife-slapping. (Stark and McEvoy, 1970: 52)

### *Suburbanization*

Blood and Wolfe also found that families living in the suburbs were more husband-dominant than those who live in the central city. This directly contradicts the popular image of suburban life as being dominated by women and, therefore, oriented toward the satisfaction of women's needs. The data showed that suburban families were more husband-dominant at every status level than their urban peers. (1960: 36) They then speculated that suburban husbands were more powerful "because suburban wives feel more indebted to their husbands for providing them a place to live which is more attractive than the industrial city of Detroit. If so, this fits the theory that power accrues to those husbands who are able to provide for their wives especially well." (1960: 36)

In a recent study on the working class in suburbia, Tallman has suggested that other factors than the wife's gratitude might be working to build up the husband's power. He constructed a profile of the working-class marriage which indicated consistently that wives tend to maintain close ties with relatives and old girl friends while husbands continue their premarital peer-group associations. Social and psychological support emanates, then, not from marriage partners, but from same-sex friends and kin of long standing and tight-knit social networks. As a consequence, there is a relatively high degree of conjugal role segmentation which is characterized in part by a lack of communication between the spouses. In general, the experiences of working-class women are more localized and circumscribed than their male counterparts. Since their security and identity depend upon their position vis-à-vis a small group of intimates, their opinions and beliefs are both dependent upon and in accord with this group. Blue-collar women have minimal experience in the external world and tend to view it fearfully. Men, on the other hand, have more frequent social contacts, in part for occupational reasons, but also because they have been socialized into male roles which define them as family representatives to the outside world.

Tallman concluded that suburban women are more isolated because of disruptions in the primary group relations. The disruption of friendship and kinship ties is not only personally disintegrating for the wife but also demands fundamental changes in the role allocations in the family. Suburban wives are more dependent upon their husbands for a variety of services previously provided by members of tight-knit networks. In brief, he found that moving to the suburbs was experienced as a disintegrative force in the lives of many working-class women, leading to a greater isolation and dependence upon the husband. (1969: 66–69)
This partial explanation of the husband's increased power in the suburbs as being due to the wife's increased isolation

and dependence seems eminently more reasonable than Blood and Wolfe's explanation that it is due to gratitude on the part of the wife. Tallman's data also indicate that the wife frequently regrets the move to the suburbs, despite more pleasant living conditions, because of its disruption of the kinship and friendship network.

*Race*

Blood and Wolfe report very little on black families, except to say that Negro husbands have unusually low power compared to whites. Their data show that white husbands are always more powerful than their black status equals and that this is true within each occupational stratum, each income bracket, and each social level.[6] They concede that "the label 'black' is almost a synonym for low status in our society—and Detroit Negroes are no exception in having less education, lower incomes, inferior jobs, and lower prestige generally than whites. Since low status white husbands make relatively few decisions, we would expect Negro husbands to exercise little power, too." (1960: 34)

What they fail to take into account (among other things) is that black women, too, are discriminated against in our society. They, too, have less education, lower incomes, inferior jobs, and lower prestige generally than whites. The fact that blacks are discriminated against does not explain power differentials within black families. To explain power differentials in black families, just as for white families, the sources of power for black men and black women must be examined and compared. Blood and Wolfe fail to do this.

Their primary purpose seems to be to demonstrate gross differences between black and white families, without bothering to report differences within black families. Andrew Billingsley in *Black Families in White America* has criticized just this approach in sociological studies. He draws attention to the fact that class variables are as important in black families as in white families. "Negro families are not only Negroes to be compared and contrasted with white families, they may also be upper-class (10%), middle-class (40%), or lower-class (50%), with urban or rural moorings, with southern or northern residence, and most importantly, they may be meaningfully compared and contrasted with each other." (1968: 8)

Billingsley accounts to some extent for what may be part of the white/black differences in overall power. He notes that black samples are dominated by low-income families and points out that even where income levels between whites and blacks are similar, the groups are not truly comparable, for the black group reflects not only its income level but its experiences with prejudice and subjugation as well.

Because both black husbands and black wives are discriminated against in this society, it is absurd to explain power differentials between them as being due to race (as Blood and Wolfe do), unless there are mitigating factors brought about by racial discrimination which operate in favor of one sex's access to sources of marital power. Since data on the black family are so sadly inadequate, I can at this point only examine some demographic data which have possible implications for power distributions in black families.

Black women comprised of 40 percent of all black workers in 1960. They earned considerably less than black men. The median earnings of black women in full-time year-round employment in 1959 was two-fifths that of black men.[7] (In 1964, it was 64.2 percent.)[8] Since 1963, the unemployment rate for black women has been higher than the unemployment rate for black men. In 1967, for Negro men aged twenty to sixty-four, the unemployment rate was 3.7. For Negro women it was 6.0. The unemployment rates for black women under twenty were also higher than the rates for black men.[9] Clearly, then, black women are not superior to black men in income.

In occupational status, we find that Negro women are most frequently in service jobs while Negro men are predominantly blue-collar workers. However, relatively more Negro women than men had professional or technical jobs, this being due primarily to their extensive employment as teachers and nurses. Of all full-time year-round Negro workers in 1960, Negro women constituted nearly all private household workers. They were more than half the number of Negroes employed as professional workers (61 percent) and other service workers (51 percent). Except for the clerical group, in which the numbers were about equal, the remaining occupational groups (sales, managers, operatives, crafts, laborers, and farmers) had fewer Negro women than men.[10]

Negro women in general had a higher median education than Negro men. (This is also true in the white population.) The median educational level of nonwhite women was 10.1 years in 1966, but for nonwhite men it was 9.4. However, at the top of the educational ladder, just as for the white population, men were more numerous.[11]

Though there are differences, we find that the power sources *between the sexes* for both blacks and whites are similar. Obviously, black men have suffered from discrimination in this society. This is evident in the figures of income, occupation, and education. However, it is also evident that Negro women have suffered discrimination, not only because of race, but also because of their sex. Thus, they are doubly oppressed. This, too, is evident in figures of income, occupation, and education.

Jesse Bernard in *Marriage and Family among Negroes* has suggested still another variable which must be taken into account in Negro family patterns. She reports that there is an extraordinarily low sex ratio (number of males per 100 females) among urban Negroes as compared to whites. The ratio is especially low (88.4) in the critical years of marriageability. Bernard conjectures that the low sex ratio means that black women are competing for a relatively scarce "good" when they look forward to marriage, being buyers in a sellers market. (1966: 69)

While this is certainly not the cause of power distributions in the black family, it does suggest a source of male power.[12] Delores Mack, in a study of black and white families, supports this contention. (1969)

What these findings suggest is that researchers have not carefully evaluated the logic of the assumptions of their hypotheses. They have looked at the white community; there they have observed that education, occupation, and income are important sources of power. . . . They have ignored the possibility that the sources of power in the Black community may be different from that in the white community. In fact, they have ignored one of the most potent forms of power in any marriage, but particularly sex power in Black marriages. Certainly researchers have noted the preoccupation of the Black male with sex. Some have viewed this preoccupation with sex as a form of escapism, failing to realize that this concentration on sexual activities may be a main source of power. The Black male is well aware, as Eldridge Cleaver notes, that he is the desired sex object for both white and Black females. He may use this power in his marriage, much as the white male uses his education and earning power as a lever in his marriage.

The threat or use of violence (as discussed above) is another factor which must be taken into account to explain power differentials in black as well as in white families. Obviously, we need to take a much harder look at the "black matriarchy." But before this can be done, a great deal of research on the differences within black families is needed, as Billingsley has suggested.

*Life Cycle*

The stages of the family life cycle also affect the marital power distribution. In the early (childless) stage of marriage, the wife is frequently working, but the pressure of social discrimination against women is already beginning to be exerted. Women are unable to procure anything but low-paying, low-status jobs as compared with their husbands. Already status background and autonomous experiences are being eroded. Though the married childless woman maintains some sort of independent social and economic status if she works, it is below that of her husband. During this period, the power of the husband is moderate.

With the birth of children, there is a substantial jump in power differentials, the husband universally gaining. (Blood and Wolfe, 1960: 41–44) There is more than a little truth in the old saw that the best way to control a woman is to "keep her barefoot and pregnant," for there is evidence that the power of the wife declines as the number of children grows. (Heer, 1958: 341–347) At this period, after the first child is born, but before the oldest child is in school, the power of the husband reaches its maximum. Many women stop working during this stage and, in doing so, become isolated and almost totally socially, economically, and emotionally dependent upon their husbands, further eroding any strength they might have gained due to earning power or participation in organizations. They lose their position, cannot keep up with developments in their field, do not build up seniority. Further, women lose that precious "organizational" experience, the growth of competence and resources in the outside world, the community positions which contribute to power in a marriage. The boundaries of her world contract, the possibilities of growth diminish. If they return to work, and most women do, they must begin again at a low-status job and usually stay there—underemployed and underpaid. As a woman's children grow up, she gradually regains some power within the family.

These data again call into question the theory of individual resources as the source of power in marriage. As David Heer pointed out, there is no reason, according to Blood and Wolfe's theory, for the power of the wife to be greater before she has borne children than when her children are preschool age. Surely the wife with preschool children is contributing more resources to the marriage than she did before their children were born. (1963: 138) Power, then, is clearly not the result of individual contributions and resources in the marriage, but is clearly related to questions of social worth; and the value of women and women's work, as viewed by society, is obviously very low. The contributions of women in the home are of little concern and are consequently little valued, as Margaret Benston explained in "The Political Economy of Women's Liberation." (1969: 3–4):

> In sheer quantity, household labor, including child care, constitutes a huge amount of socially necessary production. Nevertheless, in a society based on commodity production, it is not usually considered "real work" since it is outside of trade and market place. It is pre-capitalist in a very real sense. The assignment of household work as the function of a special category "women" meant that this group *does* stand in a different relation to production than the group "men." We will tentatively define women, then, as that group of people who are responsible for the production of simple use-values in those activities associated with the home and the family.

Since men carry no responsibility for such production, the difference between the two groups lies here. Notice that women are not excluded from commodity production. Their participation in wage labor occurs, but as a group, they have no structural responsibility in this area and such participation is ordinarily regarded as transient. Men, on the other hand, are responsible for commodity production; they are not, in principle, given any role in household labor. . . . The material basis for the inferior status of women is to be found in just this definition of women. In a society in which money determines value, women are a group who work outside the money economy. Their work is not worth money, is therefore valueless, is therefore not even real work. And women themselves, who do this valueless work, can hardly be expected to be worth as much as men, who work for money. In structural terms, the closest thing to the condition of women is the condition of others who are or were outside of commodity production, i.e., peasants or serfs.

## *The Husband: Most Likely to Succeed*

Thus it is clear that for a wife to gain even a modicum of power in the marital relationship, she must gain it from external sources, i.e., she must participate in the work force, her education must be superior to that of her husband, and her participation in organizations must excel his. Equality of resources leaves the power in the hands of the husband. However, access to these sources of power are structurally blocked for women.

In the general population, women are unable to procure anything but low-status, low-paying, dead-end jobs as compared with their husbands, be it factory or university.[13] Partly as a result of unequal pay for the same work, partly as a consequence of channeling women into low-paying jobs, the median income of women is far less than that of men workers. Black women tend to fare slightly better in relation to black men, but make only two-thirds as much as white women.

MEDIAN EARNINGS OF YEAR-ROUND FULL-TIME WORKERS, 1968[14]

| | Men | Women | Women as % of Men |
|---|---|---|---|
| White | $7,870 | $4,580 | 56.9 |
| Nonwhite | 5,314 | 3,487 | 62.4 |

In higher socioeconomic classes, the husband is more likely to excel his wife in formal education than he is among blue-collar workers. Men predominate among college graduates, regardless of race, but adult women have a higher median of education (12.1 for women, 12.0 for men in 1964).[15] (We have already seen that the educational attainment of the nonwhite population is lower [10.1 for women, 9.4 for men], reflecting the results of racial discrimination.)

All of these areas are sources of power in the marital relationship, and in all of these areas women are structurally blocked from realizing their capacities. It is not because of individual resources or personal competence, then, that husbands obtain power in marriage, but because of the discrimination against women in the larger society. Men gain resources as a class, not as individuals, and women are blocked as a class, not as individuals.

In our mutual mobility bet women (as a class) always lose in the fight for power within the marital relationship. In a system of institutionalized male supremacy, the cards are systematically stacked against women in all areas—occupational, political, educational, legal, as well as within the institution of the family. As long as the structure of society remains the same, as long as categorical discrimination against women is carried out, there is relatively little chance for most women to gain autonomy, *regardless* of how much good will there is on the part of husbands.

The equalitarian marriage as a norm is a myth. Under some conditions, individual women can gain power vis-à-vis their husbands, but more power is not equal power. Equal power women do not have. Equal power women will not get so long as the present socioeconomic system remains.

NOTES

1. Blood and Wolfe's work plays a major part in this paper because it has been one of the most influential studies of marital power in the last ten years.
2. It should be made clear that legality is not necessarily a basis for decision-making. It merely reflects the position of society as to how the power is to be distributed when such distributions are contested in the courts. This normally occurs

upon dissolution of marriage and not in an ongoing relationship.

3. "Know Your Rights," Women's Bureau (1965: 1).
4. Ideas in this section suggested by Shiela Cronan's "Marriage," The Feminists, New York.
5. Conversation with Ann Leffler, 1969.
6. Blood and Wolfe's report of the data is so skimpy that it makes interpretation difficult. For example, they say that the thirty-five high income husbands (over $4,000) have lower mean power (4.09) than their sixty-eight less affluent colleagues (4.56). This is possibly analogous to the distribution of power in the white blue-collar class, where low blue-collar husbands have more power than high blue-collar husbands. Comparisons are difficult because, for the general population, income was broken into five groups, while for black families only two were used—over $4,000 and below $4,000. They reported that "the generalization that the husband's power is correlated with occupational status also holds within the Negro race" (4.31, 4.60, no cases, and 5.00 respectively). The only mention of Negro husbands and social status was that the few white husbands in the lowest status groups differ sharply from their powerless Negro counterparts (no figures reported).
7. *Negro Women Workers*, Women's Bureau, Department of Labor (1964: 23–25).
8. Fact Sheet on the Relative Position of Women and Men Workers in the Economy (1965: 3).
9. U.S. Department of Labor, Bureau of Labor Statistics, *Employment and Earnings*, Vol. 16, No. 7 (January, 1970), Table A-1 (data under Negro heading is for "Negro and other races").
10. *Negro Women Workers*, pp. 23–25.
11. *Negro Women . . . in the Population and in the Labor Force* (1967: 1–2).
12. This has also been suggested in several articles in *The Black Woman*, edited by Toni Cade (1970), particularly "Dear Black Man" by Fran Sanders; "Who Will Revere the Black Woman?" by Abbey Lincoln; "The Black Woman as Woman" by Kay Lindsey; "Double Jeopardy: To Be Black and Female" by Frances Beale; "On the Issue of Roles" by Toni Cade; "Black Man, My Man, Listen!" by Gail Stokes; "Is the Black Man Castrated?" by Jean Carey Bond and Pat Peery.
13. *Handbook on Women Workers*, U.S. Department of Labor, Women's Bureau (1965: 34, 35).
14. Fact Sheet on the Relative Position of Women and Men Workers (1968).
15. *Handbook on Women Workers* (1965: 172).

REFERENCES

Babchuk, Nicholas, and Alan P. Bates (1963). "The Primary Relations of Middle-Class Couples: A Study in Male Dominance," *American Sociological Review*, 28: 377–384.

de Beauvoir, Simone (1968). *The Second Sex*. New York: Bantam Books.

Benston, Margaret (1969). "The Political Economy of Women's Liberation," *Monthly Review*, September, 1969.

Bernard, Jesse (1966). *Marriage and Family among Negroes*. Englewood Cliffs, N.J.: Prentice-Hall.

Billingsley, Andrew, and Amy Tate Billingsley (1968). *Black Families in White America*. Englewood Cliffs, N.J.: Prentice-Hall.

Blood, Robert O., and Donald M. Wolfe (1960). *Husbands and Wives, the Dynamics of Married Living*. New York: Free Press.

Cade, Toni (1970). *The Black Woman, an Anthology*. New York: New American Library.

Cronan, Shiela (1969). "Marriage," The Feminists, New York.

Gallen, Richard T. (1967). *Wives' Legal Rights*. New York: Dell Publishing Co.

Goode, William (1956). *Women in Divorce*. New York: Free Press.

——— (1963). *World Revolution and Family Patterns*. New York: Free Press.

——— (1964). *The Family*. Englewood Cliffs, N.J.: Prentice-Hall.

Heer, David M. (1958). "Dominance and the Working Wife," *Social Forces*, 36: 341–347.

——— (1963). "The Measurement and Bases of Family Power: An Overview," *Marriage and Family Living*, 25: 133–139.

Kanowitz, Leo (1969). *Women and the Law, the Unfinished Revolution*. Albuquerque: University of New Mexico Press.

Komarovsky, Mirra (1967). *Blue Collar Marriage*. New York: Vintage Books.

Mack, Delores (1969). "The Husband-Wife Power Relationship in Black Families and White Families," Ph.D. dissertation, Stanford University, October, 1969, unpublished.

O'Connor, Lynn (1970). "Male Dominance, the Nitty-Gritty of Oppression," *It Ain't Me, Babe*, Vol. 1, No. 8 (June 11–July 1, 1970), pp. 9–11.

Pilpel, Harriet F., and Theodora Zavin (1964). *Your Marriage and the Law*. New York: Collier Books.

Rainwater, Lee, Richard P. Coleman, and Gerald Handel (1968). *Workingman's Wife*. New York: MacFadden-Bartell Books.

Safilios-Rothschild, Constantia (1969). "Family Sociology or Wives' Family Sociology? A Cross-Cultural Examination of Decision Making," *Journal of Marriage and the Family*, Vol. 31, No. 2 (May, 1969), pp. 290–301.

Stark, Rodney, and James McEvoy, III (1970). "Middle-Class Violence," *Psychology Today*, Vol. 4, No. 6 (November, 1970).

Tallman, Irving (1969). "Working-Class Wives in Suburbia: Fulfillment or Crisis?" *Journal of Marriage and the Family*, Vol. 31, No. 1 (February, 1969), pp. 65–72.

Weisstein, Naomi (1969). "Kinde, Kuche, Kirche as Scientific Law: Psychology Constructs the Female." New York: New England Free Press.

## *United States Government Publications*

Fact Sheet on the Relative Position of Women and Men Workers in the Economy, U.S. Department of Commerce, Bureau of the Census: CPR–60, No. 66., 1968.

*1965 Handbook on Women Workers*, U.S. Department of Labor, Women's Bureau.

"Know Your Rights: What a Working Wife Should Know about Her Legal Rights," U.S. Department of Labor, Women's Bureau, 1965.

"Negro Women . . . in the Population and in the Labor Force," U.S. Department of Labor, Wage and Labor Standards Administration, December, 1967.

"Negro Women Workers in 1960," U.S. Department of Labor, Women's Bureau, 1963.

U.S. Department of Labor, Bureau of Statistics, *Employment and Earnings*, Vol. 16, No. 7, January, 1970.

III

# *Gender Differentiation and the Ambiguities of Sexual Identification*

*In the last few decades the traditional sex-role differentiation has been subjected to considerable change without approaching a point of consolidation. Harriet Holter, Professor of Social Psychology at the University of Oslo in Norway, has written extensively on sex roles and related subjects, including her recent book on* Sex Roles and Social Structure *(Oslo University Press, 1970). The article presented here is reprinted from* Acta Sociologica, *Vol. 14, 1971. She summarizes present theories of changes in sex-role differentiation, stressing that sex-role definitions are the results rather than the determinants of social change. The needs of the economic system with respect to labor and consumption are seen as the most important promoters of the change from traditional sex roles to a quasi-egalitarianism. This leads the author to some reflections on the question of strategies for sex-role changes.*

*Joachim Israel, Professor of Sociology at the University of Lund in Sweden, and his student, Rosmari Eliasson, have studied the realities of the "sexual revolution." Professor Israel, whose book on* Alienation—From Marx to Modern Sociology *has been translated into several languages, and his collaborator have found that in a permissive society the expectations of women control traditional female sex roles more than do men's expectations. If high emphasis is placed on sexuality as a goal in itself and moral pressure is exerted to engage in sexual behavior only under conditions of love, then divorce and extramarital relations are bound to increase. This result further differentiates the findings of Martha Baum presented in the preceding section. While such conflicting values apparently have a negative impact on marriage relations, the younger generation's greater permissiveness has a healthy effect on moral double standards. The more permissiveness, the fewer double standards. To a large extent the "sexual revolution" is a drastic change in attitudes rather than in behavior.*

# 7

# Sex Roles and Social Change[1]

HARRIET HOLTER

## *Introduction: Theories and Strategies*

THE FOLLOWING IS A tentative outline of perspectives on changing sex roles in present-day society. First, a brief summary of some theories on sex roles and social change is given. It is of course impossible here to give justice to the great variety and depth of sex-role theories, but attention is drawn to a few systematic descriptions of how and why sex roles are established and maintained. Second, an elaboration of important points of theoretical descriptions, as seen by this author, contains the substance of this article. The focus is here on fairly recent changes in sex roles and their links with society at large. Finally, questions of strategy, i.e., questions as to where in the social structure—in the light of theory—actions toward change should be directed in order to result in desired consequences, are discussed.

## *Some Theories of Sex-Role Change*

Most theories about change in sex roles have a global character. They are often formulated with a view to understanding the very existence of gender differentiation, and at the same time purport to explain changes in the position of women especially.

A considerable number of authors simply point to changing "traditions" or "attitudes" as the main basis for changes in sex roles. Since traditions and attitudes are among the phenomena to be explained, only theories that attempt to do so are mentioned here. Also, theories of sex roles that give constitutional features of men's and women's psychology a main explanatory status must necessarily be excluded here, since they do not lend themselves to an understanding of changes in the system.

The sociological, anthropological, and social-psychological theories all seem to point—ultimately—to changes in the requirements of the economic system as the prime moving forces of shifts in sex roles or changes in the status of women.

The American sociologist Goode, for example, points to industrialization as a main explanation for a trend toward egalitarian relations within and outside the family. The industrialized economy and its need for a mobile, flexible, labor force is best served with a small, independent family. Goode postulates a "fit" between the conjugal family and the modern industrial system, stressing the individual's right to move about and the universalistic evaluation of skills. The increasing demand for skill and mobility tends to eliminate barriers of race and sex, and, in addition, forces within the conjugal family press for equality between husband and wife.[2]

Bott, especially, has shown how the social network of a family—that is, its total web of friends and social contacts—may influence the division of tasks in the family.[3] The families with looser social ties cannot count on stand-ins in traditional roles, and husband and wife are forced to give up a traditional arrangement and to share more than the families with more close-knit networks. Mobility combined with urbanization, which is likely to produce socially isolated families, may thus develop more egalitarian relations between spouses.

"The crisis theory of women's equality" furnishes another illustration of a view of changing sex roles. Rapid modernization as well as war and crisis often seem to bring women into "male" positions, at least for some time,[4] a fact which may be interpreted as a national mobilization of all resources, even secondary ones. In times of crisis, the economic or military demands may, at least temporarily, lead to a breakdown of cultural norms and ideals pertaining to men's and women's tasks. The fact that gender differentiation is reestablished, although often in novel forms, when crisis conditions disappear does not render the "crisis theory" useless. It serves to illustrate the importance not only of material resources but also of the time necessary for changing ascribed roles. The possibilities and limitations for sex-role change inherent in a society are likewise demonstrated during crisis.

Also relevant is the notion that sex differentiation is caused by gender differences in physical strength, which suggests that when technological development renders physical strength unimportant, as in highly mechanized production, this will eventually diminish sex differentiation.

In Marxist thinking, strategy can hardly be separated from theoretical descriptions without doing injustice to both. Nevertheless, for the sake of analysis and since Marxist theory is the theory of social change par exellence, a few points concerning Marxist ideas on changes in sex roles are presented here, rather than in the last section. Marx never formulated a comprehensive view on the subject, although his works contain several references to it; traditional Marxist theory is mainly developed by Engels[5] and later by Bebel[6] and Lenin.[7] In general, Marxist analyses of sex differentiation and sex discrimination are, of course, formulated in terms of historical development, starting with changes in the material conditions. With the development of surplus capital in prehistoric times, man—who through a natural and nondiscriminating division of labor with women had access to the surplus—took possession and instituted private property. Private property again necessitates individual as opposed to collective households and rules of inheritance. This is the foundation of the patriarchical family in which the father rules, and in which women and children are subjugated to the father.

Engels as well as Lenin saw women's participation in modern, collective forms of production and the disappearance of individual household work as a condition for equality and liberation of women. Lenin strongly advocated the establishment of child-care institutions and partly collective household functions in the Soviet Union, and seemed to believe that the U.S.S.R. was on the road to the liberation of women.

It is recognized, however, also among Marxists, that important elements of traditional gender discrimination have survived in Eastern Europe, and that additional theoretical considerations must be brought to bear on Marxist ideas about the subject. Simone de Beauvoir,[8] Evelyn Sullerot,[9] Juliet Mitchell,[10] and others have started this work, bringing forth rather different conceptions of sex roles and the forces which influence them. Most important is de Beauvoir's attempt to link historical materialism to a conception of man as a being of transcendence, seeking always to dominate the other, to exercise his sovereignty in an objective fashion. Men would not have used their early material advantage to dominate women had this not been embedded in their existential condition. According to de Beauvoir, then, a change in sex roles requires not only changes in the economic and social order, but first of all women's attainment of authenticity.

Recent Marxist theories on women's position are all very vague with respect to the crucial distinction between equality in a capitalist versus a socialist society. This is perhaps most evident in Mitchell's analysis, which focuses on the situation of women with respect to production, reproduction, socialization, and sexuality. Only changes in all these four structures can bring about equality between men and women, but they are at present in different stages of development. The problem of structures in which women are *not* integrated, e.g., the political power structure, the relation between class struggle and sex equality, is left undiscussed in Mitchell's article. One is further led to forget that some of the repression and manipulations to which women are subject are shared by men.

One of the difficulties of a strict Marxist analysis of gender differentiation is that such differentiation is common to all productive relationships, but is less important than the more specific relationship expressed by social classes.[11] Gender differentiation as such cannot be linked to capitalism. The task of Marxists is to place gender differentiation as an element in the productive relationship and in the superstructure, not as a property of the productive forces. The Marxist's specific, historical elaboration of the differentiation must, however, be seen in light of the class structure, a question to which we may return in the discussion of strategy.

The mainly sociological analyses of sex roles cited above offer a natural mixture of pessimism and optimism with respect to the possibility of changes in sex differentiation in current society. The same is true of writers who have developed theories in which sex roles are seen as consequences of specific biological and sexual differences between men and women. Montagu,[12] for example, postulates women's biological superiority over men, and the unconscious striving of men to dominate and take revenge on women. The Norwegian psychologist Nissen[13] (see pp. 42–50) maintains a different sexual cycle for the two genders, and shows some of the implications of such a possibility in terms of male-dominated societies.

Such deeper psycho-social elements of sex differentiation are not discussed in the following. The present modes and the present maintenance of sex roles, rather than their ultimate origin, causes, and historical development are the themes in what follows. Furthermore, the discussion builds on the assumption, among others, that sex roles are of secondary importance as a force of social change in general. Also, the importance of basically economic forces, combined with technological developments and ideological shifts—as summarized in this section—is recognized. The analysis stresses, however, a trend toward *latent sex differentiation* and *latent discrimination* in industrial societies, as opposed to manifest differentiation in traditional society. It differs from some theories of changing sex roles in viewing sex differentiation not as something which either exists or is eliminated, but as a social arrangement which may take on different forms and functions.

## *Theoretical Elaborations*

### *Sex Differentiation and Potentials for Change*

Anthropologists have labeled gender differentiation "the primary division of labor," and with good reason. Gender differentiation is more ancient, more stable, and more widespread than any other type of social differentiation. It appears under all known economic systems and political orders. The very existence of sex roles cannot be attributed to special forms of production or subsistence conditions.

But the *extent* to which sex—or, rather, gender—constitutes a differentiating element in society varies considerably culturally and historically. This is true of the modes and substance of gender differentiation as well. It may be maintained, for example, that the degree of task differentiation between men and women has been kept stable over the last hundred years, since a number of "new" job openings for women actually are extensions into modern work life of their traditional tasks. At the same time, this shift in women's production from a primary to a secondary social frame for their work constitutes a change in the mode of sex differentiation. Such shifts also point to changes in those social forces which maintain sex differentiation.

Gender differentiation is here used primarily to include a division of tasks between men and women which is accompanied by a consistently different personality formation of the two genders. Such differentiation usually also discriminates against women, and it is the contention of the present author that discrimination of women necessarily follows from most known gender differentiations.[14]

The consequences of social changes for the extent and modes of sex differentiation practiced in a society—including degree of discrimination—is a main theme in the following discussion. It is an assumption, then, that the extent and modes of sex differentiation are more resultants than determiners of changes in other social and economic relations. This does not imply that changes in gender differentiation are without consequences for social structure and cultural conditions. The opposite is the case, since gender differentiation contributes to the maintenance of a number of other social arrangements.[15] But sex differentiation contains less of a dynamic potential for conflict and change than, for example, social classes or technological change. The very stability of sex differentiation should therefore also be exposed, at least in part, by the analysis presented here.

*Sex Differentiation and Social Structure*

The modes and degree of sex differentiation are partly a reflection of requirements of the economic system at large and of more specific demands for a suitable labor-and-consumption force. Sex differentiation is also directly influenced by technological changes, such as the invention of contraceptives. The changes in cultural values which have developed, partly in harmony with and partly in opposition to the postindustrial economic demands, sometimes have a direct bearing on the current ideas about differentiation, ideas which to a large extent are contradicted by sex-differentiating practices.

The shift from a production-oriented to a consumption-oriented economy have changed women's position more than men's, and in at least two ways. First, women's services have increasingly been extended directly to production outside the home, and employers take a novel interest in the female labor force. Second, the "consumption-and-fun ethos" has brought women into focus as consumers—and as fun. The last pattern is supported by the invention of a number of contraceptives, which has also implied new freedom for women as well as men.

A modern economy requires a mobile, partly well-trained labor force, and men are more mobile than women. Young women, however, have proved willing to move in great numbers to the urban centers, a development that has created population imbalances in the cities as well as in the rural areas. The changes in the structure and function of the family facilitate mobility for men as well as women, and the changes in the family have probably provided increased sex-role equality between husband and wife. Physical strength has become less important for unskilled and semiskilled jobs, which should tend to eliminate sex differences in the lower echelons in industry. The expansion in white-collar jobs and the stagnation in blue-collar work favor women to a certain extent; the same may be true of a shift from labor conflict and industrial struggles to an atmosphere of negotiation, human relations skills, and attempts at psychological manipulation of employers.

Most of these changes in the desired properties of the labor force should favor women in the lower positions in firms and corporations, and may in time produce a certain pattern of equality in these sectors. The development, however, has not at all been conducive to equality in the middle and higher levels of industrial work units. The demands for leadership, devotion, education, efficiency, and stress-taking, when higher level work is concerned, effectively shut out women from the business elite and other types of elite.

Women's confinement to routine and service work is balanced, as it were, by their important function as consumers who are flexible and sensitive to advertising and status consumption. Women are even increasingly consumers of education, which partly serves to solve a main problem of modern economy: the absorption of surplus.[16] This is the more evident since women to some extent make no use of their education. But there is still a large group of women who work all day, nowadays, because they have two jobs, and another group who are full-time consumers.

Women's work in the home constitutes part of the infrastructure of modern economy. Women's poorly paid, isolated work with children and family is clearly one of the conditions for the efficient, collective organization of "official" production. In both production spheres, and in the main, men still have the leadership positions, and women do the serving.

Since a large number of women are fairly isolated housewives, their conceptions of themselves and each other are mediated to them through "a third party"—especially the mass media. Such stereotyped self-images of women are less conducive to feelings of solidarity among women than direct contact and cooperation.

At the same time, new values constantly question this lack of changes in the basic differentiation according to gender. Ever since women came to be regarded as human beings, comparisons between the situations of men and women have been legitimate. Secularization and universalism have furnished new standards for such comparisons; equality, scientific rationalism, and "criticism is a duty" have strengthened these ideas.

The main effects of economic and social changes outlined

above point to some forms of increased equality, but also to strong elements of inequality and covert sex differentiation. An elaboration of the changes that have taken place in sex differentiation may furnish some explanations for this situation.

*From Traditional Sex Roles to Quasi-egalitarianism*

The first type of change to be discussed is one from an openly recognized and accepted differentiation, which is expressed in legal rules or other codes, to a more covert differentiation, a quasi-egalitarianism.[17] Present-day sex differentiation is neither officially accepted nor manifested in legal codes, but constitutes a contrast to the official ideology. This discrepancy between ideology and reality is a "modern" phenomenon, the maintenance of which is closely related to the complexity of industrialized society.

The term "quasi-egalitarianism" refers to elements of latency in present-day sex differentiation as well as to certain mechanisms for covering sex differentiation.

Latent structures are potentials for which there exists a psychological and social preparedness, and which come into operation under certain circumstances. For example, some kinds of sex differentiation in the labor market or in education appear only under conditions of scarcity. When jobs are abundant, that is, when the business cycle is rising, women are in demand and may get jobs which would be denied them under economic downturns. When parents can afford to give all children an education and they don't have to choose between sons' and daughters' education, the fact that parents would usually give priority to the education of a son is not expressed in action. There exists, nevertheless, a constant psychological propensity for sex differentiation—should the situation change.

The mechanisms of "covering" sex differentiation are numerous. An emphasis on legal definitions or official ideology may distract attention from actual practice, and the same is true of ritualized selection of women for a small number of official positions.

It may also be suggested that one of the covering processes

is a tendency to increase women's influence in institutions which are, in some respects, becoming obsolete in present-day society.

At the same time as the family has lost its importance as an economic and political institution, egalitarianism between spouses has become increasingly common. Women are today probably the main decision-makers in a large number of families in which the father is a rather absent and diffuse figure. The father's absence is dictated by the demands of his work, which again necessitates the mother's role as decision-maker. Nevertheless, this coincides with the decline of the family as an important social and political unit.

Educational institutions may furnish another example of female influence in obsolete institutions. The first years of elementary schools have—at least in Scandinavia, although similar trends are found in the United States of America[18]—changed over the last decades, from being oriented toward children's acquiring of knowledge to more diffuse purposes of primary socialization and personality formation. At the same time, the male schoolmaster or teacher has moved away from these beginner classes of the elementary school system; female teachers are now in an overwhelming majority as teachers during the first years. Later, when the "real" acquisition of knowledge is in focus, the male teacher takes over. From a strictly educational point of view, the first steps have become, if not obsolete, at least more an extension of the family's primary socialization. The fact that there are a great number of female teachers does not imply that the educational tasks are distributed in an equal manner but, rather, that female teachers continue the mother's family tasks.

One may, finally, consider certain aspects of women's political activity in the light of a hypothesis about female influence in institutions which are in the process of losing influence. In Scandinavian political discussions, it has been recurrently asserted that parliament as an institution is becoming less powerful, that important decisions to an increasing degree are made outside this body, and that the parliament is losing influence vis-à-vis a strong governmental apparatus, as well as powerful economic forces. This seems to be a typical postwar development. It is interesting to note that at the same time the percentages of women representatives are increasing in all the Scandinavian countries—although slowly. The number of women on the boards of banks, insurance companies, and industrial concerns remains nil.

### *From Unreflectedness to Self-awareness*

With respect to sex roles, the development from traditional to industrialized society is also one from unawareness to self-reflection. This is true in the sense that sex roles in older societies were seen as unproblematic, God-given and unchangeable, whereas the roles today—for example in Scandinavia—represent a constant subject of discussion, of reflection, and also of social research. The description above also suggests that some of the reasons for this change are to be found in the movement from legitimate to illegitimate differentiation. A social differentiation which is declared illegitimate but which nevertheless occurs will be reflected upon by some, although, almost by definition, covered up by others. Today there can be no doubt that the status quo is questioned, discussed, and criticized.

Such awareness of social injustices in certain groups is, however, also a more general characteristic of modern society than of traditional society. The idea that the present is not good enough permeates conservative as well as radical thought in Western society—although the premises for desires for change, as well as the changes advocated, may be quite different. It would be strange indeed if sex differentiation should be exempted from examination in this culture. It may be suggested, nevertheless, that the discrepancies between the criticism and the reality illustrate the status of opinions in current society: the lack of consequences of opinions or ideas held is apparent.

The discrepancies between ideology and reality also indicate a powerlessness on the part of the official authorities in a society. In Scandinavia, most political parties state explicitly their desire to obtain equality between men and woman, but their power to influence the development seems more limited than indicated by their programs. Furthermore, as can be seen in connection with a number of social problems, a "right" has become something which politicians, administrators, and "the law" would *like* people to have, not something people have. If this is true, rights may be increasingly generously issued to the losers in current Western society.

### *From Ideological to Psychological Maintenance of Sex Differentiation*

The development from a commonly accepted sex differentiation to an almost illegitimate one has had a number of consequences. One of them is, of course, that legal or open sanctions cannot be brought to bear upon those who deviate from the sex-role pattern. An employer is not free to fire women because they marry, no school or university may bar women's entrance, nobody could formally deny a female politician from running. Formal sanctions have been replaced by informal ones, and this has come to constitute a special pressure on psychological sex differentiation. In traditional society, *ideology, division of tasks*, and *personality formation* were to some extent harmonized for men and for women to form two distinct patterns of life, one male and one female. In industrialized society, ideology does not justify sanctioning of deviance from the essence of sex differentiation, which is differentiation of tasks. The maintenance of task differentiation has thus become heavily dependent on different personality formation of boys and girls. This does not necessarily mean that the socialization of boys and girls is more segregated now than it was before, but that those differences which are the outcome of socialization have another social significance. Conformity must, for example, be important as a general characteristic.

### *From Supernatural to Rational Premises*

The ideological changes which have accompanied an increasingly urbanized industrialized capitalist society have already been mentioned. The idea of a discrepancy between an official egalitarian ideology and actual differentiating between men and women is seen as an important aspect of sex roles in current society. The presence of an official egalitarian value system does not imply, however, that the actual practices have no ideological premises. Beliefs in sex differentiation, which are in conflict with the ideas of equality and which are more or less implicitly formulated, may sometimes be found as remnants of previous religious values. But even the ideas that constitute arguments *for* sex differentiation have undergone changes, in that more rationality, more systematic proofs and sophistication are required of them. When research indicated that the old belief in superior male intelligence had no scientific basis, this was a blow to the arguments for a social differentiation of men and women. Other psychological data have, however, furnished arguments in favor of differentiation; this is the case with research regarding the infant's need for motherly care. In addition, more or less well-founded ideas about psychological sex differences have gained in importance as support for differentiation, whereas religious beliefs have lost much of their force in this respect.

### *From Role Homogeneity to Role Heterogeneity*

The development from manifest to latent sex differentiation has a number of facets, of which only a few may be mentioned here. A shift from cultural homogeneity to cultural heterogeneity with respect to sex roles should, however, not be overlooked. Although in traditional society the substance of sex roles may have varied somewhat within a population, at least they varied in fairly predictable ways. To be a woman in the feudal lower class was probably a fairly well-established role, even if it was somewhat different from the role of an aristocratic lady. Today the variations in sex roles within subgroups are probably considerable, and this is true within and sometimes across class boundaries.

Sex differentiation has, however, always assumed a different character in different social classes and it still does. Liberation is one thing for an educated middle-class woman and another for a working-class wife with only the prospect of unskilled labor if she wants to work outside the home. The trend is, however, to increase women's influx into white-collar jobs and thus to decrease the class differences between women. On the other hand, new psychological dividing lines are separating women, such as married versus unmarried, or more subtle choices between various versions of the feminine role.

### *Shifts in the Domain of Male and Female Value Orientations*

There can be no doubt about the fact that the—in a sense somewhat limited—entrance of women into secondary institutions in present-day society has taken place on male premises. Women have accepted the dominant norms and values of secondary affairs, be it "efficiency" or "competition" or "universalism," and these very values have often in the debates provided the justifications for women's participation in work, education, and politics. No wonder, then, that male values persist in the face of female participation.

In primary relations, however, there seems to be a decline in the influence of traditional male values. As maintained by Dahlström,[19] a feminization or humanization of the relations in the family, in the classroom, and in the work group may be observed.

The development may thus be interpreted as an increased polarization of male and female values, feminization of primary values being compensated, as it were, by an increased dominance of male values in secondary affairs. If this interpretation is reasonable, it indicates that the structure of primary groups is such that even with an influx of male participation, traditional female orientations not only prevail but are strengthened. In the same vein, the structure of secondary institutions is kept more or less unchanged in the face of increased female participation.

### *Strategies of Sex-Role Change*

In questions of sex roles and especially changes in sex roles, problems of strategy often take precedence over problems of theory, and sometimes, but not always, to the advantage of the two.

The first question to be asked concerns, of course, the aims of the movements toward equality between men and women. Whereas there is general agreement about the insufficiency of formal equality, expressed in laws and administrative rules or in "empty rights" of women, the content of equality is still vague.

One may roughly distinguish at least between equality within the framework of the present Western societies, on the one hand, and equality in a radically changed society, on the other. The first may be termed equality on masculine premises, or briefly, "masculine equality"; the other—or others—is equality in a qualitatively different society, that is, a society which is not dominated by masculine values as we know them.

Masculine equality would be a situation accomplished in the present type of economy and political order, expressed as a 50/50 distribution of men and women in almost all positions, be it care of home and children or the business elite. Such a goal, combined with an assumption that present society and institutions remain by and large intact, obviously requires women to become more similar to current masculine ideas of efficiency, profit, competition, and power, according to which Western societies operate. Half the power, so to speak, would have to be handed over to women, with the burden which is implied in male power today—and in the female tasks that would be taken over by men.

The main strategies for attainment of this situation would be awakening of women's political consciousness and an increase in women's educational level, but above all an introduction of a number of specific detailed laws and regulations which would secure for women the possibility and ability to to compete, fight, and exercise power.

The thesis that obtaining equality is first and foremost a question of women seizing half the power which men now have has a ring of reasonableness, but is nevertheless an expression of a static view.

It is still a question whether equality in a reasonable sense can at all be attained within a society that builds on a capitalist economy, and perhaps at all in a society which is not both socialist *and* above a certain level of technology. The interests of children as a group would be contradictory to, and heavily set aside under, a combination of market economy and gender equality. The practicality of full equality under the present economy must be questioned.

A long-range perspective on equality contains the establishment of an economy subordinated to the goal of equality. In addition, a number of political and educational measures would be necessary.

Starting with today's economy, however, and with an eye to the description of sex differentiation offered above, two examples of problems to be attacked may be mentioned. One is the problem of latent or covert sex differentiation; the other consists of breaking the psychological maintenance of sex roles. Both are closely related to the question of women's self-respect and ability to advance their own interest. The covert discrimination leads to a feeling of defeat, since the official rights are all there, and gives the illusion that it is a matter of the single woman's ability and energy to use the rights. The psychological maintenance of sex differentiation also consists of encouraging women's devaluation of themselves in various ways, a devaluation which is clearly reflected in the wages paid for women's work.

The money and prestige paid for one's work are in current society the main road to self-respect for men. Women have been advised to seek their rewards in love and child-rearing, which may be inherently as valuable—if it were paid and respected. To get out of this vicious circle for women, all work with children, especially in child-care institutions, should be paid somewhat more than, say, the production and maintenance of cars. This would increase the self-respect of large groups of women and, in addition, change radically the desirability of child-care work. Such a manifestation of changes in a society's values and priorities would lower the prestige of competitiveness and technological advancement.

Increased higher education for women is another road to changes in women's working conditions and in their self-respect. Various Norwegian data indicate that women with a higher level of education are more politically active, report less submissiveness, less conflict avoidance, and more gender-egalitarian norms than do women with lower education. Higher education may not, however, be especially conducive to the development of solidarity among women. And higher education alone is not enough for women to gain power.

The analyses in the preceding paragraphs show that the time has come to see the premises on which women work outside the home as more important than such work itself. Work outside the home as a policy must be judged in terms of pressure toward equal wages and working conditions and the avoidance of a female reserve labor force. The question of consequences in terms of solidarity formation on the part of women—and men—is also relevant.

The last point has become very clear in statements from young Western European Marxists: if the struggle for equality between men and women is a struggle *between* men and women, then this would lead to a weakening of the solidarity of the working class and must at present be given low priority. Marxist groups offer other reasons as well for taking a conservative stand in the question of married women's work, such as the extra exploitation of women, and the pressure on men's wages in general.[20]

If sex differentiation and sex discrimination are mainly the results of social forces and not deeply rooted antagonism between men and women, the solidarity between men and women is probably less served by women being isolated housewives than industrial employees. Under certain circumstances, however, men and women will compete for jobs under more equal working conditions, in ways which may decrease their loyalty toward each other. The problem is then more to counteract competition among employees who have long-range interests in common, especially since splits in the labor movement are a much more serious and widespread problem than only the hypothesized conflict between male and female workers. More of a danger to a solidary labor movement lies in the tendency of women to go into low-paid white-collar work which offers little stimulus for consciousness about equality and political work. This too, however, represents a more general problem than women's participation itself.

If the "premises of work" is one strategic point for changing current sex roles, the "premises of consumption" is another. This contains a wide variety of problems related to sex differentiation, but ultimately it is a question of the direction of production. For example, from the point of view of equality, it is more important to build houses in a new way and on a sufficient scale than to produce a broad range of the commodities which today dominate the consumers and which are necessary for production to be kept up. The housing industry should be nationalized and put in the service of reasonable, more or less collective types of housing, building for flexible families and for the needs of children.

As has been shown by the above summary and elaboration of theoretical descriptions, the breakdown of sex differentiation is not only an economic question. The privatizing and latency of sex roles require a "consciousness-raising," in small groups as well as in the existing women's organizations. In particular, training in groups with young couples who try to share work in a new way should be attempted. It is on this level of attitude changes that the question of cooperation between women and between men and women has a direct bearing.

The point is of special importance, since it is sometimes maintained to be related to the all-important question of women's solidarity toward each other.

Solidarity and identification with one's own and the opposite gender are feelings that obviously are sensitive to social circumstances. The social devaluation and isolation of women have proved dangerous to their solidarity with each other, and their overidentification with man, the stronger, is a problem to any attempt at liberation of women as well as men. Some of these psychological states may be broken down in the individual's work with herself and others, but this will often be a fight against society.

Individual men may be antagonistic to equality between the genders, but even this is a result of social circumstances. The view that the more or less hopeless and bitter fight between man and woman within the four walls of a home can bring about a revolution in sex roles is denied by all reasonable analysis of the forces of revolution as well as of sex differentiation.

The individual consciousness of the problems of sex differentiation is, however, one of the initiators of change and this consciousness must be brought to bear on social as well as psychological maintenance of the system. The ambivalence of the situation constitutes a temptation to passivity, for the individual man or woman who attempts to change current sex roles moves in a field of ambivalence, not only socially but also psychologically. The tension between practicing equality, which may be the individual's intention (the "project," to use Sartre's word), on the one hand, and his "embeddedness" in past experiences, emotions, learned norms, and values, on the other,[21] is expressed in the institutional setting as well.

NOTES

1. I am indebted to stud. mag. art. Annemor Kalleberg and stud. mag. art. Lars Hem for discussion and criticism of my views on sex roles and social change.
2. W. J. Goode, *World Revolution and Family Patterns* (New York: The Free Press, 1963).
3. E. Bott, *Family and Social Network* (London: Tavistock Publications, 1957).
4. E. Boulding, *The Road to Parliament for Women*, International seminar on the participation of women in public life. Rome 1966, Mimeo.
5. F. Engels, *The Origin of the Family, Private Property and the State* (New York: International Publishing Company, 1942).
6. A. Bebel, *Die Frau und der Sozialismus* (Berlin: Dietz Verlag, 1946).
7. V. Lenin, *Marx-Engels-Marxisme* (Oslo: A/S Norsk Forlag Ny Dag, 1952).
8. S. de Beauvoir, *The Second Sex* (New York: Bantam Books, 1970).
9. E. Sullerot, *Kvinden og fremtiden* (Demain des femines) (København: Gyldendal, 1969).
10. J. Mitchell, "Women: The Longest Revolution," *New Left Review*, No. 40, 1966.
11. L. Hem, *Kjønnsdifferensiering og kvinneunderdrykkelse* (Sex Differentiation and Suppression of Women), Kontrast, 1971.
12. A. Montagu, *The Natural Superiority of Women* (New York: Macmillan, 1968).
13. I. Nissen, "The Role of the Sexual Constellation," *Acta Sociologica*, No. 1–2, 1971.
14. H. Holter, *Sex Roles and Social Structure* (Oslo: Universitetsforlaget, 1970).

15. *Ibid.*
16. L. Hem, *Forsøksgymnaset. En studie av forandring* (The Experimental Gymnasium. A Study of Change). Oslo: University Press, 1971.
17. H. Holter, *op. cit.*
18. J. Henry, *Culture against Man* (London: Tavistock Publications, 1966).
19. E. Dahlström, "Analys av kønsrollsdebatten." In *Kvinners liv og arbeid* (Stockholm: Studiesällskapet Näringsliv och Samhälle, 1962).
20. K. Ohrlander, *Kvinner som slaver* (Women as Slaves) (Stockholm: Bonniers, 1969).
21. L. Hem, *op. cit.*

# 8

# Consumption Society, Sex Roles, and Sexual Behavior

JOACHIM ISRAEL & ROSMARI ELIASSON

## *1. Capital Accumulation and Puritanism*

THERE SEEMS TO BE A relationship between rapid capital accumulation and a puritan moral norm system.[1] In brief, this relationship can be described in the following way. The earliest phases of the process of industrialization can be characterized by a discrepancy between the amount of capital available and the amount of capital needed in order to carry through industrialization. The necessary capital can be acquired in two ways: (1) by import from outside a given economic system; or (2) by the extreme exploitation of human labor and the reinvestment of the values created—for example from the agricultural sector—in industry. At the same time consumption has to be kept at a low level, which means that the working class not only has had to defer need gratification, but to a certain extent abstain from it. Rapid capital accumulation means renouncement in favor of following generations.[2]

If we look at the process of industrialization in Western Europe, in particular England, we will find that it occurred under social conditions of great deprivation and self-denial: long working hours, hard physical labor and toil often carried to the point of exhaustion, child labor, dangerous working conditions, miserable wages, exposure to arbitrary and authoritarian treatment by management, etc.

Such working and living conditions can be created by (1)

coercion, suppression, and the absence of democratic rights, like organization in trade unions, and (2) by the creation and internalization of moral norms, making work man's foremost duty, and the repression of needs the second but not less important demand. By creating such a moral norm system, external coercion can be transformed into internal moral duty.

Thus in any puritan moral system work as man's foremost duty ranks high. During the process of industrialization organized within the frame of a capitalist economic system, norms are added concerning abstention from the fruits of one's own work.

Max Weber has analyzed the relationship between capitalistic development and the puritan moral. He talks about "*innerweltliche Askese*" (mundane asceticism) which characterizes the spirit of capitalism and which in turn is anchored in the Protestant ethic. This Protestant ethic is characterized by emphasis on moral duty in general, work as a moral duty in particular, and puritan attitudes toward sexuality: everything which does not serve the basic process of production should be repressed. Sexuality therefore becomes acceptable only as far as it functions in the service of reproduction. In all other aspects sexuality—e.g., sexual gratification as a goal in itself—is repressed. The social repression of sexual needs in turn can be used as means for social control in general: repression of basic needs leads to the development of such personality characteristics which facilitate the acceptance of authoritarian structures within the family, the place of work, and even within the social system as a whole.[3]

The relationship between early and rapid capital accumulation and the puritan moral is not only a feature of the process of industrialization within a capitalist economic system. The relationship can also be observed in societies which carry out their process of industrialization in a noncapitalist manner. Examples are the puritan moral in the Soviet Union from the twenties which still is prevailing. We can refer to the work moral and the ethics of "revolutionary purity" in China and we can find examples of the same type in Cuba today.[4] Socialist work moral is an economic necessity, perhaps sharpened by the division of the world into highly industrialized and less developed nations.

When the process of industrialization reaches a certain level and transgresses a certain threshold, the basic production process changes. Human toil is replaced by machines, working hours are reduced, conditions of working and living improve. High standards of living and the associated high level of consumption become preconditions for further industrial development and are at the same time made possible through modern technology and—this must be stressed—the exploitation of countries in the underdeveloped world.

In addition, the consumption society has no need for a puritan moral demanding that need gratification should be deferred. Instead the moral of the consumption society supports a tendency to transform man into a reified consumer,[5] which means not only that existing needs must be satisfied but also that new ones be created. Thus the moral of the consumption society is highly nonpuritan. This does not necessarily mean that it is especially favorable toward sexual need satisfaction. In the United States of America, hypocritical attitudes toward sexuality are still widely prevalent and emphasis is placed on need satisfaction achieved by the consumption of material goods. In addition, the norm system of the United States of America traditionally has facilitated the expression of aggression and brutality, whereas in Scandinavian countries greater inhibitions are placed on aggression than on sexual behavior.[6] Thus the repression of sexual needs in the consumption society can be transformed into and channeled through the expression of aggression and violence.

This is only a short discussion indicating in which areas differences between Scandinavian societies and other consumption societies like the United States of America can be sought. However, sexual behavior and its change can not only be explained within the framework of changes in the basic process of production. These changes in turn have affected other aspects of the social structure. A few may be briefly mentioned: (1) Urbanization leading to the breakdown of *informal* social control and its substitution by *formal* social control. That transformation especially influences sexual norms and behaviors. Norm change is also facilitated by the anonymity caused by living conditions in metropolitan areas. (2) The change in family structure and function as a consequence of the industrialization process. (3) The changed role of sexuality by the separation of sexual behavior and reproduction, made possible, for instance, through the development of and access to contraceptives. (4) The change in authority relations and the breakdown of traditional authoritarian norms in the family, the place of work, and within the social structure in general. (5) The process of secularization, implying decreased influence of the church on attitudes and behavior. (6) The development of an adolescent society as a special age group, partly as a consequence of prolonged education and delayed entrance into the production process. (7) Last but not least, changes in sex roles, especially with regard to the female sex role.[7]

## 2. *Sex Roles and Sexuality in the Consumption Society*

Sex roles usually do not function independently but, rather, in a special social context. Thus varying norms concerning sex-role behavior exist in different social classes. In addition, sex roles and other roles often are interdependent.

One example of the last-mentioned phenomenon is the interaction of sex and age roles with regard to sexual behavior in our society. It is acceptable today for a man of—let us say—forty years of age to have sexual relations with and marry a woman half his age, while there still exist sanctions against women having sexual relations with men far younger than themselves. Obviously there are no biological reasons for this state of affairs, especially in a society where sexuality and reproduction are or can be held separate. It is characteristic, however, for relations between classes or groups of people with varying degrees of power in the social structure. Thus the factual right of access to sexual partners of one's own choice or the demand for such rights is one of the signs of a class of people occupying superior power positions. The same right usually is denied those who factually occupy inferior positions or are perceived as such. That holds for ethnic groups like black people in a racist society as well as for women in our society. Of course consequences may vary.

One reason for the interaction between sex and age roles may have to do with the actual economic situation. Men, at least in middle-class occupations or professions, tend to improve their economic position with increasing age whereas women do not. In fact, there may be a reversed trend for women. Therefore older men in our society have certain actual possibilities to acquire sexual partners, especially since the economic situation and prospects as criteria for male sexual attractiveness are supported by existing norms.

Three additional reasons may be mentioned, all of which are interrelated: (1) Women are in our society often looked upon as sexually passive *objects*, whereas men, according to the same role-expectations, are seen as *active subjects*, with the possibility of choosing sexual partners. The tendency to view women as passive objects is still perpetuated and reinforced by several factors. First, we have the increasing amount of advertisement and commercial propaganda using women as *means* for the sale of commodities. Second, the role of women as passive objects is strengthened by mass media like TV, cinema, and weekly magazines, which probably have a strong indoctrinating effect. Also the free sale of pornography may have had a similar effect, since women often are presented here as traditional objects.[8]

(2) Women as objects are in our society not only perceived as *means* for the sale of commodities. Since our social system is built upon a market economy, there is a strong tendency to transform everything to commodities to be bought and sold on the market. This not only holds true for traditional prostitution but applies even to sexual attractiveness in general.

(3) Mass media have the tendency to create standardized ideals with regard to female sexual attractiveness, whereas the same does not hold true for men. Thus certain characteristics are promoted as sexually attractive, as for example, age, figure, bosom, etc. These characteristics then acquire a special exchange value. Since characteristics of attractiveness are not developed to the same extent in the case of men, norms have evolved for exchange relationships where women exchange their beauty (or that which is normatively con-

sidered as beauty) for men's economic capacity. In summary, then, norms in our society further an exchange relationship in which women can cash in on their looks and sexual attractiveness: the economic and intellectual status and power of the man are transferred upon the woman in the man's company—and women in turn become status objects.

Thus female sexual attractiveness is a commodity, whereas male sexual attractiveness is not, at least not to the same extent, and is in turn dependent on other factors. One important reservation should be made. What has been said is probably more valid for upper-middle- and upper-class behavior and less for working class.

So far we have mentioned factors concerning traditional sex-role expectations with regard to sexuality. We will consider now a few factors which may act in the direction of greater equality between men and women.

First we have the development of political equality as exemplified by women's voting rights, introduced in Sweden in 1919. Also in the legal field there have been certain developments such as the legal competence of married women, the law concerning equal pay for men and women in the civil service, laws prohibiting the dismissal of female employees on account of marriage, pregnancy, childbirth, etc.

Furthermore, an increasing number of women participate in the process of material production and therefore have a possibility to acquire economic independence. In addition, labor market policies make it possible for women to be retrained independently of the husband's work potential.

Another factor contributing to the trend toward equality is the increased number of women receiving an education and especially a higher education.

These factors mentioned above contribute to the greater independence of women and may therefore *indirectly* also contribute to greater equality with men in the field of sexual relations. The access to reliable contraceptives—especially the pill—makes it possible to separate sexual activity from (undesired) pregnancy. Therefore for the first time it is possible for women to engage in sexual activities without fearing undesired consequences. Also the greater availability of legal abortions works in the same direction.

## 3. *Some Empirical Data from a Study of Metropolitan Youth*

The figures presented here emanate from a study carried out in 1966–67. A total of 1,297 persons in the age group sixteen to twenty-five, living in Stockholm, were interviewed with regard to their sexual behavior, norms, and attitudes. Of the randomly selected sample, 93 percent participated in the study; 663 were men, 634 were women. A sample of similar size, comprised of people having venereal diseases, also were interviewed.

### 3.1. *Permissiveness and Equality*

We are going to present some data pertaining to sex-role expectations and their influence on factual sexual behavior.

The fact that women have been considered as sexual objects has given rise to double standards with regard to the desirability of premarital sexual relations, the number of sexual partners, extramarital activity, etc.

The first type of double standard has been measured by two attitude questions, presented separately in the interview. The results were combined in an index. The statements were formulated in the following way: "It is good for a man to have sexual experience before marriage" and "It is good for a woman to be a virgin when she marries." The following results were obtained.

The majority of all men and of all women express norms permitting premarital sexual relations for both sexes. If we add those who advocate abstinence for both sexes to the permissive group, there are 71 percent among the interviewed men and 75 percent among the women who reject double standards.

Those who express double standards as well as those who favor abstinence for both sexes seem to be significantly more represented in American and English studies.[9]

If we compare our data with Zetterberg's study,[10] comprising a national representative sample of the Swedish population, we find a somewhat higher degree of double standards in his upper age groups than in his lower age

*Table 1*
INDEX OF SEXUAL STANDARDS

| | Men (n = 660) | Women (n = 625) |
|---|---|---|
| *Traditional double standard:* Sexual experience is good for men, virginity is good for women | 20% | 13% |
| *Equalitarian—permissive standard:* Sexual experience is good for men, virginity is *not* good for women | 64% | 69% |
| *Equalitarian—restrictive standard:* Sexual experience is *not* good for men, virginity is good for women | 7% | 6% |
| *Reversed double standard:* Rejecting both items (including "don't know" responses to one of the two items or both) | 9% | 12% |

groups and in our sample. Thus we assume that with increasing permissiveness toward premarital and sexual activity in general, a decrease of double sexual standards occurs.

The rationale for such a hypothesis would be that restrictions with regard to sexual activity are more strictly applied to those who factually are or are conceived of as being inferior. Therefore greater permissiveness may lead to greater equality (which *strict* enforcement of restrictions also may). We have some data supporting this hypothesis, referring to attitudes.

We developed attitude scales which were factor-analyzed. Among the factors, two will be mentioned. The first was labeled "pragmatic puritanism," measuring a puritanical, restrictive attitude toward sexual behavior founded not on moral but on pragmatic grounds, e.g., risks involved with sexual intercourse.[11] Among male as well as female subjects, only weak support of "pragmatic puritanism" could be found. No sex differences existed. There is a positive correlation between acceptance of a traditional double standard and a puritanical attitude.[12]

We find a positive correlation between a traditional double moral standard and a restrictive attitude also if we use another scale, called "romantic love moral." This scale refers to attitudes stressing the necessity to be in love with one's sexual partner.[13]

### 3.2. *Romantic Love and Sexual Behavior*

Another feature of this scale should be stressed. "A romantic love moral" is highly correlated with the sex of the interviewee, but not with social background factors. Thus significantly more women support a romantic love moral than men do.

We have found a tendency in literature to stress that a romantic love moral is widespread in Scandinavia, that it is the predominant moral standard.[14] Our data, however, indicate that at least among metropolitan male youth, the majority rejects the restrictions imposed by a romantic love moral. In general, we doubt whether a romantic love moral ever has been a dominant and accepted standard, especially among men in Sweden. In the agrarian society of seventy to one hundred years ago, it certainly did not play a major role, since marriage and family relations were to a large degree based upon economic criteria.

First in the small nuclear family living in urbanized areas love is perpetuated as a more important factor. However, even there it plays a greater role for the *selection* of partners for marriage than for the *maintenance* of existing marital relations. In fact the propagation of a romantic love moral has a self-defeating effect. If one maintains that sexual relations should be established only if the partners are in love with each other, then such a moral demand can usefully be applied only for *premarital* sexual relations. If it is also applied to marital relations, then, if love wanes in marriage—which it often does—one has four possibilities: (1) to accept sexual relations as a marital privilege or duty, (2) to establish extramarital relations where love still plays this role, (3) to get a divorce, (4) to live in sexual abstinence during prolonged periods of marriage. Thus romantic love may be a useful criterion for the selection of sexual partners. It is with a high probability not an especially useful criterion for maintaining sexual relations.

Among our female subjects we also find a variation with regard to the acceptance of "a romantic love moral." Another of our attitude scales measures "acceptance of traditional sex-role expectations." This scale concerns not sexual behavior but attitudes toward authority, division of labor in the home, and emotional characteristics of men and women. We found that the less a subject has traditional sex-role expectations, the less she supports a romantic love moral. Thus we conclude that traditional sex-role expectations support moral standards based on romantic love and the latter in turn may reinforce traditional sex-role expectations.[15]

In addition, we find a positive correlation between "pragmatic puritanism" and traditional sex-role expectations.[16] Thus in general a restrictive attitude toward sexual activity is correlated with an acceptance of traditional sex-role expectations. So much for attitudes. What relations do we find between attitudes and factual sexual activity? Due to lack of space, we will go into detail only with regard to the treatment of the relationship between the typically feminine attitude "romantic love moral" and factual sexual activity.[17]

We will begin with the relation between age at first sexual intercourse and "romantic love moral." The findings are summarized in the following table.

*Table 2*

"ROMANTIC LOVE MORAL" AND AGE AT FIRST INTERCOURSE

| Degree of "Romantic Love Moral" | | Age at First Intercourse: ≦15 % | 16–17 % | ≧18 % | (n = 100%) | No Coitus (n) | % |
|---|---|---|---|---|---|---|---|
| *Men* | low | 42 | 32 | 26 | (200) | (20) | 9 |
| | middle | 29 | 37 | 34 | (254) | (95) | 27 |
| | high | 25 | 32 | 43 | (56) | (34) | 38 |
| *Women* | low | 21 | 32 | 47 | (66) | (5) | 7 |
| | middle | 17 | 37 | 46 | (249) | (64) | 20 |
| | high | 10 | 39 | 51 | (163) | (79) | 33 |

*Gamma* Men: .22 $p<1\%$
Women: .10 n.s.

This table indicates that especially among men—but even among women—there is a positive relationship: the less the respondents accept "a romantic love moral," the younger they were when they started their heterosexual activities. The same correlations hold true for the onset of varying petting activities and "romantic love moral."

There is probably a mutual influence between a romantic love moral and amount of sexual experience: having a strictly romantic love moral may lead to a postponement of the onset of heterosexual activities, which in turn may reinforce a romantic love moral.

Our data also indicate that the more sexual experiences our subjects have the less prone they are to accept romantic love standards.

For instance, we found correlations for women as well as for men between "romantic love moral" and "sexual *exten-*

*Table 3*

"ROMANTIC LOVE MORAL" AND PERCENTAGE (OF RESPONDENTS WITH COITAL EXPERIENCE) WHO HAVE HAD FOUR OR MORE COITAL PARTNERS

| | | Degree of "Romantic Love Moral": | | | | |
|---|---|---|---|---|---|---|
| Age Group | Sex | Low % | Middle % | High % | All Together % | Gamma |
| 16–20 | Men | 64 | 56 | 24 | 54 | —.32 p<1% |
| | Women | 52 | 20 | 10 | 21 | —.36 p<1% |
| | Diff | +12 | +36 | +14 | +33 | |
| 21–25 | Men | 80 | 55 | 33 | 64 | —.50 p<1% |
| | Women | 59 | 40 | 26 | 38 | —.28 p<1% |
| | Diff | +21 | +15 | + 7 | +26 | |

*Table 4*

"ROMANTIC LOVE MORAL" AND PERCENTAGE (OF RESPONDENTS WITH COITAL EXPERIENCE) WHO HAVE HAD TWO OR MORE COITAL PARTNERS IN THE LAST TWELVE MONTHS

| | | Degree of "Romantic Love Moral": | | | | |
|---|---|---|---|---|---|---|
| Age Group | Sex | Low % | Middle % | High % | All Together % | Gamma |
| 16–20 | Men | 59 | 41 | 24 | 44 | —.23 p<1% |
| | Women | 33 | 16 | 15 | 18 | —.25 n.s. |
| | Diff | +26 | +25 | + 9 | +26 | |
| 21–25 | Men | 53 | 27 | 15 | 37 | —.43 p<1% |
| | Women | 36 | 13 | 7 | 14 | —.46 p<1% |
| | Diff | +17 | +14 | + 8 | +23 | |

*siveness*" as measured by total number of sexual partners, number of sexual partners during the last twelve months, and number of short-term heterosexual relations.

*Table 5*

"ROMANTIC LOVE MORAL" AND PERCENTAGE (OF RESPONDENTS WHO HAVE HAD TWO OR MORE COITAL PARTNERS) WHO HAVE HAD ONE OR MORE SHORT-TERM HETEROSEXUAL RELATIONS

| Age Group | Sex | Degree of "Romantic Love Moral": Low % | Middle % | High % | All Together % | Gamma |
|---|---|---|---|---|---|---|
| 16–20 | Men | 82 | 65 | 44 | 68 | $-.36$ $p<1\%$ |
| | Women | 45 | 22 | 24 | 28 | $-.29$ $p<1\%$ |
| | Diff | +37 | +43 | +20 | +40 | |
| 21–25 | Men | 82 | 61 | 43 | 70 | $-.39$ $p<1\%$ |
| | Women | 45 | 26 | 15 | 26 | $-.41$ $p<1\%$ |
| | Diff | +37 | +35 | +28 | +44 | |

In order to measure the partial effects of age, sex, and "romantic love moral," we have performed a multivariate analysis according to Coleman's model.[18] Since this type of analysis is built upon dichotomic data, the "high" and the "in-between" categories of attitudes were combined. The results are presented in Table 6.

*Table 6*

EFFECTS OF "ROMANTIC LOVE MORAL," SEX, AND AGE ON THREE MEASURES OF SEXUAL ACTIVITIES

| | Total Number of Coital Partners ($\geq 4$) | Number of Partners in the Last Twelve Months ($\geq 2$) | Short-term Sexual Relations ($\geq 1$) |
|---|---|---|---|
| $a_1$ = Effect of (low degree of) "romantic love moral" | .26 | .23 | .22 |
| $a_2$ = Effect of (male) sex | .21 | .20 | .37 |
| $a_3$ = Effect of (being 21–25 years of) age | .11 | −.05 | −.01 |
| r = Random shocks in the same direction as $a_1$–$a_3$ | .22 | .10 | .22 |
| s = Random shocks in the opposite direction | .20 | .42 | .18 |

The age of the subject has an insignificant effect on the behavioral measures except on the total number of partners. That depends on the trivial fact that the chances of increasing the total number of sexual partners grows the older a subject becomes.

The sex of the interviewees, however, contributes as much as "romantic love moral" and, in fact, more with regard to short-term sexual relations. Men state that they have had more partners than women do and they particularly admit more short-term sexual relations than do women. The question is whether these differences totally are *factual* ones or whether the *answers* are influenced by the subjects' sex-role expectations.

One argument in favor of the second type of explanation is the following. We find quite large differences between men and women with regard to number of partners and the other extensity measures. However, our sample is a representative one. Assuming that heterosexual relations are to a high degree performed within the age groups studied and occur within the same geographical area, namely Stockholm, then we would expect similar measures of extensity for both sexes, since sexual intercourse demands at least two partners. The reasoning is correct provided that not a large number of men have sexual relations with a small number of women or vice versa. Since in our material sexual relations between men and prostitutes practically do not occur (one would not have expected it in our age groups living in a permissive society) and since more men than women admit an excessive number of sexual partners, we must suspect that the answers are influenced by sex-role expectations. We are strengthened in this belief by the fact that the differences between female and male subjects with regard to having had sexual intercourse at all are very small or nonexistent in the different age groups. This is what one would expect in a random sample limited to certain age groups and a certain geographical area. Therefore answers to the question of whether or not one has had sexual intercourse are probably less dependent on sex-role expectations than are questions concerning the number of partners and other extensive sexual activities.

A final word about sex differences and the "romantic love

moral." Our data show that differences in extensity measures *decrease the more restrictive the attitude.* In other words, men and women who accept "a romantic love moral" are more similar with regard to extensity measures than men and women who reject "romantic love moral." Both men and women who accept "a romantic love moral" have had few partners, etc. The extensity curve for men increases more steeply than the curve for women with increasing rejection of "romantic love moral." An example of this is illustrated in Figure 1.

*Figure 1*

SEX, "ROMANTIC LOVE MORAL," AND PERCENTAGE WHO HAVE HAD FOUR OR MORE COITAL PARTNERS (AGE GROUP: 21–25 YEARS)

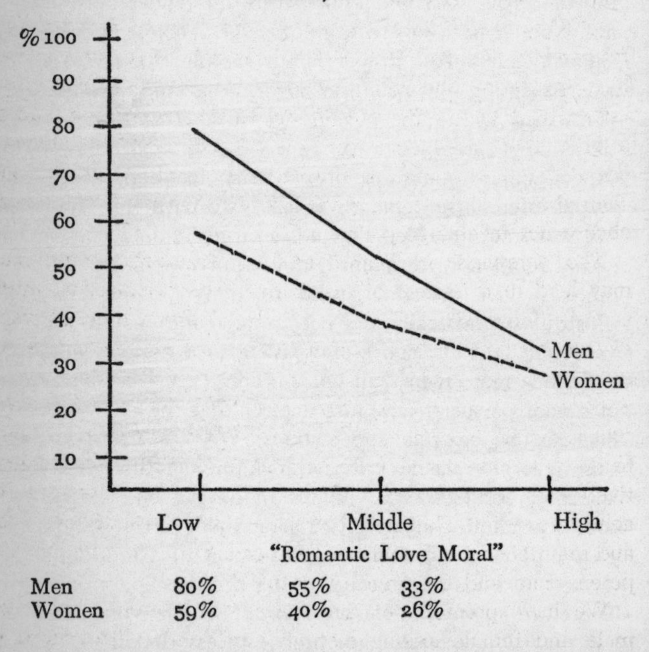


Several explanations can be given in addition to the one cited above, namely that responses are influenced by sex-role expectations.

1. *Both sexes have the same possibility to choose*, but women prefer to have fewer partners than do men. Thus even women who do not accept "romantic love moral" are more selective with regard to sexual partners than are men.

2. *The possibilities to choose are more limited for women than for men.* Women have fewer opportunities to change partners even if they would like to, since they often have to take care of children, have smaller economic resources, are generally more tied to their homes, and are in addition exposed to a stricter social control. The first-mentioned factors may not really influence our subjects too much. Only a minority—*ca.* 20 percent of the women—are married and/or have children. However, women, even in the age groups studied by us, probably meet more negative reactions to "promiscuous" activities than men do.

3. *The possibilities to choose are more limited for men than for women.* According to certain sex-role expectations men have to prove their "potency" and to apply quantitative criteria to sexual activity. Women, on the other hand, can to a greater degree prove their sexual ability by qualitative criteria, for example experience and intensity of orgasm. Therefore as long as these criteria are satisfied, women may choose not to change partners.

The emphasis on quantitative performance among men may lead to a neglect of qualitative aspects of sexual intercourse. Thus W. Reich has made a distinction between *ejaculative* and *orgastic* potency. The first can be measured *quantitatively* by counting the number of ejaculations within a given time period. The second has to be measured *qualitatively* by the experience of intensity of orgasm. If men learn to stress a quantitative criterion and to disregard the qualitative, one consequence will be difficulties for women to achieve orgasm. That may be the reason for the development and maintenance of what has been called "the myth about the potent man and the frigid woman."[19]

We have pointed out that there are differences between male and female among metropolitan youth with regard to stated number of sexual partners, etc. A look back at Tables 3 to 5, however, indicates that most differences between extreme groups *within* each sex are greater than the total differences *between* the two sexes, a fact which ought to be stressed.

### 3.3. *Sex-Role Expectations and Sexual Behavior*

We will now briefly treat another attitude scale, namely, the scale mentioned earlier measuring sex-role expectations. In contrast to the "romantic love scale," this scale is significantly correlated with education.[20] Sex-role expectations are in our material not correlated with sexual *extensity*, measured in the same way as mentioned before. However, there are a few other significant correlations which we want to mention. First, there exists a significant correlation between age at first intercourse and sex-role expectations among women only. There is a tendency for girls with traditional sex-role expectations to start *earlier* than those who have more equalitarian sex-role expectations. This correlation may partly be due to the relation between education and sex-role expectations, since age at first intercourse and education also are correlated.[21]

Another explanation would stress the fact that girls in the adolescent society are exposed to clothes, cosmetics, etc., especially designed for this age group by commercial interests to exploit this special category of consumers with a high buying power. Girls with traditional sex-role expectations can, earlier than before, make use of these offered paraphernalia. Therefore they can at an early age begin to play the role of sexual objects for men, who through their reactions may create and strengthen a self-image of being a sexual object. That in turn may lead to sexual activity.

Among the motives mentioned for having first intercourse, one pertains especially to sex-role expectations among women. We refer to the statement that a main motive for first sexual intercourse was the subject's own desire. The more equalitarian sex-role expectations women have, the more they state that they themselves wanted the first intercourse.

Women with equalitarian expectations also to a greater degree than women with a traditional outlook admit that they have desired intercourse with another partner during the period they have been together with their present partner.

With regard to desired number of intercourses with the present partner, women with an equalitarian outlook state that they want to have intercourse more often than what women with traditional expectations assert. The same tendency is also found among men.

One important aspect of sexual behavior related to sex-role norms has traditionally been the question of who should take the initiative to sexual intercourse. We asked our subjects who they thought should take the initiative to sexual intercourse. In the next table we present the relationship between sex-role expectations and the response category stating that both partners ought to take initiative.

*Table 7*

SEX-ROLE EXPECTATIONS AND OPINION ABOUT INITIATIVE TO SEXUAL INTERCOURSE

| Degree of Conventionalism | Percentage Stating That Both Partners Should Take Initiative | | | |
|---|---|---|---|---|
| | Men | | Women | |
| | % | (n = 100%) | % | (n = 100%) |
| Low | 82 | (101) | 87 | (152) |
| Middle | 67 | (188) | 59 | (172) |
| High | 55 | (177) | 58 | (113) |
| All Together | 62 | (587) | 63 | (552) |
| | Chi Square = 21.46 2*f* $p<0.1\%$ | | Chi Square = 35.87 2*f* $p<0.1\%$ | |

The more equalitarian the subjects—men and women—are, the more they state a norm of equality also with regard to initiating intercourse. More than 60 percent of the respondents state that both should take the initiative. It is therefore interesting to know how these expressed attitudes coincide with factual behavior.

In one of our questions we asked: "Who took the initiative for the first coitus?" The results are presented in the next table.

In answer to the question, 14 percent of the male and 7 percent of the female interviewees state that it was the woman who initiated the first intercourse. Interestingly, there are more men than women who assert female initiative. To a certain degree that depends on the fact that many males

*Table 8*

SEX ROLE EXPECTATIONS AND INITIATIVE TO FIRST INTERCOURSE

| Degree of Conventionalism | | "Who took the initiative?" No one % | Respondent % | Partner % | Both % | (n = 100%) | |
|---|---|---|---|---|---|---|---|
| *Men* | Low | 2 | 46 | 24 | 28 | (83) | Chi Square = 15.18 |
| | Middle | 1 | 63 | 14 | 22 | (166) | 2f |
| | High | 6 | 68 | 9 | 17 | (155) | $p < 0.1\%$ |
| All Together | | 4 | 61 | 14 | 21 | (467) | |
| *Women* | Low | 4 | 8 | 68 | 20 | (127) | Chi Square = 1.30 |
| | Middle | 4 | 5 | 71 | 20 | (140) | 2f |
| | High | — | 8 | 79 | 13 | (100) | n.s. |
| All Together | | 2 | 7 | 73 | 18 | (425) | |

state that their first partner was experienced. In fact, more than half of the men and three-fourths of the women stated that their first partner had experienced sexual intercourse before. That holds true especially for those subjects who had their first experiences at a relatively early age.

Furthermore, the table indicates a correlation between sex-role expectations and women's initiating activity, at least in the responses given by men.

We also found quite a stability in these patterns when we asked about who took the initiative to the first intercourse with the present partner. In both instances there are about 30 percent of the total number of interviewees who state that both or the woman alone took the initiative. The difference between the stated norm (see Table 7) and the factual behavior as presented by the subjects is rather large. However, our questions concerning initiative only dealt with *first* intercourse with the first or present partner. It should be clear that the more the partners know each other, the more both will be in a position to initiate sexual activity. If, in addition, there exist sex-role expectations which favor this type of behavior, the probability increases that it will occur.

### 3.4. *Sex Roles and Interviewer Effect*

Our last problem will be dedicated to the question of reliability of the answers given by our subjects. Among several measures taken and computations carried out, we also investigated whether or not the sex of the *interviewer* influenced the responses of the interviewee.[22] The sex of the interviewer was correlated with thirty-two variables concerning sexual behavior and sexual norms as stated by male and female subjects. Among the sixty-four correlations, four were such that differences between male and female interviewers were statistically significant.

The first two significant differences occurred in the responses to the question concerning who ought to take the initiative. The results are presented in Table 9.

Male subjects tell male interviewers more often than female interviewers that men should take the initiative.

*Table 9*

SEX OF INTERVIEWER AND OPINION ABOUT INITIATIVE TO INTERCOURSE

| Sex of Respondent | Sex of Interviewer | "Who should take initiative?" Neither % | Men % | Women % | Both % | (n = 100%) | Level of Significance |
|---|---|---|---|---|---|---|---|
| *Men* | Male Interviewer | 3 | 39 | 3 | 55 | (179) | $p < 5\%$ |
| | Female Interviewer | 3 | 29 | 3 | 65 | (405) | |
| *Women* | Male Interviewer | — | 31 | — | 70 | (154) | $p < 1\%$ |
| | Female Interviewer | 4 | 35 | 1 | 61 | (392) | |

Female subjects, on the other hand, tell female interviewers more often than male interviewers that men ought to take the initiative and less often that both ought to do it. Therefore we can conclude that traditional sex-role expectations have influenced the answers to this normative question. Both male and female subjects give different answers to interviewers of different sex. However, male subjects give more traditional answers to male interviewers and female subjects do the same to female interviewers. Thus the case of the same sex of interviewer and interviewee seems to have strengthened the responses in the traditional direction.

The other two significant correlations concern only female respondents. The first of them was found in answers to the question: "Who took the initiative at the first intercourse?" The results are presented in Table 10.

When interviewed by women, female subjects tend to respond also to this question more in accordance with traditional sex-role expectations. The same tendency was observed finally in a question concerning how many intercourses the subjects had during the last thirty days.

If female subjects did not want to appear seductive to our male interviewers, then they tried to give female interviewers an impression of lower sexual activity, which is in accordance with traditional norms. The interesting lesson from these figures, however, is the hypothesis that among metropolitan female youth, traditional sex-role behavior seems to be reinforced by persons of the same sex. If we could get some evidence for this hypothesis, then it really would mean a social change: girls do not believe that men have traditional expectations concerning sexual behavior to the same degree as women. Thus female oppression—with regard to sexual behavior and norms in this field—would have its sources in one's own sex. When it comes to economic questions, however, such as equal pay for equal work and in the area of consumption, men are probably more eager to uphold traditional norms and behavior patterns. Usually they are in positions of power and therefore are those who want to keep the status quo, which, among other things, includes upholding traditional sex-role standards in the economic field.

*Table 10*

SEX OF INTERVIEWER AND INITIATIVE AT FIRST INTERCOURSE (FEMALE RESPONDENTS ONLY)

| Sex of Respondent | Sex of Interviewer | "Who took the initiative?" No one % | Respondent % | Partner % | Both % | (n = 100%) | Level of Significance |
|---|---|---|---|---|---|---|---|
| *Women* | Male Interviewer | 5 | 17 | 67 | 11 | (125) | $p < 1\%$ |
| | Female Interviewer | 2 | 3 | 75 | 21 | (296) | |

*Table 11*

SEX OF INTERVIEWER AND NUMBER OF INSTANCES OF INTERCOURSE IN THE LAST THIRTY DAYS (FEMALE RESPONDENTS ONLY)

| Sex of Respondent | Sex of Interviewer | Number of Instances of Intercourse 0 % | 1 % | 2–4 % | 5–10 % | 11+ % | (n = 100%) | Level of Significance |
|---|---|---|---|---|---|---|---|---|
| *Women* | Male Interviewer | 22 | 5 | 25 | 36 | 12 | (125) | $p < 5\%$ |
| | Female Interviewer | 32 | 9 | 21 | 27 | 11 | (300) | |

NOTES

1. See also J. Israel *et al.*, "Sexuelle Verhaltungsformen der Schwedischen Grosstadtjugend," in *Modelfall Skandinavien?* (Reinbek: Rohwolt Taschenbuch Verlag, 1970).
2. It is interesting to note the contrary attitudes developed in the so-called consumption society. There the immediate need-satisfaction is a main goal. Consideration for future generations has been abandoned, as can be shown by the pollution and destruction of the environment.
3. These theories have been developed by Wilhelm Reich. For a discussion of his theories see P. A. Robinson, *The Freudian Left* (New York: Harper Colophon Books, 1969).
4. Cuba is an extremely interesting example of the process of early capital accumulation as exemplified with the enormous efforts to achieve a large sugar harvest, the result of which is intended to be used in the process of industrialization. Puritan morals in Cuba are anchored in the tradition of Catholic ethics, which dominated the moral aspects of the superstructure of the Cuban society.
5. For the analysis of the process of reification see J. Israel, *Alienation: From Marx to Modern Sociology* (Boston: Allyn and Bacon, 1971).
6. As one example only of these differences, we can refer to the functioning of film censorship. In Sweden, as long as it functioned, it concentrated mainly on brutality and violence, whereas sexual behavior was accepted. The tendency in the United States has been exactly the opposite.
7. A more detailed description of these factors is to be found in J. Israel, "Sociologiska faktorer kring sexualiteten," in J. Israel (ed.), *Sexologi* (Stockholm: Almqvist & Wicksell, 1970).
8. There seems to be a tendency in pornography to change content and to picture women more actively.
9. See M. Schofield, *The Sexual Behavior of Young People* (London: Longmans, 1965), and I. Reiss, *The Social Context of Premarital Sexual Permissiveness* (New York: Holt, Rinehart and Winston, 1967).
10. H. Zetterberg, *Om sexuallivet i Sverige*, S.O.U. 1969: 2.
11. Examples of items forming the scale are: "The risk for undesired pregnancy makes it necessary to abstain from sexual intercourse before marriage" and "The aim of intercourse is having children and not achieving pleasure."
12. Using Chi Square the differences are significant at the 0.1% level for both men and women.
13. Examples of items forming this scale are: "One ought only to have sexual intercourse with somebody one loves" and "Sexual intercourse without love is filthy." The following table indicates the correlation between "romantic love moral" and a traditional double standard.

| Degree of "Romantic Love Moral": | | Low | Middle | High | |
|---|---|---|---|---|---|
| % Traditional Double-Standard Responses | *Men* | 13 | 22 | 30 | Chi Square = 14.16 2f $p < 0.1\%$ |
| | *Women* | 1 | 10 | 22 | Chi Square = 26.81 2f $p < 0.1\%$ |

14. Zetterberg, *op. cit.*, and I. Reiss, *Premarital Sexual Standards in America* (London: The Free Press of Glencoe, 1960).
15. The correlations between "romantic love moral" and traditional sex-role expectations are, using a gamma-coefficient, .06 for men and .16 for women. For women this correlation is significant at the 1% level.
16. The correlations between pragmatic puritanism and traditional sex-role expectations are, using a gamma-coefficient, .16 for men and .22 for women, both significant at the 1% level.
17. The reader is referred to a forthcoming thesis by Rosmari Eliasson.
18. J. Coleman, *Introduction to Mathematical Sociology* (New York: Free Press, 1965).
19. J. Israel, *Välfärdssamhället—och därefter?* (Stockholm: Aldus/Bonniers, 1969).
20. The following table indicates the correlations:

| Degree of Conventionalism | | Low | Middle | High | Gamma |
|---|---|---|---|---|---|
| % Having More Than Primary School Education | *Men* | 54 | 35 | 35 | −0.20 $p < 1\%$ |
| | *Women* | 54 | 41 | 26 | −0.37 $p < 1\%$ |

21. Keeping education constant does not eliminate the correlation.
22. The results are presented by P. Howard, "Problems of Refusal and Interviewer-Effect in Surveys," dissertation (Uppsala: Institute of Sociology, 1969). Mimeo.

# IV

# Liberation and the Politics of the Body

*Part of the so-called sexual revolution is a new wave in women's struggle for equal rights. In this chapter the women's liberation movement is seen in the larger context of class conflict and in the light of a new element, sensuousness, which has entered these conflicts through the protest movements of the late sixties. Jo Freeman, an Assistant Professor of Political Science at the University of Chicago, presents an overview of the origins, structures, and ideas of the women's liberation movement. She describes the different factions of the movement and emphasizes that the struggle for liberation in the future cannot be separated from equal rights now. Her article is published for the first time in this volume.*

*Branka Magaš is an editor of the* New Left Review, *from which her article on "Sex Politics: Class Politics" is reprinted (Vol. 66, 1971). Presently completing her doctorate in the philosophy of science at Chelsea College of Technology in London, she has been active in the women's liberation movement for some time. Her article reviews the most important literary contributions to the movement, i.e., Kate Millett, Germaine Greer, Eva Figes, and argues from a Marxist point of view that sex politics cannot be separated from the class struggle.*

*Using a different perspective derived from a critical phenomenology, John O'Neill comes to a similar conclusion. His article "On Body Politics," which was written for this volume, presents the first coherent view of the sensual quality displayed by recent protest movements. Even though the author does not deal specifically with the family or sexual problems, the implications for the struggle of the sexes are clear. John O'Neill is Professor of Sociology, York University, Toronto. His publications cover a vast range of topics including a monograph on the French phenomenologist Merleau-Ponty.*

# 9

# The Women's Liberation Movement: Its Origins, Structures, and Ideas

JO FREEMAN

SOMETIME IN THE 1920S, feminism died in the United States. It was a premature death. Feminists had only recently obtained their long-sought-for tool, the vote, with which they had hoped to make an equal place for women in this society. But it seemed like a final one. By the time the granddaughters of the women who had sacrificed so much for suffrage had grown to maturity, not only had social mythology firmly ensconced women in the home, but the very term "feminist" had become an epithet.

Social fact, however, did not always coincide with social mythology. During the era of the "feminine mystique" when the percentage of degrees given to women was dropping, their absolute numbers were rising astronomically. Their participation in the labor force was also increasing—even while their position within it was declining. Opportunities to work, the trend toward smaller families, plus changes in status symbols from a leisured wife at home to a second car and TV, all contributed to a basic alteration of the female labor force from one of primarily single women under twenty-five to one of married women and mothers over forty. Added to these developments was an increased segregation of the job market, a flooding of traditional female jobs (e.g., teaching and social work) by men, a decrease of women's percentage of the professional and technical jobs by a third, and a commensurate decline in their relative income. The result was the creation of a class of highly educated, underemployed women.

In the early sixties feminism was still an unmentionable, but its ghost was slowly awakening from the dead. The first sign of new life came with the establishment of the Commission on the Status of Women by President Kennedy in 1961. Created at the urging of Esther Petersen of the Women's Bureau, in its short life the commission came out with several often radical reports thoroughly documenting women's second-class status. It was followed by the formation of a citizen's advisory council and fifty state commissions.

Many of the people involved in these commissions became the nucleus of women who, dissatisfied with the lack of progress made on commission recommendations, joined with Betty Friedan in 1966 to found the National Organization for Women.

NOW was the first new feminist organization in almost fifty years, but it was not the sole beginning of the organized expression of the movement. The movement actually has two origins, from two different strata of society, with two different styles, orientations, values, and forms of organization. In many ways there were two separate movements, which only in 1970–71 began to merge sufficiently for the rubric "women's liberation" to be truly an umbrella term for the multiplicity of organizations and groups.

The first of these I call the older branch of the movement, partially because it began first, and partially because the median age of its activists is higher. In addition to NOW it contains such organizations as the PWC (Professional Women's Caucus), FEW (Federally Employed Women), and the self-defined "right wing" of the movement, WEAL (Women's Equity Action League).

The participants of both branches tend to be predominantly white, middle class and college-educated, but the composition of the older is much more heterogeneous than that of the younger. In issues, however, this trend is reversed, with those of the younger being more diverse. While the written programs and aims of the older branch span a wide spectrum, their activities tend to be concentrated on the legal and economic difficulties women face. These groups are primarily made up of women who work and are substantially concerned with the problems of working women. Their style of organization has tended to be formal, with numerous elected officers, boards of directors, bylaws, and the other trappings of democratic procedure. All started as top-down organizations lacking in a mass base. Some have subsequently developed a mass base, some have not yet done so, and others don't want to.

In 1967 and 1968, unaware of and unknown to NOW or the state commissions, the other branch of the movement was taking shape. Contrary to popular myth it did not begin on the campus; nor was it started by SDS. However, its activators were, to be trite, on the other side of the generation gap. While few were students, all were "under thirty" and had received their political education as participants or concerned observers of the social-action projects of the last decade. Many came direct from New Left and civil rights organizations where they had been shunted into traditional roles and faced with the self-evident contradiction of working in a "freedom movement" but not being very free. Others had attended various courses on women in the multitude of free universities springing up around the country during those years.

At least five groups in five different cities (Chicago, Toronto, Detroit, Seattle, and Gainesville, Florida) formed spontaneously, independently of each other. They came at a very auspicious moment. In 1967 the blacks kicked the whites out of the civil rights movement, student power had been discredited by SDS, and the New Left was on the wane. Only draft-resistance activities were on the increase, and this movement more than any other exemplified the social inequities of the sexes. Men could resist the draft. Women could only counsel resistance.

There had been individual temporary caucuses and conferences of women as early as 1964, when Stokely Carmichael made his infamous remark that "the only position for women in SNCC is prone." But it was not until 1967 that the groups developed a determined, if cautious, continuity and began consciously to expand themselves. In 1968 they held their first, and so far only, national conference, attended by over two hundred women from around the United States and Canada on less than a month's notice. They have been expanding exponentially ever since.

This expansion has been more amoebic than organized because the younger branch of the movement prides itself on its lack of organization. Eschewing structure and damning the idea of leadership, it has carried the concept of "everyone doing her own thing" almost to its logical extreme. The thousands of sister chapters around the country are virtually independent of each other, linked only by the numerous journals, newsletters, and cross-country travelers. Some cities have a coordinating committee which attempts to maintain communication between the local groups and channel newcomers into appropriate ones, but none has any power over group activities, let alone group ideas. One result of this style is a very broad-based, creative movement, which individuals can relate to pretty much as they desire with no concern for orthodoxy or doctrine. Another result is a kind of political impotency. It is virtually impossible to coordinate a national action, assuming there could be any agreement on issues around which to coordinate one. Fortunately the older branch of the movement does have the structure necessary to coordinate such actions, and is usually the one to initiate them, as NOW did for the August 26, 1970, national strike.

It is a common mistake to try to place the various feminist organizations on the traditional left/right spectrum. The terms "reformist" and "radical" are convenient and fit into our preconceived notions about the nature of political organization, but they tell us nothing of relevance. As with almost everything else, feminism cuts through the normal categories and demands new perspectives in order to be understood. Some groups often called "reformist" have a platform which would so completely change our society it would be unrecognizable. Other groups called "radical" concentrate on the traditional female concerns of love, sex, children, and interpersonal relationships (although with untraditional views). The activities of the organizations are similarly incongruous. The most typical division of labor, ironically, is that those groups labeled "radical" engage primarily in educational work while the so-called reformist ones are the activists. It is structure and style rather than ideology which more accurately differentiate the various groups, and even here there has been much borrowing on both sides. The older branch has used the traditional forms of political action, often with great skill, while the younger branch has been experimental.

The most prevalent innovation developed by the younger branch has been the "rap group." Essentially an educational technique, it has spread far beyond its origins and become a major organizational unit of the whole movement, most frequently used by suburban housewives. From a sociological perspective the rap group is probably the most valuable contribution so far by the women's liberation movement to the tools for social change.

The rap group serves two main purposes. One is traditional; the other is unique. The traditional role is the simple process of bringing women together in a situation of structured interaction. It has long been known that people can be kept down as long as they are kept divided from each other, relating more to those in a superior social position than to those in a position similar to their own. It is when social development creates natural structures in which people can interact with each other and compare their common concerns that social movements take place. This is the function that the factory served for the workers, the church for the southern civil rights movement, the campus for students, and the ghetto for urban blacks.

Women have been largely deprived of a means of structured interaction and been kept isolated in their individual homes, relating more to men than to each other. Natural structures are still largely lacking, though they have begun to develop, but the rap group has created an artificial structure which does much the same thing. This phenomenon is similar to the nineteenth-century development of a multitude of women's clubs and organizations around every conceivable social and political purpose. These organizations taught women political skills and eventually served as the primary communications network for the spread of the suffrage movement. Yet after the great crusade ended, most of them vanished or became moribund. The rap groups are taking their place and will serve much the same function for the future development of this movement.

They do more than just bring women together, as radical an activity as that may be. The rap groups have become mechanisms for social change in and of themselves. They are structures created specifically for the purpose of altering the participants' perceptions and conceptions of themselves and society at large. The means by which this is done is called "consciousness raising." The process is very simple. Women come together in groups of five to fifteen and talk to each other about their personal problems, personal experiences, personal feelings, and personal concerns. From this public sharing of experiences comes the realization that what was thought to be individual is in fact common; that what was thought to be a personal problem has a social cause and probably a political solution. Women learn to see how social structures and attitudes have molded them from birth and limited their opportunities. They ascertain the extent to which women have been denigrated in this society and how they have developed prejudices against themselves and other women.

It is this process of deeply personal attitude change that makes the rap group such a powerful tool. The need of a movement to develop "correct consciousness" has long been known. But usually this consciousness is not developed by means intrinsic to the structure of the movement and does not require such a profound resocialization of one's concept of self. This experience is both irreversible and contagious. Once one has gone through such a "resocialization," one's view of oneself and the world is never the same again, whether or not there is further active participation in the movement. Even those who do "drop out" rarely do so without first spreading feminist ideas among their own friends and colleagues. All who undergo "consciousness raising" virtually compel themselves to seek out other women with whom to share the experience, and thus begin new rap groups.

There are several personal results from this process. The initial one is a decrease of self and group depreciation. Women come to see themselves as essentially pretty groovy people. Along with this comes the explosion of the myth of individual solution. If women are the way they are because society has made them that way, they can only change their lives significantly by changing society. These feelings in turn create the consciousness of oneself as a member of a group and the feeling of solidarity so necessary to any social movement. From this comes the concept of sisterhood.

This need for group solidarity partially explains why men have been largely excluded from the rap groups. It was not the initial reason, but it has been one of the more beneficial by-products. Originally, the idea was borrowed from the black power movement, much in the public consciousness when the women's liberation movement began. It was reinforced by the unremitting hostility of most of the New Left men at the prospect of an independent women's movement not tied to radical organizations. Even when this hostility was not present, women in virtually every group in the United States, Canada, and Europe soon discovered that the traditional sex roles reasserted themselves in the groups regardless of the good intentions of the participants. Men inevitably dominated the discussions, and usually would talk only about how women's liberation related to men, or how men were oppressed by the sex roles. In segregated groups women found the discussions to be more open, honest, and extensive. They could learn how to relate to other women and not just to men.

Unlike the male exclusion policy, the rap groups did not develop spontaneously or without a struggle. The political background of many of the early feminists of the younger branch predisposed them against the rap group as "unpolitical" and they would condemn discussion meetings which "degenerated" into "bitch sessions." This trend was particularly strong in Chicago and Washington, D.C., which had been centers of New Left activity. Meanwhile, other feminists, usually with a civil rights or apolitical background, saw that the "bitch session" obviously met a basic need. They seized upon it and created the consciousness raising rap group. Developed initially in New York and Gainesville, Florida, the idea soon spread throughout the country, becoming the paradigm for most movement organization.

To date, the major, though hardly exclusive, activity of the younger branch has been organizing rap groups, putting on conferences, and putting out educational literature, while that of the older branch has been using the "channels" and other forms of political pressure to change specific situations in inequity. In general, the younger branch has been organized to attack attitudes and the older branch to attack structures.

While the rap groups have been excellent techniques for changing individual attitudes they have not been very successful in dealing with social institutions. Their loose informal structure encourages participation in discussion and their supportive atmosphere elicits personal insight; but neither is very efficient in handling specific tasks. Thus, while rap groups have been of fundamental value to the development of the movement, the more structured groups are the more visibly effective.

Individual rap groups tend to flounder when their members have exhausted the virtues of consciousness raising and decide they want to do something more concrete. The problem is that most groups are unwilling to change their structure when they change their tasks. They have accepted the ideology of "structurelessness" without realizing the limitations of its uses. This eventually caused an organizational crisis within the movement because the formation of rap groups as a major movement function is becoming obsolete. Due to the intense press publicity that began in the fall of 1969, as well as the numerous "overground" books and articles now being circulated, women's liberation has become a household word. Its issues are discussed and informal rap groups formed by people who have no explicit connection with any movement group. Ironically, this subtle, silent and subversive spread of feminist consciousness is causing a situation of political unemployment. With educational work no longer such an overwhelming need, women's liberation groups have to develop new forms of organizations to deal with new tasks in a new stage of development. This is necessitating a good deal of retrenchment and rethinking. Cities undergoing this process often give the impression of inactivity, and only time will tell what will be the result.

Initially there was little ideology in the movement beyond a gut feeling that something was wrong. NOW was formed under the slogan "Full equality for women in a truly equal partnership with men" and specified eight demands in a "Bill of Rights." It and the other organizations of the older branch have continued to focus around concrete issues, feeling that attempts at a comprehensive ideology have little to offer beyond internal conflict.

In the younger branch a basic difference of opinion developed quite early. It was disguised as a philosophical difference, was articulated and acted on as a strategical one, but actually was more of a political disagreement than anything else. The two sides involved included essentially the same people who differed over the rap groups, but the split endured long after the groups became ubiquitous. The original issue was whether the fledging women's liberation movement would remain a branch of the radical left movement or be an independent women's movement. Proponents became known as "politicos" or "feminists," respectively, and traded arguments about whether "capitalism was the enemy," or the male-dominated social institutions and values. They also traded a few epithets, with politicos calling feminists politically unsophisticated and elitist, while in turn being accused of subservience to the interests of left wing men.

With the influx of large numbers of previously apolitical women an independent, autonomous women's liberation movement became a reality instead of an argument. The spectrum shifted to the feminist direction, but the basic difference in orientation still remained. Politicos now also call themselves feminists, and many have left the left, but most see women's issues within a broader political context while the original feminists continue to focus almost exclusively on women's concerns. Although much of the bitterness of the original dispute has subsided, politicos generated such distrust about their motives that they prejudiced many women against all concerns of left ideology. This has led some feminists to the very narrow outlook that politicos most feared they would adopt.

Meanwhile, faced with a female exodus, the radical left movement has forsaken the rhetoric of its original opposition without relinquishing most of its sexist practices. Embracing the position that women are a constituency to be organized, most New Left (and some Old Left) organizations have created women's caucuses to recruit women to "more important activities." These are very different from the women's caucuses of the professional associations that have also mushroomed into existence. The latter are concerned with raising feminist issues within their organizations. The New Left women's groups serve much the same function as traditional ladies auxiliaries.

The widely differing backgrounds and perspectives of the women in the movement have resulted in as many different interpretations of women's status. Some are more developed than others, and some are more publicized, yet as of 1972 there is no comprehensive set of beliefs which can accurately be labeled women's liberationist, feminist, neofeminist, or radical feminist ideology. At best one can say there is general agreement on two theoretical concerns. The first is the feminist critique of society, and the second is the idea of oppression.

The feminist critique starts from entirely different premises than the traditional view, and therefore neither can really refute the other. The latter assumes that men and women are essentially different and should serve different social functions. Their diverse roles and statuses simply reflect these essential differences. The feminist perspective starts from the premise that women and men are constitutionally equal and share the same human capabilities. Observed differences therefore demand a critical analysis of the social institutions which cause them.

The concept of oppression brings into use a term which has long been avoided out of a feeling that it was too rhetorical. But there was no convenient euphemism and discrimination was inadequate to describe what happens to women and what they have in common with other groups. As long as the word remained illegitimate, so did the idea and it was too valuable not to use. It is still largely an undeveloped concept in which the details have not been sketched, but there appear to be two aspects to oppression which relate much the same as two sides of a coin—distinct, yet inseparable. The social-structural manifestations are easily visible, as they are reflected in the legal, economic, social, and political institutions. The social-psychological ones are often intangible; hard to grasp and hard to alter. Group self-hate and distortion of perceptions to justify a preconceived interpretation of reality are just some of the factors being teased out.

For women, sexism describes the specificity of female oppression. Starting from the traditional belief of the difference between the sexes, sexism embodies two core concepts.

The first is that men are more important than women. Not necessarily superior—we are far too sophisticated these days to use those tainted terms—but more important, more significant, more valuable, more worthwhile. This value justifies the idea that it is more important for a man, the "breadwinner," to have a job or a promotion, than for a woman, more important for a man to be paid well, more important for a man to have an education and in general to have preference over a woman. It is the basis of the feeling by men that if women enter a particular occupation they will degrade it and that men must leave or be themselves degraded; and the feeling by women that they can raise the prestige of their professions by recruiting men, which they can only do by giving them the better jobs. From this value comes the attitude that a husband must earn more than his wife or suffer a loss of personal status, and a wife must subsume her interests to his or be socially castigated. From this value comes the practice of rewarding men for serving in the armed forces and punishing women for having children. The first core concept of sexist thought is that men do the important work in the world and the work done by men is what is important.

The second core concept is that women are here for the pleasure and assistance of men. This is what is meant when women are told that their role is complementary to that of men; that they should fulfill their natural "feminine" functions; that they are "different" from men and should not compete with them. From this concept comes the attitude that women are and should be dependent on men for everything, but especially for their identities, the social definition of who they are. It defines the few roles for which women are socially rewarded—wife, mother, and mistress—all of which are pleasing or beneficial to men, and leads directly to the "pedestal" theory, which extols women who stay in their place as good helpmates to men.

It is this attitude which stigmatizes those women who do not marry or who do not devote their primary energies to the care of men and their children. Association with a man is the basic criterion for participation by women in this society, and one who does not seek her identity through a man is a threat to the social values. It is similarly this attitude which causes women's liberation activists to be labeled as man-haters for exposing the nature of sexism. People feel that a woman not devoted to looking after men must act this way because of hatred or inability to "catch" one. This second core concept of sexist thought is that women's identities are defined by their relationship to men and their social value by that of the men they are related to.

The sexism of our society is so pervasive that we are not even aware of all its inequities. Unless one has developed a sensitivity to its workings, by adopting a self-consciously contrary view, its activities are accepted as "normal" and justified with little question. People are said to "choose" what in fact they never thought about. A good example is what happened during and after the Second World War. The sudden onslaught of the war radically changed the whole structure of social relationships as well as the economy. Men were drafted into the army and women into the labor force. Now desperately needed, women's wants were provided for as were those of the boys on the front. Federal financing of day-care centers in the form of the Landham Act passed Congress in a record two weeks. Special crash training programs were provided for the new women workers to give them skills they were not previously thought capable of exercising. Women instantly assumed positions of authority and responsibility unavailable only the year before.

But what happened when the war ended? Both men and women had heeded their country's call to duty to bring the war to a successful conclusion. Yet men were rewarded for their efforts and women punished for theirs. The returning soldiers were given the GI Bill and other veterans' benefits, as well as their jobs back and a disproportionate share of the new ones created by the war economy. Women, on the other hand, saw their child-care centers dismantled and their training programs cease. They were fired or demoted in droves and often found it difficult to enter colleges flooded with ex-GIs matriculating on government money. Is it any wonder that they heard the message that their place was in the home? Where else could they go?

The eradication of sexism and the practices it supports, like those above, is obviously one of the major goals of the women's liberation movement. But it is not enough to destroy a set of values and leave a normative vacuum. They have to be replaced with something. A movement only begins by declaring its opposition to the status quo. Eventually, if it is to succeed, it has to propose an alternative.

I cannot pretend to be even partially definitive about the possible alternatives contemplated by the numerous participants in the women's liberation movement. Yet from the plethora of ideas and visions feminists have thought, discussed, and written about, I think there are two basic ideas emerging which express the bulk of their concerns. I call these the Egalitarian Ethic and the Liberation Ethic, but they are not independent of each other, and together they mesh into what can only be described as a feminist humanism.

The Egalitarian Ethic means exactly what it says. The sexes are equal; therefore sex roles must go. Our history has proved that institutionalized difference inevitably means inequity, and sex-role stereotypes have long since become anachronistic. Strongly differentiated sex roles were rooted in the ancient division of labor; their basis has been torn apart by modern technology. Their justification was rooted in the subjection of women to the reproductive cycle. That has already been destroyed by modern pharmacology. The cramped little boxes of personality and social function to which we assign people from birth must be broken open so that all people can develop independently, as individuals. This means that there will be an integration of social functions and life-styles of men and women as groups until, ideally, one cannot tell anything of relevance about a person's social role by knowing the sex of the person. But this increased similarity of the two groups also means increased options for individuals and increased diversity in the human race. No longer will there be men's work and women's work. No longer will humanity suffer a schizophrenic personality desperately trying to reconcile its "masculine" and "feminine" parts. No longer will marriage be the institution where two half-people come together in hopes of making a whole.

The Liberation Ethic says this is not enough. Not only must the limits of the roles be changed, but their content as well. The Liberation Ethic looks at the kinds of lives currently being led by men as well as women and concludes that both are deplorable and neither are necessary. The social institutions which oppress women as women also oppress people as people and can be altered to make a more humane existence for all. So much of our society is hung upon the framework of sex-role stereotypes and their reciprocal functions that the dismantling of this structure will provide the opportunity for making a more viable life for everyone.

It is important to stress that these two ethics must work together in tandem. If the first is emphasized over the second, then we have a women's rights movement, not one of women's liberation. To seek for only equality, given the current male bias of the social values, is to assume that women want to be like men or that men are worth emulating. It is to demand that women be allowed to participate in society as we know it, to get their piece of the pie, without questioning the extent to which that society is worth participating in. This view is held by some, but most feminists today find it inadequate. Those women who are more personally compatible in what is considered the male role must realize that that role is made possible only by the existence of the female sex role; in other words, only the subjection of women. Therefore women cannot become equal to men without the destruction of those two interdependent, mutually parasitic roles. The failure to realize that the integration of the sex roles and the equality of the sexes will inevitably lead to basic structural change is to fail to seize the opportunity to decide the direction of those changes.

It is just as dangerous to fall into the trap of seeking liberation without due concern for equality. This is the mistake made by many of the left radicals. They find the general human condition to be so wretched that they feel everyone should devote energies to the Millennial Revolution in the belief that the liberation of women will follow naturally the liberation of people.

However, women have yet to be defined as people, even among the radicals, and it is erroneous to assume their interests are identical to those of men. For women to subsume their concerns once again is to ensure that the promise of liberation will be a spurious one. There has yet to be created or conceived by any political or social theorist a revolutionary society in which women are equal to men and their needs duly considered. The sex-role structure has never been comprehensively challenged by any male philosopher, and the systems they have proposed have all presumed the existence of a sex-role structure to some degree.

Such undue emphasis on the Liberation Ethic has also often led to a sort of Radical Paradox. This is a situation the politicos frequently found themselves in during the early days of the movement. They found repugnant the possibility of pursuing "reformist" issues which might be achieved without altering the basic nature of the system, and thus, they felt, only strengthen the system. However, their search for a sufficiently radical action and/or issue came to naught, and they found themselves unable to do anything out of fear that it might be counterrevolutionary. Inactive revolutionaries are a good deal more innocuous than active "reformists."

But even among those who are not rendered impotent, the unilateral pursuit of liberation can take its toll. Some radical women have been so appalled at the condition of most men, and the possibility of becoming even partially what they are, that they have clung to the security of the role they know, to wait complacently for the revolution to liberate everyone. Some men, fearing that role reversal was a goal of the women's liberation movement, have taken a similar position. Both have failed to realize that the abolition of sex roles must be continually incorporated into any radical restructuring of society and thus have failed to explore the possible consequences of such role integration. The goal they advocate may be one of liberation, but it does not involve women's liberation.

Separated from each other, the Egalitarian Ethic and the Liberation Ethic can be crippling, but together they can be a very powerful force. Separately they speak to limited interests; together they speak to all humanity. Separately they are but superficial solutions; together they recognize that while sexism oppresses women, it also limits the potentiality of men. Separately neither will be achieved because its scope does not range far enough; together they provide a vision worthy of our devotion. Separately these two ethics do not lead to the liberation of women; together they also lead to the liberation of men.

# 10

# Sex Politics: Class Politics

BRANKA MAGAŠ

IN THE COURSE OF 1970, three books were written by women on women's oppression and liberation.[1] *The Female Eunuch* and *Patriarchal Attitudes*, although not written from within the women's liberation movement, are nevertheless valuable contributions to it. They try to grapple with a number of problems related to the current growth of consciousness among women and, in their treatment of the present as well as their suggestions for the future, reflect the strengths and weaknesses of the present stage. The author of *Sexual Politics* is an active member of the American women's liberation movement, and this book is the most recent attempt to articulate the components of sexual politics and put them into a social and historical context. In this sense it is a continuation of the project started by Simone de Beauvoir in 1949. The three books illustrate the range of problems as well as the scope of the effort necessary to construct a theory of women's position in society. They all suffer from one fundamental weakness: a failure to link sexual with class politics. But if one thing is clear about the women's liberation movement as it has developed in the last few years, it is its organic relationship with the other forms which the class struggle has taken (above all in the United States): militant opposition to the imperialist war in Vietnam, the upsurge of revolutionary activity among the black population, radicalization of large sections of youth and students.

## *Woman as Noble Savage*

A female human infant gains admission to the society which "has been lying in wait for her since before her birth and seizes her before her first cry, assigning to her her fixed destination." Although this process gives her a certain room to maneuver, so to speak, enough room to make disastrous mistakes as well as achieve spectacular successes, it is nevertheless in almost every detail determined by the particular culture into which she is born.

Greer's premise is that a woman successfully socialized into patriarchal society is a spectacular failure as a human being, a tragic negation of all that she could be; she is, in short, defined by her castration.

From childhood, woman's upbringing, both physically and intellectually, is characterized by the contradiction between her feminine conditioning and the male order that suffuses the world around her. The castration of women is "carried out in terms of a masculine-feminine polarity, in which men have commandeered all the energy and streamlined it into an aggressive conquistadorial power, reducing all heterosexual contact to a sado-masochistic pattern." This results in love perverted by altruism and self-interest, and turned into an obsession produced by the bourgeois myth of love and marriage. This syncretism of body and soul is the stereotype, the myth of the Eternal Feminine. Perverted love comes to involve hate. The way out lies not in "rebellion" but in "revolution." *The Female Eunuch* is therefore structured around three dichotomies: body/soul, love/hate, and rebellion/revolution.

The section of the book dealing with sex shows Germaine Greer to be magnificently and militantly antipuritan: here she is at her most convincing. She quotes from ballad literature to portray a time when women could describe their sex as that "lusty wench" did in the seventeenth century:

> You'l find the Purse so deep,
> You'l hardly come to the treasure.

Samuel Collins's *Systema Anatomicum*, published in the same century, "described the vagina so lovingly that any woman who read his words must have been greatly cheered. . . . Collins's description is an active one: the vagina *speaks, throws,* is *tense* and vigorous." The debunking of the illusory vaginal orgasm has been an advance, argues the author, but the pendulum has now swung to the other extreme and "the substitution of the clitoral spasm for genuine gratification may turn out to be a disaster for sexuality." The spate of manuals on sexual techniques is probably welcome, but they try to persuade one that "there is a statistically ideal fuck which will always result in satisfaction if the right procedures are followed." If female sexual response becomes localized in the clitoris, the same limitation will be imposed on it as that which has stunted male sexuality.

"The ideal marriage as measured by the electronic equipment in the Reproductive Biology Research Foundation laboratories is enfeebled—dull sex for dull people. The sexual personality is basically antiauthoritarian. If the system wishes to enforce complete suggestibility in its subjects, it will have to tame sex. Masters and Johnson supplied the blueprint for standard, low-agitation, cool-out monogamy." Women "must hold out not just for orgasm but for ecstasy." Greer quotes from Blake's *Jerusalem*:

> Embraces are comminglings from the Head even to the Feet,
> And not a pompous High Priest entering by a Secret Place.

Germaine Greer's vision of the world, and woman's role in it, contains many almost Rousseauesque elements in that she believes that civilization has corrupted man and his return to nature will be a return to a stage of sexual innocence and love. Our civilization has been marked by disastrous consequences brought about by the polarization of the sexes; for in concentrating on the penis it has castrated women and deformed men. "The world has lost its soul, and I my sex" quotes the author at the start of the book—the result is a world that will "run to its lunatic extremes at ever-escalating speed." Woman, like the Noble Savage, dear to the *philosophes* of the eighteenth century, has remained closer to nature because of her lack of education, and so it is woman who can, for this reason, in regaining her self-respect save the world. "What is the arms race and the cold war but the condition of male competitiveness and aggression brought into the inhuman sphere of computer-run institutions? If women are to cease producing cannon fodder for the final holocaust, they must rescue men from the perversities of their own polarization."

For Rousseau, aggression was not an inherent characteristic of man, but one that civilization had imposed on him. The prime virtue of the natural man was pity, a feeling that resulted from his awareness of his own vulnerability, and which philosophy and reason were to distort as society developed. But this pity can still be found in creatures weaker than man—in women and animals. Greer is but an echo! "If women would only offer a genuine alternative to the treadmill of violence, the world might breathe a little longer with less pain." "If women understand by emancipation the adoption of the masculine role then we are lost indeed. If women can supply no counterbalance to the blindness of male drive the aggressive society will run to its lunatic extremes at ever-escalating speed. Who will safeguard the despised animal faculties of compassion, empathy, innocence and sensuality?"

Here the basic, and determinant, contradiction of her work comes to the surface. There is an ambiguity already involved in the term "female eunuch" and now it obtains clarification. The ambiguity is that this concept is, in a certain sense, suspended between a negation: woman is a not-man—and a void—for what is a noncastrated woman? To show that woman is socialized to conform to an order not of her making, but made by man, or to number instances in which her socialization proceeds differently from man's, both of which the author does, inevitably defines woman in terms of man. (Indeed, unless women seize the male-dominated culture and turn it into an instrument of the liberation, thereby ensuring that the culture based on domination of one sex over the other will be destroyed together with its concomitant sexual polarization, women will continue to be defined in terms of men.) This ambiguity means that she must either reject the stereotype that parades itself as woman (thus also rejecting the sentiments tied to it) or embrace its qualities and, with them, confront those associated with men. In attempting to turn "all the defects which it defines into advantages," Greer embraces the stereotyped woman and, in rejecting the world of today, turns her into a Noble Savage—an image of the past for the sake of the future.[2]

But the implications of this choice are not fully integrated in the book, and, as a result, we are continuously involved in a dilemma: women are castrated into something other than themselves but only by remaining so can they liberate themselves—and men too. Women are oppressed by men, but they should not confront them with violence—in the interest of the world of tomorrow. "The way forward is unknown, just as the sex of the uncastrated female is unknown"—but women's liberation can only mean sexual liberation as "sex is the principal confrontation in which new values can be worked out." Women, in confronting men, "perpetuate estrangement of the sexes and their own dependency."

"Woman's oceanic feeling for the race has little opportunity for expression," Greer writes. "It is grotesquely transmogrified in organized works of charity, where her genius for touching and soothing has dwindled into symbolic attitudinizing." The female mind that "flows on gossamers for deduction," that "rejects the misguided masculine notion that men are rational animals," this female mind represents a breakthrough. Now that "most information is not disseminated in argumentative form, but is assimiliated in various non-verbal ways for visual and aural media, clarifications and virtues of disputation are more and more clearly seen to be simply alternative ways of knowing, and not the only or the principal ones," the female mind can come into its own.

## *"Rebellion" and "Revolution"*

Given the terrible state of the world,[3] women could not do worse than choose violence. For this violence would be turned against men and "it is not a sign of revolution when the oppressed adopt the manners of the oppressors and practice oppression on their own behalf." "That women should seek a revolution in their circumstances by training themselves as a fighting force is the most obvious case of confusing reaction or rebellion with revolution. . . . Women who adopt the attitudes of war in their search for liberation condemn themselves to acting out the last perversion of dehumanized manhood, which has only one foreseeable outcome, the specifically masculine end of suicide."

Greer's recommendation for the future is a reverie of wishfulness. "It would be a genuine revolution if women would stop loving victors in violent encounters. . . . If women were to withdraw from the spectatorship of wrestling matches, the industry would collapse; if soldiers were certainly faced with the withdrawal of all female favors, as Lysistrata observed so long ago, there would suddenly be less glamour in fighting. . . . The male perversion of violence is an essential condition of degradation of women. The penis . . . has become a gun. . . . Women cannot be liberated from their impotence by the gift of a gun. . . . The process to be followed is the opposite: women must humanize the penis, take the steel out of it and make it flesh again. . . . The . . . female attitude to violence is inseparable from this problem."

Starting from her view of the world as distorted and to be rejected, and given the fact that for her its principal contradiction is that between man and woman, Greer is forced to accept the female stereotype. Only by understanding her position can we understand why she castigates *all* attempts by women to organize merely as reaction and why her revolution insists ultimately on the passivity of women. The confrontation between women and men/the world is for her purely symbolic—unless it is dissolved in a sexual encounter.[4] She insists on the role of consciousness in the process of women's liberation: "She should begin . . . by reassessing herself." This is one of the strengths of the book. *The Female Eunuch* is an effective propaganda text, in the best sense of what she says about literature as communication: "The love of fellows is based upon understanding and therefore upon communication. It was love that taught us to speak, and death that laid its fingers on our lips." But the reassessment is seen as individual, is conducted in a void. Women can change the world for the better, she argues, and she is right—women's liberation is revolutionary precisely because it involves the liberation of all humanity—but in her view women could do it almost by default: the world would crumble before their indifference.

Women's liberation will abolish the nuclear family, thus abolishing the necessary substructure of the authoritarian state, argues Greer, after which communism will necessarily follow. But instead of the nuclear family she would like to import peasant communities into industrial society, a return to the past. The vagueness of her concrete proposals for the abolition of the state is accompanied by the most detailed instructions for communal living: buy in bulk, buy second-hand clothes, make your own cosmetics. Her radicalism disintegrates into moralizing: in the whirlwind of absurdities and half-truths that her revolution represents, it is often difficult to know if she wants to liberate women or improve the moral standards of the nation.[5]

So it is not surprising that Germaine Greer fails to identify herself with the women's liberation movement insofar as it is trying to organize masses of women and work out a theory of woman's position: suspended between the rejection of the present and a vision of the future she is reduced to impotence. Her criticism of the current women's lib contains much truth, but it is not criticism offered sympathetically: in zigzagging between left and right it dismisses the entire political experience of women's lib today without replacing it with anything but reveries.

*The Female Eunuch* has much in common with Betty Friedan's *The Feminine Mystique*: both focus on the plight of women at home, on popular culture as the source of propaganda for the status quo, and on biased "scientific evidence" evoked in its defense. And yet, Betty Friedan's NOW is a vehicle of reformism, working for amelioration within the system. Germaine Greer is at least more radical in tone: "The conservatives who saw women's liberation as the undermining of our civilization and the end of the state and marriage were right after all; it is time for the demolition to begin."

## Emile *versus the* Social Contract

The political demand for women's rights was born during the struggle for power between the French bourgeoisie and nobility in the course of the French Revolution. But the revolution, even in its most radical moment, failed to include rights for women in its political program. Eva Figes in her *Patriarchal Attitudes* calls this a betrayal, an effect of Rousseau's misogynist ideology. Unlike Greer, who offers only a superficial account of the rise of capitalism, mainly to illustrate her view that it pulled the family out of production with detrimental effect on all concerned, Figes puts forward more ambitious theses which require an answer.

According to her, "woman shared in the prosperous heyday [of England's renaissance] and no doubt her social position was aided by the fact that England was ruled by a strong queen, unaided by a male consort." The Reformation put the accent on marriage as a lifelong partnership and friendship, she goes on with approval.[6] The household was a working and productive unit and a wife's labor was necessary to her husband. The craftsman's wife helped her husband and supervised the domestic chores, and was often engaged in a business of her own. With the later development of capitalism, the rich man's wife became an idle plaything while women lower down the social scale provided cheap labor. The increasing difference between men and women was reflected in their education. "Compare Shakespeare's heroines to the ladies of the Restoration and you see the change that has taken place in under a century."[7] Women became increasingly dependent on men economically, a process that went together with a growing division between the sphere of work and that of home. Religious taboos were thereby weakened and "sexual license" increased. Some means of ensuring authentic paternity for the purposes of inheritance became essential. This was the root cause of the "romantic revolution"—and its instigator was Jean Jacques Rousseau.

Rousseau's role is contrasted with that of other men of literary fame in the eighteenth century who were "in favor of women getting a broader education. Dr. Johnson approved of educated women and said that men who did not were frightened of being outstripped by their womenfolk: Richardson, Daniel Defoe and Addison pleaded for a more comprehensive education for women. . . . The famous salons of Paris in the seventeenth and eighteenth centuries found a more modest counterpart in London." However, a reaction came which "attacked both the social inequality on which this life was based, and the values implicit in this urban way of life, and the prime instigator was Jean Jacques Rousseau. At the same time . . . he put women firmly back in the home."

"The whole gamut of reactions and attitudes which we now cover under the umbrella 'Romantic Revolution' is directly attributable to Rousseau," states the author. " 'A man is born free, and everywhere he is in chains,' thunders the inspiring if philosophically unsound first line of the *Social Contract*, and if one had not read any of his other works one might remain under the blissful illusion that when he uses the word 'man' he means 'mankind.' " In emphasizing woman's role as mother, Rousseau celebrated moral virtue as well as confinement to the bounds of home. "See that mothers deign to nourish their own babies," Eva Figes quotes from *Emile*, "and morals will be reformed of themselves, and the sentiment of nature will be wakened in all hearts. . . . The appeal of the domestic life is the best counterpart to bad morals. . . . When the family is lively and animated, the domestic chores are the dearest occupation of the wife and the most delightful entertainment to the husband."

Figes's rejection of this image is not entirely unsympathetic to it: "Note that domestic life is still somehow 'entertainment' for men, a pleasurable diversion and not a central preoccupation. The image that Rousseau fosters would not have been a bad one, had it not been based on fundamental inequality, and this is particularly ironic when one considers that Rousseau also preached a radical egalitarianism." Rousseau proclaims: "To renounce one's liberty is to renounce one's quality as a man, the rights and also duties of humanity." But, Figes argues, liberty, perhaps humanity itself, is an all-male affair, for *Emile* has the following to say about women: "They must be trained to bear the yoke from the first, so that they may not feel it, to master their own caprices and to submit themselves to the will of the others."

Given that the *Social Contract* was "the Bible of the French Revolution, illogical as the book now seems to us" and that Robespierre was Rousseau's most devout disciple, it comes as no surprise to the reader of Figes to learn that "the women of revolutionary France were thoroughly conned." For, although women played a significant role in the French Revolution at all social levels, "once the groundwork was done the position of women changed: in 1793 the National Convention suppressed all women's political clubs and societies, closed the salons, and denied women all political rights. This was in fact not only a betrayal but represented a position even worse than before the Revolution, since during the *ancien régime* women with certain property qualifications had been able to vote and occasionally even sit in provincial assemblies. Later Napoleon decreed that a woman should obey her husband, that the father had sole authority over her children, and that a woman could not go to law without her husband's consent."[8] The thesis is unambiguous: the French Revolution betrayed women, owing to Rousseau's influence and his unsound and illogical philosophy.

The betrayal of women by the Jacobins is contrasted by Figes with the progress made by them up to the eighteenth century and in contemporary England. However, her historical presentation in fact shows women at first engaged in productive work centered around the home but later—with the development of capitalism that breaks up the idyll of the family as a productive unit and of husband-wife partnership—divorced from productive work. Moreover she is, of course, unable to point to any actual political rights of women or indeed of most men in England at the time when French women were arresting their king. In fact, without giving credit where it is due, Figes is criticizing Rousseau, and the Jacobins, from the standpoint of the *Social Contract*. She is pitting the *Social Contract* against *Emile*.

Because of her basic premise (history seen in terms of man-woman conflict) and her method (history is reduced to a few texts extrapolated from both their literary context and that of their time—a method which allows her to slide from one author to another, from one century to another, from one class to another) she does not grasp the issues at stake, the economic and political forces of living history. However, she brings to the surface (and that is half the work done) a crucial problem: why bourgeois radicalism as advanced as that of the Jacobins failed to take up the question of women's rights at the time when it advocated rights for men. Indeed, this contradiction is found explicitly in Rousseau's opus. How do we reconcile *Emile* with the *Social Contract*?

## *Rousseau and the French Revolution*

The *Social Contract* was written as an answer to Thomas Hobbes.[9] Hobbes argued that men had to choose between being free, but not civilized, or living in civil society, under authority. Rousseau argued that, on the contrary, men can be both free *and* live in civil society. Indeed, only through living in society can man experience his fullest freedom and realize his own nature as man. True, society has corrupted men but it is a bad one and should be changed. The solution to Hobbes's problem is a simple one: a people can be free if it retains sovereignty over itself. Hobbes argued that sovereignty, based on nature or divine right, is transferred from the people to the ruler by a social contract; on the contrary, argued Rousseau, no such transfer need take place. Sovereignty not only originates with the people, it ought also to stay there.

This was the revolutionary scope of Rousseau's ideas. They helped to inspire a revolution of unprecedented radicalism: the Jacobin Republic attempted to carry the ideas of equality and people's sovereignty into practice—thereby putting the relationship between freedom, equality, and property into sharp focus.

Events between 1789 and 1794 showed a series of shifts in power from the right to the left, reflected in the political manifestos of the period. The 1789 Declaration of the Rights of Man and Citizen insisted on the right to own property as natural and inviolable. It expressed belief in a constitutional and secular state, with civil liberties and guarantees for private enterprise, a government of taxpayers and property owners that excluded half of the adult male population. The following protest by women was put to the assembly of the Estates General in that year: "Nous ferons mouvoir l'Église, nous animerons la Noblesse, nous dériderons la magistrature, nous affranchirons le Tiers-État; et quand il s'agira des intérêts des trois corps réunis, on refusera de nous appeler. Assez longtemps, les femmes l'ont souffert: la fin de leur esclavage est arrivée et il ne sera plus dit que, des vingt-quatre millions d'individus qui peuplent la France, la moitié n'aura pas le droit d'être représentée aux États généraux!"[10] The Jacobin Republic of 1793 went further: it proclaimed universal male suffrage, the right to work, the right to education, the right to insurrection, abolition of slavery in the French colonies. These ideas, as well as the mass participation in politics characteristic of the Revolution, frightened the European ruling class into military intervention. They were also the inspiration of working-class radicalism in the early nineteenth century, and of the precursors of the suffragette movement.[11] Mary Wollstonecraft, who in 1790 defended the French Revolution against Burke, was two years later to produce *A Vindication of the Rights of Woman* in which she argued against Rousseau's views on women and demanded for them the education he had envisaged for Emile.

However, the suffrage proclaimed by the Jacobins in 1793 did not include women. A demand for women's rights was indeed posed in 1791 by Olympe de Gouges, who put forward a manifesto *Droits de la Femme* in seventeen articles with an argument that was unanswerable: "If women have the right to mount the scaffold, they have the right to mount the tribune."[12] Her struggle in favor of women's rights as well as against the violence of the Convention led her to the guillotine in November, 1793. The Jacobin Terror struck right and left, men and women. A few days later, Mme Roland, an active supporter of the Gironde, perished in the same way. The Convention now proceeded to prohibit all women's associations and, as women protested against this injustice, denied them access to the Convention and all public assemblies—thus effectively depriving them of *de facto* as well as *de jure* political rights.

Let us now—against this background—examine Rousseau's ideas more closely. He ends his *Discourse on the Origin of Inequality among Men* with a statement that "there is hardly any inequality in the state of nature [inequality of individual men], all the inequality that now prevails owes its strength and growth to the advance of the human mind, and becomes at last permanent and legitimate by the establishment of property and laws." Therefore almost all inequality is due to "property and laws." In contrast to this, he writes in *Emile*: "Others [among women] not content to secure their rights lead them to usurp ours: for to make women our superior in all the qualities proper to her sex and to make her equal in all the rest, what is this but to transfer to the woman the superiority that nature has given to her husband?"[13] Nature? But "nature" stands here for "bourgeois reason," as can be seen from the following passage: "Women do wrong to complain of the inequality of man-made laws; this inequality is not of man's making, or, at any rate, it is not a result of mere prejudice, but of reason. She, to whom nature has entrusted the care of children, must hold herself responsible for them to their father. . . .When she gives her husband children who are not his own, she is false to him and to them, her crime is not infidelity but treason. To my mind, it is the source of dissension and crime of every kind."[14] Here the limits of bourgeois right can be clearly seen. If children are man's property and woman is contracted into his service (Rousseau saw marriage as a "civil contract"), then upsetting property relations becomes crime and treason. Equality is in fact dependent on one's position in the particular social hierarchy based on property. As Rousseau was to explain in his *Social Contract*: ". . . as for equality, this word must not be taken to imply that degrees of power and wealth should be absolutely the same for all, but rather that power shall stop short of violence and never be exercised except by virtue of authority and law, and, where wealth is concerned, that no citizen shall be rich enough to buy another and none so poor as to be forced to sell himself; this in turn implies that the more exalted persons need moderation in goods and influence and the humbler persons moderation in avarice and covetousness." (And in a footnote: "Do you want coherence in the state? Then bring the two extremes as close together as possible; have neither very rich men nor beggars, for these two estates, naturally inseparable, are equally fatal to the common good; from the one class come friends of tyranny, from the other, tyrants. It is always these two classes which make commerce of the public freedom: the one buys, the other sells.")[15]

The economic structure that underlies Rousseau's political philosophy can be seen to be petty commodity production and exchange, in which the economic unit is not the free individual, free to sell his labor, but the *family*, in which the man *is* the patriarchal master and of which the *Communist Manifesto* writes: "Modern industry has converted the little workshop of the patriarchal master into the great factory of the industrial capitalist."[16] The most radical layer of the Jacobin Republic, the Sansculottes, was an amorphous conglomeration of small craftsmen, shopkeepers, artisans, petty entrepreneurs—in short, a combination of "small master" elements. They combined a respect for (small) property with hostility for the rich; they dreamed of a world of small farmers and artisans undisturbed by bankers—or industrialists. One might conclude that at the time of the French Revolution the *political* and *economic* forces were not ripe for the legal emancipation of women.[17]

The completion of the bourgeois program—to make all equal before the law, ultimately symbolized by the right to vote irrespective of the size of one's property—took (for both men and women) a long and tortuous path over the next 130 years. While the eighteenth century gave birth to a political demand for legal equality of women, the nineteenth century provided the economic base. The industrial revolution introduced a large section of women into public production and turned them into proletarians; in general, it provided women with the opportunity to work outside the family. The nineteenth century saw the emergence of a militant suffrage movement among women—though in the end it was not their militancy that earned them the vote, but, rather, their service in the First World War. The nineteenth century also saw the correct posing, at the theoretical level, of the problem of women's historical subjugation, in the works of Marx and Engels. Moreover, Marxist theory posed the whole question of equality in a new light. "The equality of the bourgeoisie (abolition of class [or sex] privileges)," writes Engels in *Anti-Dühring*, "is very different from that of the proletariat (abolition of *classes themselves*)."

Figes goes on to discuss the patriarchal ideology that identifies women with nature and men with reason, the ways in which women are brought up to feel themselves inferior, as well as their situation today. Other bourgeois thinkers: Hegel, Darwin, Freud—theoreticians who represent the classical revolutionary bourgeois tradition—are seen as ideologues of oppression. The point is that her historical conception does not provide any means for their proper evaluation, and their role in uprooting the system that produced them is therefore entirely lost. This incapacity to grasp "the march of modern history" means that in the end she can only offer a series of reforms designed to take account of the cash nature of marriage, and dissolve it.

"The harsh fact of the matter is that the institution of marriage we are now trying to reform so unsuccessfully is based not on love, sentiment or compatibility, but on economic necessity. . . . The idea of people being tied together not by love, but by economic necessity, is abhorrent to us. It smacks of prostitution."[18] Why should you "tie yourself to a woman when you can have her anyhow, why pay through the nose for what you can have for free?" In her view the state ought to become the financial mediator between parents and children: "A man who paid tax to the state (then repaid to the mother in the form of a child allowance, unless the father or some other person had the care of the child) would at the same time have his paternal rights officially recognized." But she does not seem to have much hope; "perhaps it is asking too much . . . and we must wait for its meaning [that of marriage] to be gradually eroded over the next 50 years."[19]

## *Sexual Politics and Class Politics*

By the end of the eighteenth century the British mercantile bourgeoisie was in control of most of the world's markets and raw material. The industrial revolution, provoked by this concentration of capital and resources, took off in the last decades of that century and accelerated over the next years until, by 1830, it produced a new class in history: a large and radical proletariat. The basis of the industrial revolution in its first stage was cotton. By 1834 two-thirds of British textile workers were women.

The industrial bourgeoisie was now strong enough, by forming a bloc with its mercantile counterpart, to secure independent political rights with the Reform Bill of 1832. The world by then seemed a different place. Free trade and competition were replacing old feudal, religious and patriarchal ties. This presupposed individuals who could freely dispose of their activity. To create such "free" and "equal" persons was one of the tasks of capitalist production. In this new conception of social relations, marriage became a business contract. If freedom was required to conduct business, was it not also required to contract marriage?

This is the attitude behind John Stuart Mill's *On the Subjection of Women.* His argument for women's suffrage was that women should be able to dispose of themselves and their talents under the auspices of free competition. What is characteristic of this new world, argues Mill, is that human beings are no longer born into their place in life. Women are the only exception to this general rule. "The disabilities, therefore, to which women are subject for the mere fact of their birth, are solitary examples of this kind in modern legislation." If women have a greater natural inclination for one thing rather than another, there should be no law or social persuasion to tell them which: "what they can do, but not so well as men who are their competitors, competition suffices to exclude them from." Whatever "women's services are most wanted for, the free play of competition will hold out the strongest inducements to them to undertake."[20]

Mill was thus arguing for the right of women to compete with men—but they were already doing so in thousands, in industry, on the land, and in domestic service. Mill's project related to something different: the bourgeois woman could not dispose of her property, gain higher education, engage in business or control various aspects of her marriage without gaining legal rights. In 1866 Mill presented a petition to Parliament demanding suffrage for women of the class whose men already held the vote—and thus inaugurated the first phase of what Kate Millett calls the Sexual Revolution.[21]

In *Sexual Politics* Kate Millett argues that between 1830 and 1930 the world saw the coming and the passing of the first phase of the Sexual Revolution. The precursor of that revolution was Mill, in particular his work *On the Subjection of Women.* (The oscillations in the dating here are Kate Millett's own.) In her view, Mill not only gave an extremely lucid and realistic account of the position of women (enslavement of their body and mind, differential education, marriage based on sale or enforcement), he also argued that the subjugation of women is the psychological foundation of other forms of oppression. No love can be founded on a family in which man and woman are not equal. He therefore urged complete emancipation of women not only for the sake of an "unspeakable gain in happiness to the liberated half of the species, the difference to them between a life of subjection to the will of the others and a life of rational freedom," but also for the enormous benefit to humanity in having its talents doubled. The time has come, Mill said in 1869, for "the most fundamental of the social relations" to be "placed under the rule of equal justice."

## *Engels versus Mill*

But, Millett argues, Mill was "a liberal [who] saw no further back in time than a universal rule of force and who took the subjugation of women to be an eternal feature of human life which 'progress' and moral persuasion might alleviate, as he felt they had tyranny and slavery." Mill did urge women's right to work, enter professions, etc., but he imagined most of them would stay at home. He also thought that legal rights would be sufficient. In contrast to him, Millett points out, Engels was much more radical and revolutionary. First of all, he "preferred instead to regard institutions as man-made and hence capable of radical, sudden, even violent alteration, should a conscious revolutionary humanity so desire. Having seen the connection between the patriarchal family and private property, Engels believed he had found the origins of property in the subjugation and ownership of women upon which patriarchy was founded."

"What Mill had thought to be a primordial evil, the inevitable consequence of man's original slavery, Engels's historical account transformed into an oppressive innovation, an innovation which brought with it innumerable other forms of oppression, each dependent upon it. Far from being the last injustice, sexual dominance became the keystone to the total structure of human injustice." This means that the end of male economic domination, the entrance of women into the economic world on a perfectly equal basis, would do away with the need for sexual love to be based on financial coercion, dissolve the patriarchal family, and bring women independence, that is, would bring about social revolution.

While Millett is right to draw a dividing line between Engels and Mill, and indeed uses the former for a lucid critique of the latter, she nevertheless draws that line not at the origin of the difference between them but at its secondary aspect. For Millett's persuasive account of Engels's position contains one important and fundamental misunderstanding which underpins the whole book, its structure as well as its theory. Whereas Engels really argued that the development of productive forces gave rise to private property, resulting in the subjugation of women as well as the subjugation of most men, Millett's Engels argues that it is the subjugation of women that gave rise to private property (ownership of women being its first form) and thereafter to "the total structure of human injustice."[22] According to her, both Mill and Engels saw the subjugation of women as the cause of other forms of oppression, and therefore she can argue that once this oppression disappears all other forms will do so as well. The class history of mankind is thereby turned into the sex theory of history. Two concepts, so crucial to Engels's theory, "private property" and "class" (in particular, the proletariat, which Millett replaces by "conscious revolutionary humanity"), play no role in her analysis. (Nor in that of Mill, needless to say.)[23]

In fact, Engels was adamant on this point. "That woman was the slave of man at the commencement of society is one of the most absurd notions that have come down to us from the period of the Enlightenment of the 18th century." History in fact proceeded quite differently. "According to the division of labor then prevailing [in early history] in the family, the procuring of food and the implements necessary thereto fell to the man; he took them with him in case of separation just as woman retained the household goods." This division of labor does not at this stage imply any dominance of one sex over the other. However, "the domestication of animals and breeding of herds had developed a hitherto unsuspected source of wealth and created entirely new social relationships." It separated the family from the *gens* as well as changed the family itself. According to the above division of labor "the man was also the owner of the new sources of foodstuffs."

"In an old unpublished manuscript," continues Engels further on, "the work of Marx and myself in 1845 [*The German Ideology*], I find the following: 'The first division of labor is that between man and woman for child breeding.' And today I can add: The first class antagonism which appeared in history *coincides with* the development of the antagonism between man and woman in a monogamous marriage, and the first class oppression [coincides] with that of the female sex by the male. Monogamy was a great historical advance, but *at the same time* it inaugurated, *along with slavery and private property*, that epoch lasting until today, in which every advance is likewise a relative regression, and in which the well-being and development of the one group are attained by the misery and repression of the other."[24]

The subjugation of women by men came as a result of the development of surplus wealth due to the development of production: at the same time other forms of class oppression (slavery) came into being. The antagonism between men and women, as expressed by sexual politics, is therefore historically determined by the appearance of private property. Two related conditions for the liberation of women follow, according to Engels: (1) reintroduction of the entire female sex into public industry (*public* production as against the *private* nature of housework); (2) abolition of the family as the economic unit so that *all* its functions become public (in contrast to *private* responsibility *of women*). But this does not sum up women's liberation—any more than the abolition of private property sums up communism. It is its *precondition*, its premise, as Engels said.[25]

Thus the foundation of Millett's position is as follows. Society today is based ultimately on the subjugation of women. It was caused by history—not nature: it can therefore be changed if humanity so desires. With the disappearance of female subjugation all other forms of oppression will crumble. This will happen when women are economically independent, and legally and socially equal to men. In this process the patriarchal family will disappear. Sexual love, based on voluntary association of men and women, will be independent of coercion. The path to this goal is called Sexual Revolution. There are two concepts that are not part of this tableau: property and class.

"The term 'politics,'" Millett writes, "shall refer to power structured relationships, arrangements whereby one group of persons is controlled by another." Given the fact that men dominate women, "sex is a status category with political implications." Recent developments in the United States have convinced us that the relationship between races is a political one—the same can be shown for the relationship between sexes. Sexual politics has achieved a most ingenious form of "interior colonization," sturdier than any other form of segregation; every avenue of power is in the hands of men. It obtains consent, based on the needs and values of the dominant sex, and is elaborated in terms of the conduct, gesture, and attitude of each sex. The patriarchal family is therefore *the* agent of the patriarchal society. In the past, the patriarchal system used to grant the man nearly total ownership of women (and children); modern patriarchy has modified this through a series of legal reforms granting divorce, protection, citizenship, and property to women.[26] In class terms some women do appear to have a higher social status than some men, but in the last instance "the caste of virility triumphs over the social status of wealthy and educated women." In fact "one of the chief effects of class within patriarchy is to set one woman against another." Women have less investment in the class system, although, because of their economic dependence, "middle-class women identify their economic survival with the prosperity of those who feed them." Indeed, "one of the most efficient branches of the patriarchal government lies in the agency of its economic hold over its female subjects." Most women are engaged in work which is not paid—when they work outside the home they enjoy only half of the average income of men. When patriarchy is exposed and questioned, the system begins to change.

## *The Suffragette Movement and Its Heritage*

This first happened, the author goes on, around the 1830s, when political organizations on issues of sexual politics appeared and excited public controversy. The movement for sexual revolution that developed in England and the United States during the next hundred years in the end did not succeed in abolishing patriarchy. "The chief weakness of the movement's concentration on suffrage, the factor which helped it to fade, disappear and even lose ground when the vote was gained, lay in its failure to challenge the patriarchal ideology at a sufficiently deep and radical level to break the conditioning process of status, temperament and role." "Because the opposition was so strong and unrelenting, the struggle so long and bitter, the vote took on a disproportionate importance. And when the ballot was won, the feminist movement collapsed in what can only be described as exhaustion." So "the phase ended in reform rather than revolution." The official resistance, she goes on, cannot completely account for the subsequent counterrevolution. In most places "the sexual revolution collapsed from within." Patriarchy remained in force simply because it lived on "in the mind and heart."

Kate Millett tries to justify the failures of the suffragette movement by reducing them to tactical mistakes induced by the nature of the opposition they faced. A proper examination of "sexual revolution" would, however, require concepts that are not found in her theoretical vocabulary: those that describe economic and political forces not only in terms of sexual political ones. Her theoretical system fails, in fact, to account for any of the development she discusses. Why did the sexual revolution start in 1832? What was the social base of the movement? Its ideology? What was the historical situation in which it operated?

Compare what Waltraud Ireland wrote in *Leviathan*: While the women's rights movement initially "stood on the principle of universal suffrage, with the coming of the industrial age [to the United States of America], the influx of large masses of poor immigrants and the rise of a terribly exploited working class, middle-class feminists, like their men, began worrying about what might happen if the downtrodden got the vote. Elizabeth C. Stanton [one of the founders of the movement] in her old age favored an educational voting requirement, which was adopted by the unified suffrage movement in 1903.[27] Since the white native American women outnumbered the immigrant, uneducated vote, the women appealed to the worst race and class prejudices of men in arguing in favor of women's suffrage. . . . In 1903, with the tacit toleration of some and the active collaboration of the older abolitionists, the Northern-based suffrage movement formed an alliance with the white Southern suffragists movement, although the Southern women were arguing that the vote should be given to women in order to ensure white supremacy. (This argument was advanced as early as 1867 by an old abolitionist, Henry B. Blackwell[28] together with his wife, Lucy Stone, leader of the Conservative AWSA [American Women's Suffrage Association]. Blackwell argued that by giving the vote to women, the white electoral majority would be increased, ensuring the preservation of white supremacy.)"[29] In England, a notable spokesman of the movement, Frances Power Cobb, declared: "The difference, nay, rather the contrast should be insisted on between proposals to admit dregs of population to franchise, and those to admit mothers, daughters and sisters of those who already exercise it."[30]

No doubt these views were not universally shared, but they are not insignificant either; they belong to the very founders of the movement. Kate Millett may call them "patriarchal ideology" or present them merely as "unsavory dealings," but they have a more precise name: racial and class hatred.[31] The truth is that, in the last instance, class loyalty prevailed over sex loyalty: the education requirement voted by the unified American suffrage movement in 1903 unambiguously excluded a large majority of women, in line with the refusal to demand the vote for the "dregs of society."

The women's suffrage movement was fundamentally limited by the fact that many of the women inside it identified with the "patriarchal society," but this does not mean that it was unimportant. Just as the specific character of the economic oppression of the proletariat only stands out more sharply after juridical equality of classes has been established (this equality in no way abolishing the antagonism between them) so too the peculiar character of man's domination of woman is brought out more clearly once the two are equal before the law. Moreover, the demand for suffrage provided a political arena upon which women could *organize* as women. Indeed the militancy of the suffragette movement at times surpassed that of the working class.

Just as we are given no realistic account by Millett of why "sexual revolution" started, we are even less clear why counterrevolution occurred, particularly as, we are told, the suffrage movement collapsed from within. When she comes to describing counterrevolution there is nothing within her theoretical structure which can indicate how very special Nazi Germany and the Soviet Union under Stalin were. And yet, it is in dealing with these two exceptional cases that we find her groping for criteria other than those supplied by her theory.

## *The 1920s and 1930s*

There was a sharp dislocation between the ideology and the practice of Nazi Germany, which Millett reveals most impressively. On the one hand, the Nazi propaganda machine daily hammered out the theme that German women were to dedicate themselves to motherhood and family. This ideology was supported by a series of measures to strengthen the family. On the other hand, the number of women employed rose sharply under Nazi rule. Although Hitler made it clear that the Nazis desired "no women to throw grenades," most of the new female labor force was employed in the armament industry. At the same time women were being withdrawn from higher jobs and education and thrown back onto the labor market as unqualified workers.

The second case discussed (without any transition) is the Soviet Union. The author contrasts Russia under Lenin with its subsequent development and here her argument becomes perceptibly more complex. "After the Bolshevik revolution," she writes, "every possible law was passed to free the individual from the claim of the family: free marriage and divorce, contraception, abortion on demand. Most material of all, the women and children were to be liberated from the controlling economic power of the husband. Under the collective system, the family began to disintegrate along the very lines upon which it had been built."

In December, 1917, and October, 1918, Lenin passed two decrees "which invalidated the prerogatives of males over their dependents and affirmed the complete right to economic, social and sexual self-determination in women, declaring it a matter of course that they freely choose their own domicile, name and citizenship. . . . One cannot legislate a sexual revolution by decree, as Lenin was aware, and efforts were made to make the financial independence of both women and children a reality: nurseries were to be established, housekeeping was to be collectivized . . . maternity leave would be granted, and women welcomed on an equal footing into the labor force. . . ."

And yet, the sexual revolution lost to counterrevolution.

"The chief causes appear to be the difficulty in establishing a complete social revolution when one is overwhelmed, as the Russians were, with both political . . . and economic problems (women were declared economically independent but this scarcely made them so, particularly in the NEP period of unemployment)." The communal housekeeping and creches failed to materialize. The burden of child-care and housework was left to women alone, as fathers often neglected their responsibilities. Urged into employment, women found themselves being awarded a triple responsibility: job, children, housework.

In fact "the great masses of women, illiterate, submissive after centuries of subordination, with little realization of their rights, could scarcely take advantage of the new freedoms to the degree that men could." Marxist theory, as Millett correctly observes, "failed to supply a sufficient ideological base for a sexual revolution." Soviet leadership "made the family defunct in a society composed entirely of family members, whose entire psychic processes were formed in the patriarchal family of Tsarist Russia." A proper integration of sexual into social revolution failed mainly for economic reasons, but also as a result of inadequate theoretical (and political) preparation.

This explanation raises a number of questions. To start with, it raises the whole question of equality again. The Bolshevik revolution gave women equal rights—for the first time in history. It in fact succeeded in putting into practice something which bourgeois ideology has preached for more than a century—the equality of all people irrespective of their sex, religion, nationality, etc.—but which bourgeois society was unable to execute, due to its unwillingness to transgress the limits of private property. And yet, in practice this equality often imposed further hardship on women. Given the social structure of Russia and the nature of women's oppression there, one is bound to conclude that the problem of women demanded an *inequality* of treatment with respect to men.

Marx wrote in a relevant passage in the *Critique of the Gotha Program* that equal right is by its very nature a right of inequality, like every other right, because it applies an equal standard to different individuals (or sexes); the unequal individuals are measured by an equal standard insofar as they are viewed from one angle only, e.g., as workers.[32] Thus for revolution to liberate women not only is a large women's movement a precondition, but also the inequality of women—the *specificity* of their oppression—must be fully understood.

The second question raised by Kate Millett's account is that of what she calls "psychic processes." If the Bolsheviks failed because, among other things, they tried to abolish the family in a society "composed entirely of family members, whose entire psychic processes were formed in the patriarchal family of Tsarist Russia," what implications does this have for the revolution in a capitalist society, which will have the task of dismantling the family in a society composed entirely of family members whose "psychic processes" have been formed in the "patriarchal family" of that society?

The patriarchal family, claims Millett, is *the* agent of the patriarchal order in that it socializes the individual along the stereotyped lines of sexual categories. But the family does more than that: it educates the child to fit into the existing social structure and its authority, system of values, modes of relation between people, attitudes to property, etc. All these become the very foundation of the individual personality because, from a strategic point of view, the family is extremely well placed: it seizes the individual from the very moment of birth. The specific mechanisms of this process were only identified with Freud. "One of the 'effects' of the humanization of the small biological creature that results from human parturition: there in its place is the object of psychoanalysis, an object which has a simple name: *the unconscious.*" Psychoanalysis has, therefore, as its object "the 'effects' prolonged into the surviving adult, of the extraordinary adventure which from birth to the liquidation of the Oedipal phase transforms a small animal conceived by a man and a woman into a small human child. . . . This object is no business of the biologist's: this story is certainly not biological!—since from the beginning it is completely dominated by the constraint of the sexed human order that each mother engraves on the small human animal in maternal 'love' or hatred."[33] Althusser points to the importance of a "discussion of the forms of *familial ideology*, and the crucial role they play in initiating the functioning of the instance that Freud called 'the unconscious,' but which should be re-christened as soon as a better form is found. This mention of the forms of familial ideology (the ideology of paternity-maternity-conjugality-infancy and their interactions) is crucial, for it implies the following conclusion . . . that *no theory of psychoanalysis can be produced without basing it on historical materialism* (on which the theory of the formation of familial ideology depends, in the last instance)."[34]

"To fill the needs of conservative societies and population too reluctant or too perplexed to carry out a revolutionary change . . . a number of new prophets arrived upon the scene," writes Millett. "The most influential of these was Sigmund Freud, beyond question the strongest individual counterrevolutionary force in the ideology of sexual politics during the period." This view of Freud as an *enemy* is extremely widespread in the women's liberation movement today. But, at the same time, this movement, like the Gay Liberation movement, has in fact integrated the conclusions of Freud's science into its ideology—even if such an appraisal at the level of theory is still absent. Psychoanalysis has, in a way, become a part of common sense. The women's liberation movement today, in its preoccupation with the family as the key socializing agency, is a testimony to the revolutionary scope of Freud's theory.

The revolt of the blacks, students, women and "the poor" may, Millett argues, produce another sexual revolution. But women are in alliance with them, it seems, as long as they are all *passive* objects of exploitation and oppression. Once they take up the method of violent confrontation with the social order, whether the state or various capitalist institutions, Kate Millett parts company with them. Violence in her mind is male. In an interview that she gave after the publication of her book she declared: "Women's lib is going to be the greatest revolutionary movement in history because it is going to avoid all the fascist traps of the male mind. But not unless we face the resurgence of all that masculine shit that's coming out of women who have learned politics from men." Asked if she envisaged a violent revolution, Millett replied: "I'm talking about a change in the way we live. If you want a violent revolution, O.K., go and buy your guns, I'll go over and do feminism in England or someplace else. We have fascism already. We get it from being stupidly violent. . . . *A revolutionary is a changer, a teacher.* Somebody who hangs in and keeps at it and keeps loving people, until they change their heads. . . . The trouble is all these women want to play war because their boyfriends do and they think it's radical. . . . We've got to get rid of it, or we're not going to make it. . . . There'll just be more of the same old garbage."[35] Once again we find the familiar equation: men = violence; women = love.

## *Conclusion*

In this review I have tried to isolate certain basic themes in the three books under discussion; this has inevitably meant that I have not been able to do them full justice. Greer, for example, gives an eloquent description of the miseries of family life. Millett does much to dispel the piety with which literary figures such as D. H. Lawrence, Henry Miller, and Norman Mailer are often viewed; her sardonic and scrupulous textual analysis exposes the vulgar fantasy and crude male chauvinism which characterize their treatment of sex. Figes shows how many of the most iconoclastic masters of bourgeois thought—Rousseau, Hegel, Nietzsche, Darwin, Freud—were incapable of going beyond a banal conformism on the subject of the social position of women. But the themes which I have attempted to isolate indicate some of the fundamental weaknesses in all three books.

The premise, common to Greer, Figes, and Millett, that the man-woman antagonism is the *primary* one leads them inevitably into a theoretical and practical impasse: either moralism (and hence strategic impotence), or reformism. Both Millett and Greer accept the stereotyped image of women, and counterpose "female" qualities to "male" ones. They recognize that a drastic change in the social order is necessary to liberate women, but they do not identify this "change" with anything as concrete as the overthrow of capitalism. Indeed, they fail to pose in any serious fashion the problem of how the "change" can be brought about at all—Millett contenting herself with calling for a "revolution in consciousness," Greer with wishful fantasies, and both short-circuiting discussion in a common rejection of "violence." Figes has the merit of being free from such ultimately romantic ideas on women. She correctly refuses any "equal but different" status as an objective for women, and insists on the possibility of, and necessity for, integral equality between men and women. But because she constructs a history of ideas divorced from any real historical context, her history becomes an undifferentiated sea of rampant male chauvinism, and the amelioration of women's position is seen in terms of gradual reform over time; this perspective does not involve her in even the romantic rejection of the existing social order which characterizes Greer and Millett.

The women's liberation movement poses difficult theoretical and practical problems for Marxists, both inside the movement and outside it. Perhaps hardest, and most crucial, of all is to develop an analysis which at once recognizes the immense potential of this new and growing radicalization of significant sectors of the female population in the advanced capitalist countries, and at the same time faces up to the overwhelmingly non-Marxist, often explicitly and bitterly anti-Marxist, ideology which characterizes the women's liberation movement. To some extent, this is a response to the failure of Marxism itself to develop a fully worked-out and adequate theory of the role of the family in advanced capitalism, or of the specificity of women's oppression. Nevertheless, it is not therefore something which Marxists should refrain from confronting, and indeed a critique of the dominant ideology of the women's liberation movement and the development of a more adequate theory of the family and of female oppression must inevitably go hand in hand. It is in this spirit that I have tried to discuss certain of the central themes in these three books. It should be clear that all three books will be valuable weapons for the women's liberation movement itself, and will help to radicalize many women—as well as men.

NOTES

1. Germaine Greer, *The Female Eunuch* (London, 1970); Eva Figes, *Patriarchal Attitudes* (London, 1970); Kate Millett, *Sexual Politics* (New York, 1970).
2. "A book on radical feminism that did not deal with love would be a political failure," writes Shulamith Firestone. "For love, perhaps even more than childbearing, is the pivot of women's oppression today. I realize this has frightening implications: Do we want to get rid of love? . . . Women and Love are [cultural] underpinnings. Examine them and you threaten the very structure of culture" (*Dialectic of Sex: The Case for Feminist Revolution*, William Morrow and Co., New York, 1970).
3. Given the terrible state of the world plagued by the evils of violence, consumerism, and pollution. In a recent interview on the B.B.C. (*Listener*, 1/21/71) Greer declared: "If we are going to sort out this situation, this poor old polluted world, then women must step in with a special kind of wisdom which is not connected with achieving prestige and importance in a masculine way, but which is just as energetic in the exercise of something like tenderness and esteem and care for life."
4. "If you are going to touch one, you might as well make love to him" (interview with Greer, *Rolling Stone*, 1/7/1970).
5. One of her proposals is that middle-class women could achieve a revolution "in consciousness" by marrying working-class men. As women intellectuals are being turned by their education into "arrogant, aggressive, compulsive and intense" beings, they lose touch with "more innocent recreations." Married to their truck drivers they would "need to shed their desperate need to *admire* a man, and accept the gentler role of loving him. . . . The alternative to conventional education is not stupidity, and many a clever girl needs the corrective of a humbler soul's genuine wisdom." The added advantage of such an arrangement would be that "a learned woman cannot castrate a truck driver like she can her intellectual rival, because he has no respect for her bookish capabilities." This class snobbery and belief in salvation through "more innocent recreations" reminds one very much of D. H. Lawrence. A devastating treatment of D. H. Lawrence's views is given by Kate Millett, *Sexual Politics*, pp. 237–93.
6. Compare Greer's opinion: "Protestant moralists sought to redeem marriage from the status of a remedy against fornication by underplaying the sexual component and addressing the husband as wife's friend" (*The Female Eunuch*, p. 209).
7. According to Greer, and more correctly, "one of the most significant apologists of marriage as a way of life and a road

to salvation was Shakespeare. . . . The new ideology of marriage needed its mythology and Shakespeare supplied it" (*The Female Eunuch*, pp. 207–9).

8. But if the point of the Code Napoléon was to ensure the correct father for inheritance purposes, as she suggests, then it sadly failed, for Article 312 decreed: "l'enfant conçu pendant le mariage a pour père le mari." Previously based on moral conviction, paternity of children was now assured by law.
9. Both *Emile* and the *Social Contract* were published in the same year, 1762, and promptly burned by the Geneva government, which immediately issued a warrant for the author's arrest.
10. Quoted by *Le Monde*, February 7, 1971, from the archives of Bibliothèque Marguerite Durand, which is one of the most complete centers of documents in Europe. It is extremely difficult to obtain a coherent idea of the role of women in the French Revolution from secondary sources—this history still remains to be written.
11. "Although it is beyond question that the culture of eighteenth-century France had much to do with the suggestion that democracy apply in sexual as well as class politics . . . and as even the reforming influence of the French Revolution was throttled in England until the danger of revolution had passed, and consequently did not emerge in any fullness until the 1830's, it seems appropriate to begin this chapter's discussion [of sexual revolution] in the nineteenth century" (Kate Millett, *Sexual Politics*, p. 65).
12. Quoted by August Bebel in *La Femme et le Socialisme* (Dietz Verlag, Berlin, 1964).
13. Quoted by Eva Figes, p. 29.
14. Quoted by Eva Figes, p. 77.
15. These are truly prophetic words, a hint of times to come. Rousseau was himself aware of this, for he goes on to say: "Such equality, we are told, is a chimera of theory and could not exist in reality. But if abuse is inevitable, ought we not at least to control it? Precisely because the force of circumstances tends always to destroy equality, the force of legislation ought always to tend to preserve it" (*The Social Contract*, Penguin, 1968, pp. 96–97).
16. The above is offered only as a guide to Rousseau's positions. For a wider discussion, the reader is in particular directed to Althusser's "Sur le 'Contrat Social,'" in *Cahiers pour l'analyse*, No. 8. There is one point of "disagreement" relevant to my analysis. Althusser writes: "Rousseau invoque comme solution practique à son problème (supprimer l'existence des classes sociales) une *régression économique* vers un des phénomènes de la dissolution du mode de production féodal:

le petit producteur indépendant, l'artisanat urbain ou rural, ce que le second *Discours* décrit sous le concept de 'commerce indépendant' (indépendance économique universelle permettant un 'libre' commerce, c'est-à-dire de libres relations entre les individus)." The point I want to make is that "le petit producteur indépendant" is not an individual but the family, represented in the political and civil society by the male head (paterfamilias). None of the recent Marxist critics of Rousseau (Althusser, Della Volpe, Colletti) attempts to integrate Rousseau's position of women into his political philosophy.

17. Later Proudhon and his followers in the First International would argue against legal emancipation of women on the grounds that it would lead to the dissolution of the family—which they saw as the fundamental unit of society and wanted to preserve.
18. "The bourgeoisie has, historically, played a most revolutionary part. . . . [it] has torn away from the family its sentimental veil and has reduced family relations to a mere money relation" (*Communist Manifesto*).
19. Both Figes and Greer have lost their faith in this civilization—but not Shulamith Firestone: "Thus in terms of modern technology, a revolutionary ecological movement would have the same aim as the feminist movement: control of the new technology for human purposes, the establishment of a beneficial 'human equilibrium' between man and the new artificial environment he is creating, to replace the destroyed 'natural balance'" (*op. cit.*, p. 220).
20. Mill argued that the English were particularly called upon to recognize women's rights as they were "farther from a state of nature than any other modern people" and "more than any other people, a product of civilization and discipline."
21. "Under whatever conditions, and within whatever limits, men are admitted to the suffrage, there is not a shadow of justification for not admitting women under the same. The majority of women of any class are not likely to differ in political opinion from the majority of men in the same class . . ." (*The Subjection of Women*, Everyman, p. 268).
22. This position has some structural similarities with the old Greek and Hebrew myths (of which Eva Figes gives an enjoyable account). Just as Pandora (an active female) by opening her box lets loose all evil onto the world, Kate Millett's female (a passive one) does the same by allowing herself to be subjugated. Why did she? Engels, for instance, argued that women accepted exclusive sexual possession as a not unwelcome "penalty" for "becoming exempt from the ancient community of men." Millett justifiably points out that Engels, like his age, was ignorant of the nature of female sexuality.

23. Marx had an accurate description of Mill when he said: "On the plain, simple mounds look like hills; and the imbecile flatness of the present bourgeoisie is to be measured by the altitude of its greatest intellects" (*Capital*, I, p. 518).
24. The italics are mine. The German original for "to coincide with" is *zusammenfallen mit*. Although it suggests coincidence in time from the context of the paragraph female subjugation and slavery were more closely interlinked. Engels here quotes Marx: "The modern family contains in embryo not only slavery (*servitus*) but serfdom also, since from the very beginning it is connected with agricultural services. It contains within itself *in miniature* all the antagonisms which later develop on a wide scale within society and its state."
25. The historical existence of matriarchy has hardly a supporter in modern anthropology. However, the outcome of this debate does not ultimately determine the validity of Engels's argument. His contribution consists in seeing the family as a socioeconomic formation, which therefore changes historically, and in connecting the oppression of women with the existence of private property rather than with their biological specificity. These theses represent in fact the classical Marxist position on the family and women. His text, however, falls short of a rigorous analysis of the family as the basic unit of civil society.
26. The 1964 American Civil Rights Act, which forbids discrimination in employment on the basis of sex is "the first and only federal legislative guarantee granted to women since the vote." As Kate Millett points out, it is not enforced, has not been enforced since its passage, and was not enacted to be enforced. The inclusion of "sex" in the Act was "half a joke and half an attempt on the part of Southern congressmen to force Northern industrial states to abandon the passage of the bill" (p. 41).
27. Kate Millett argues that "nearly inevitable factors contributed to its [the movement's] too frequently middle-class character; generally only women of this class enjoyed the leisure and education necessary for the endless effort the suffrage battle demanded." The membership of the movement therefore depended ultimately on education. This was also E. Stanton's view.
28. Henry Blackwell appears in Millett's book as "a liberal gentleman and abolitionist" who abdicated his rights over his wife in a document full of "period charm."
29. "The Rise and Fall of the Suffrage Movement," *Leviathan*, May, 1970.
30. Felicity Trodd, "Why Do We Want to Be Liberated?" *Socialist Woman*, November–December, 1970.
31. An attempt to show how racial, class, and sex ideologies interlock has been made by Mary Kelly, "National Liberation and

Women's Liberation," *Shrew*, December, 1970. This article is only the beginning of a wider theoretical project.

32. In *State and Revolution* Lenin comments on this passage in Marx: "Equal right we certainly have here, but it is still a 'bourgeois right' . . . really a violation of equality and an injustice. . . . The first phase of communism, therefore, cannot yet produce justice and equality; but the exploitation of man by man will become impossible because it will be impossible to seize the means of production . . . as private property."
33. Louis Althusser, "Freud and Lacan," *New Left Review* 55.
34. *Ibid.*
35. *University Review*, No. 11 (New York, 1970).

# 11
# On Body Politics

JOHN O'NEILL

WE SHOULD AVOID THE obsession with America. This, more than anything, contributes to the illusory generalizations of much of our sociology. It is, however, a practice that has become normative in the face of America's world interference, which demands that we either construct our own image of America or else indulge its narcotic dream. America is no place to grow old, no place to be poor or black or young or a woman. America is no place at all—it is a state of mind, a dream, a myth, a trip. To some, the dream is real—their trip is the moon. To others, the dream is a nightmare, acid-sweet. Ordinarily, America, like any other society, has an official daydream, which makes deviant other visions, drawing them into the house of madness, loneliness, and prison. Today America is no longer certain of the borders of its own sanity, and so it bombards them, all the way from Vietnam to Chicago, Berkeley, and Kent State. There was a time when the automobile policed the streets of America, everyone going west, each one alone, all together in the iron game of individualism. Today there are people in the streets of America's cities, arousing the old populist enthusiasm in religious and erotic gatherings of the body politic. The cops retreat behind masks, sticks, guns, shields, cannons, and gas—they even ride in the sky. The cop is out of sight anywhere but at bank robberies, and body games like football or basketball—there he is indulgent, daydreaming of his own American boyhood and the determination of all American men to remain boys.

Human embodiment is more than ever the experience of

modern times; the invitation to eroticism, the politics of sexual equality, genocide, and the convulsions of pollution. The glory and misery of American culture takes its toll upon the body, whether it is in embryonic voyages through outer space or the latest discovery that perspiration cannot be localized, but needs a total body spray, to advance happiness and social security in the jingles of North America. The body norms of affluence meanwhile destroy those who age in a youth culture, those who die in the now generation, those whose skins are anything but white, or suntanned while others are pale, and those who are hungry and sick amid their obese and overdoctored fellow men. Modern man thrives at the expense of world populations, with whom he maintains only the sentimental ties of starvation and disease, and to whom he has still to communicate the uncertainty of the air he breathes, in the last of all charities.

Increasingly we are forced to question the values of modern knowledge and to turn to our visceral knowledge of ourselves and our relations to our fellow men for an understanding of the times and circumstances which confront us. In the West, at least, the subordination of the body belongs to a long tradition of metaphysics and morals, which has in turn determined our notions of social comportment and political order. Of course, there have always been philosophers, poets, and artists to reject the mind-body dualism and to celebrate the harmony of spiritual embodiment. Nowadays, as we shall see, the culture of mind-body harmony is part of a revolutionary, chemical and psych-idyllic attack upon the dominant reality-split between socially committed (family, work) energy and libidinal freedom. With the computer-emigration of mind, the body languishes for new connections, new sensations, new social groups; and to the old-world hunger and disease there is added the new-world aesthetic commiseration.

But for the most part, and until recently, the custom has been to ignore our body knowledge, to denigrate it, to put it out of play. At best it comes to mind with the inevitabilities of sickness and death, on ski slopes or in bed. Generally, we reduce our body knowledge to an involuntary mechanism—where it does not atrophy—or we revive it only through metaphors and body English. Recently, however, there has been an enormous expansion of literature on body games and body knowledge. This literature, like cookbooks, shows every sign of becoming a standard of household furniture, completing the cycle of interest from what happens in the kitchen to what happens in the front room and the bedroom. The literature is now so vast that it is essential, in order to achieve any orientation, to neglect its pseudo-scientific and anthropological qualities in favor of the existential question of one's own interest in the human body.[1]

We may adorn our bodies simply through heightened movements, gestures, dance and song, as well as skin paint, jewelry, and robes. The history of cosmetics begins with burial practices, at least as much as the battle of the sexes. But it may have just as much to do with the religious functions of adornment in the expression of the threshold between the sacred and the profane. In every case, the body is the means of its own transcendence, its "altered state," and in this sense, its external settings are just as important as alterations of its internal states. Thus a religious ceremony on Machu Picchu exalts its participants by reason of its extraordinary natural setting, and this must be taken into account as much as the effects of wine or drugs in establishing the bond between embodiment and ecstasy. Again, whether it is in the expression of the threshold between the secular and the profane, or the boundaries between social classes, status groups, and castes, the human body is the essential means, through the variety of its physical comportment, dress, and living conditions, of expressing the social and cosmological order to which we belong.

These observations may serve to describe the *cosmological* and *social* dimensions of bodily transcendence, and to differentiate them from what we may call the *technological* and *individual* dimensions of bodily transcendence, which is the focus of the literature on the history of human sex, sexual techniques, and sexual politics. This is, of course, a typological distinction which I am using to convey my own sense of the orders of bodily experience, at least as much as to further any sociological generalization. In practice, the technological literature pays deference to cosmological and social experience, inasmuch as for its own recommendations it attempts to clear the ground of any charges of deviance—achieved by showing that sexually there is nothing new under the sun—and also promises cosmic union, if the gymnastics and vibrators are well-enough mastered. Having made this distinction between the *cosmological* and the *technological* body orders, it is necessary to understand that in practice both literatures may serve their clients as exercises in *body politics*, where, in turn, it is necessary to distinguish the *collective* and the *individual* ideologies implicit in their respective grammars. In this essay I shall not treat of the so-called sexual revolution, since, in terms of the distinctions I have just drawn, much of it turns upon individualistic and technological solutions to the achievement of orgasm. In particular, it reinvents the rhetoric of possessive individualism, reducing love's body to a fetishistic privacy, and virtually abandons love's children.

In order to be clearer about the structures of bodily experience, we should develop at least the conventional and vernacular sociological account of them, which we derive from Freud and Marx. In general terms, every society has to deal with the civilizational problem of the dialectic of the commitment and withdrawal of its libidinal energies. In the most economic terms, this problem is solved, under varying historical conditions, by transforming the anaclitic mother-child bond into a socially sanctioned pattern of achieved and roundabout, i.e., emotionally and physically capitalized, satisfactions. The transvaluation of the mother-child bond into the order of the social division of labor, in turn variously subject to the frameworks of kinship and rational legal sanctions, is possible precisely because of the largely *symbolic* nature of human embodiment and reproduction. Thus the traumas of union and separation are repeated in the symbolic languages of the psychic and political orders, and thereby furnish the fundamental categories of alienation, exchange, and communion.

The themes of domination and liberation are major themes of modern body politics, inspired by the basic insights of Marx and Freud. What is basic in Marx and Freud is that human culture, politics, and economics are related to the human body, or the humanization of the body. They regarded the humanization of the body as a historical process[2] which moves toward an ideal of the polymorphous play of the human senses, liberated from the dominance of genital sexuality, which is tied through the family to economic organization and the politics of class and adulthood. *In One-Dimensional Man,* Marcuse has formulated the relationship between the forms of socioeconomic organization predicated upon the domination of external nature and the internal sociopsychic organization of the individual ego. He argues that Freud's hypothesis on the Oedipal origins and perpetuation of guilt is a psychological version of a wider sociological dynamic, in which the instinctual processes of individual repression are anonymously generalized, through incorporation into a hierarchical economic and political division of labor. In other words, the logic of domination, which Freud located in the instinctual processes, must also be understood as a historical process, which achieves its most universal form in the processes of technological rationality. "In the social reality, despite all change, the domination of man by man is still the historical continuum that links pre-technological and technological reason. However, the society which projects and undertakes the technological transformation of nature alters the base of domination by gradually replacing personal dependence (of the slave on the master, the serf on the Lord of the manor, the Lord on the donor of the fief, etc.) with dependence on 'objective order of things' (on economic laws, the market etc.). To be sure, the 'objective order of things' is itself the result of domination, but it is nevertheless true that domination now generates a higher rationality—that of a society which sustains its hierarchic structure while exploiting ever more efficiently the natural and mental resources, and distributing the benefits of this exploitation on an ever-larger scale."[3]

Marcuse's analysis of the logic of advanced industrial society is a principal factor in the self-knowledge of the protagonists of body politics. Marcuse has furnished an awareness of the cosmological, psychic, and political levels of domination perpetrated by the seemingly civilized operations of the steel-and-glass corporate bureaucracies. "As soon as civilized society establishes itself the repressive transformation of the instincts becomes the psychological basis of a threefold domination: first, domination over one's self, over one's own nature, over the sensual drives that want only pleasure and gratification; second, domination of the labor achieved by such disciplined and controlled individuals; and third, domination of outward nature, science and technology."[4] The triple domination of nature, society and man defines the three areas of countercultural attack upon corporate society. In each of these areas, the interpenetration of cosmic, biological, and political repression derives from the symbiosis between bureaucratic rationality and violence, which is the framework of the modern politics of experience. This is the matrix of what we call body politics.

Hitherto the concept of rationality has provided the dominant focus of the production and maintenance of institutional order, making alternative conceptions of society seem utopian and irrational. However, the repressive functions of corporate rationality[5] have inevitably led to a search for a new political symbolism, whose dominant imagery may be conveyed through a more articulated analysis of the classical concept of the body politic. The body politic is the fundamental structure of political life, which provides the ground of ultimate appeal in times of deep institutional crisis, of hunger and alienation, when there is need to renew the primitive bonds of political authority and social consensus. The appeal to the logic of the body, the human body and the body politic, contains a critique of the legitimacy of technological and bureaucratic knowledge in terms of the values of common sense and libidinal knowledge, of the streets and parks.[6]

Hannah Arendt has discussed the historical sources of the crisis of authority in the West in terms of the tendency of the technique of knowledge to degenerate into the violence of knowledge, which undermines the erotic and libidinal bonds of the republic. I shall develop this argument briefly, in order to provide the historical framework and continuity that may enable us to understand the contemporary scenarios and happenings of the body politic in its struggle against the domination of technical rationality. The argument will also serve to illustrate Marcuse's thesis in terms of the classical grammar of political philosophy.

To the Greeks the human body was a symbol of the political order, because of a certain analogy between the harmony that must be embodied in the life of the individual and the corporate order which is the life of the body politic. The analogy of the body politic should not be treated as incidental to the Platonic discussion of the intrinsic grounds of authority and reason in the polis. Indeed, it underlies the transition in the *Republic* from a poetic politics based upon the Form of the Beautiful to an expert politics determined by the Form of the Good. Plato's discussion in the early books of the *Republic*, in which he differentiates the first and second cities, or the *organic* and *sensible* levels of the body politic, is guided by the Form of the Beautiful, or the *libidinal* body politic. It is only in the Sixth Book that Plato turns away from a politics of being to a utilitarian politics based upon instrumental rationality. Arendt argues that in the Allegory of the Cave the philosopher goes in search of the truth of being, without any thought of returning to impose the truth of his vision upon other men. It is only under the compulsion to return to earth that the philosopher reinterprets his contemplative vision of the Forms of Beauty, Goodness, Truth, and Justice in terms of the analogy of the technical and ruling arts.

For the original function of the ideas was not to rule or otherwise determine the chaos of human affairs, but in "shining brightness," to illuminate their darkness. As such, the ideas have nothing whatever to do with politics, political experience, and the problem of action, but pertain exclusively to philosophy, the experience of contemplation, and the quest for the "true being of things." It is precisely ruling, measuring, subsuming, and regulating that are entirely alien to the experiences underlying the doctrine of ideas in its original conception. It seems that Plato was the first to take exception to the political "irrelevance" of his new teaching, and he tried to modify the doctrine of ideas so that it would become useful for a theory of politics. But usefulness could be saved only by the idea of the good, since "good" in the Greek vocabulary always means "good for" or "fit." If the highest idea, in which all other ideas must partake in order to be ideas at all, is that of fitness, then the ideas are applicable by definition, and in the hands of the philosopher, the expert in ideas, they can become rules and standards, or as later in the *Laws*, they can become laws.[7]

It cannot be my purpose here to show how this instrumental conception of rationality has determined the history of social science knowledge and its internal dialectic of domination and recognition.[8] It must suffice to indicate the isomorphism between the triple structures of domination analyzed by Marcuse, to which we have referred, and the present triple structure of political experience, in which the needs of the organic body politic (the first city) play into a dialectic of alienation (the sensible order of utilitarian instrumental rationality) and the transcendence of the libidinal body politic (under the form of the Beautiful).

On the basis of these general indications of the conflict between politics based upon instrumental rationality and a body politics in which the organic and libidinal sources of reason are preserved, I want now to consider the style of contemporary political happenings.[9] Contemporary body politics is *politics as juvenile delinquency*. At first sight, it represents a break with the tradition of political philosophy, and yet there is a line of mythic continuity between the primal group, the plebeian secession from Rome, the social contract and the be-ins which culminated in Woodstock and Strawberry Fields.

Politics made out of delinquency: All brothers in crime: all equal as sinners. "To expand the population, Romulus followed the model of other founders of cities; he opened an asylum for fugitives. The mob that came in was the first step to the city's future greatness." "The remission of sins which makes us citizens of the Heavenly City was faintly adumbrated when Romulus gathered the first citizens of his city by providing a sanctuary and immunity for a multitude of criminals." The Heavenly City is also only an asylum for fugitives. Or as social contract thinkers see it, the social contract establishes corporate virtue as an asylum for individual sin, making an immoral society out of immoral men; men whose natural inclination according to Hobbes and Freud is murder. The social contract establishes the general will to counter the will of each—that general will which Freud called the super-ego. The super-ego is supra-individual; even as the crime, so also conscience is collective.[10]

Today, world violence is by and large the violence of industrial societies. This is not obvious to the fun-loving culture of affluence at home and innocence abroad. Yet there are the dark shadows of race, colonialism, and the ghetto which the comfortable distraction of conflict with Russia or China fails to dissipate, and even prolongs. Still there is a persistent conspiracy to externalize all threats to the American social and economic order, so that expressions like "the war on poverty" are used to cover the endemic nature of poverty and racism in American society. Beneath such expressions it is possible to detect the underlying violence of the social contract, which systematically excludes large sectors of the population and then turns upon them with missionary and colonialist zeal. There are, however, signs that the American System is losing its power to co-opt and cajole. American violence is being met with violence at home and abroad. There are internal migrations, which break with the corporate reality-principle, questioning, ridiculing, and sabotaging the great American celebration. The phenomena of violence in the ghettos, on campuses and in the streets, of mass demonstrations and sit-ins in the offices of authority are all grounded in the basic logic of the body politic not to endure the unendurable, not to suffer inhuman denials of recognition, and in ultimate crises to "come together," so that authorities can "see" what the people want. This is a palpable logic which is pre-ideological and rests on the simple and visceral faith men and women have in the renewal of justice and community. It is exercised in open places and in people's meetings because it breaks with the privatization of experience and suburbanity, which are the sanctions of the liberal order. Its scenarios therefore appear "irrational" and violent to the liberal ideology, in which two is either a crowd or a fight to the death. Indeed, the greatest of ironies is when the people's violence, which has been provoked by the historically most sophisticated techniques of rationality, is attributed to a primally aggressive nature which never allows civilization to be anything more than skin-deep. But the attempt to reduce the violence which seizes the body politic from time to time to bio-politics can only be successful where the processes of dehumanization have reduced men to abject slavery and outrage. It is only where men see no prospect of action that their sense of injustice and rage at alterable inhuman conditions atrophies, or is turned against themselves. In short, violence and rage must be understood as integral motives in the grammar of body politics, so long as the institutions of political conduct are open to human initiative and the call for freedom and justice. Thus Hannah Arendt has recently warned against the tendency to place the human emotions in opposition to "rationality" when in fact these emotions only become "irrational" when they sense reason itself is distorted.[11] Indeed, so much of what outrages contemparary rationality in the "antics" of body politics is nothing but the outrage of a more humane reasonableness driven to expose the sham of establishment rationality.

Fanon and Cleaver, the black poets of body politics, have shown as clear as ice how the rhetoric of mind-body dualism suits the grammar of racial exploitation and colonial revolt. Cleaver grasps instinctively the mind-body connections that threaten to reverse the ideal and material orders of American civilization.

> If the separation of the black and white people in America along the color line had the effect, in terms of social imagery, of separating the Mind from the Body—the oppressor whites usurping sovereignty by monopolizing the Mind, abdicating the Body and becoming bodiless Omnipotent Administrators and Ultrafeminines; and the oppressed blacks, divested of sovereignty and therefore of Mind, manifesting the Body and becoming mindless Supermasculine Menials and Black Amazons—if this is so, then the 1954 U.S. Supreme Court decision in the case of *Brown v. The Board of Education*, demolishing the principle of segregation of the races in public education and striking at the very root of the practice of segregation generally, was a major surgical operation performed by nine men in black robes on the racial Maginot Line which is embedded as deep as sex or the lust for lucre in the schismatic American psyche. This piece of social surgery, if successful, performed without benefit of any anesthetic except God and the Constitution, in a land where God is dead and the Constitution has been in a coma for 180 years, is more marvelous than a successful heart transplant would be, for it was meant to graft the nation's Mind back onto its Body and vice versa.[12]

Worse still for American white male supremacy, it was a black muscleman who betrayed its fears—Muhammad Ali spouting poetry, floating like a butterfly, stinging like a bee.

Since Cassius Clay affected poetry, the Word is no longer white property, to teach blacks the lessons of submission and the great white dualism of race, class, and the mind-body split.

Like Cleaver, Fanon, too, has the gift of revealing the structure of racist mind-body dualism as a landscape, a language, a dream of the body in which black and white confront each other as the sides of a single soul. In the white man's dream, the black man figures as the force of life that is drying up in himself. In his own dream, the black man dreams that language, knowledge, power, and beauty are all white and only to be defiled in him. Thus the black and white man each require the violence of the other.

> The settler-native relationship is a mass relationship. The settler pits brute force against the weight of numbers. He is an exhibitionist. His preoccupation with security makes him remind the native out loud that there he alone is the master. The settler keeps alive in the native an anger which he deprives of outlet; the native is trapped in the tight links of the chains of colonialism. But we have seen that inwardly the settler can only achieve a pseudo-petrification. The native's muscular tension finds outlet regularly in bloodthirsty explosions—in tribal warfare, in feuds between septs and in quarrels between individuals.[13]

It is in the context of what we have called the symbiosis of corporate rationality and violence that we must try to understand the rhetoric of creative or therapeutic violence and the renewal of the body politic, while recognizing its occasional abortive exercise, as well as the dangers of excess driving further and further away from the goal of construction. It is important to recognize the potentially antipolitical nature of violence, inasmuch as it is a technique of law and order to define violence precisely in antipolitical terms, thereby driving it into terrorism, in ever more desperate attempts to expose the political and social segregation of the issues of poverty, race and war. This cycle is in turn aggravated where the establishment power is exercised through bureaucracies, which increasingly privatize the contexts of meaning and action, impoverishing and undermining the political realm. The result is frequently a certain pathological symbiosis between bureaucratic rationality and the resort to vocabularies and scenarios of creative violence, of psychic migration and communal utopias, which destroy genuine political speech and public action.

The issues at this point may be phrased in terms of an argument between Marcuse and Norman O. Brown. The question is whether the violence and street antics of vulgarity, graffiti, and yippie put-ons belong merely to what Marcuse has called repressive desublimation, or to Norman O. Brown's politics of revelation and the renewal of love's body. As Marcuse sees it, corporate capitalism succeeds in creating a total containment of the contradictory forces within itself. Its macro-madness, seen from within, appears rational, inasmuch as the destruction and waste of wealth produces employment otherwise unavailable, and unnecessary production can be disposed of through the creation of equally unnecessary wants. Indeed, what is even more shocking to critical reason is that this irrational and violent economic order is able to appear quite beneficent through a technique of splitting behavior and fantasy in the packaging of its goods. To consider a trivial example, the girl who is not free to resist the mass-market miniskirt fashion is sold with it her sexual and female liberation, in a vicarious fantasy of admiration and conquest which is split off from the everyday miniscenes in which nothing happens to her or the men around her. "The Pleasure Principle absorbs the Reality Principle; sexuality is liberated (or rather liberalized) in socially constructive forms. This notion implies that there are repressive modes of desublimation, compared with which the sublimated drives and objectives contain more deviation, more freedom, and more refusal to heed the social taboos. It appears that such repressive desublimation is indeed operative in the sexual sphere, and here, as in the desublimation of higher culture, it operates as the by-product of the social controls of technological reality, which extend liberty while intensifying domination."[14] Through its technique of neutralized domination, monopoly capitalism is able to deepen its hold on the individual's psychic space, while seeming perfectly compatible with the liberal ideology of individual sovereignty. This technique is in turn a socially acceptable way of living out the collapse of genuine individual privacy while extending the economic space of the capitalist system, without altering its class features.

Norman O. Brown rejects Marcuse's deadly entropy, rekindling the body politic in pentecostal tongues. In *Life Against Death*, he undertook a psychoanalytical history of capital accumulation as an unnatural concentration of libido in particular bodily organs—"concentrations engineered by the negativity of the morbid death instinct, and constituting the bodily base of the neurotic character disorders in the human ego."[15] The conclusion of his historical investigations turns Brown into the mystical paths of the resurrection of the body, and drives Marcuse into Freudian skepticism and political realism! The argument between Marcuse and Norman O. Brown is the left version of the generation gap.[16] Marcuse's civilization of self, person, and property balks at Brown's communism based upon libidinal use-values. Brown sweeps away conventional reality as illusion, mystification, and dream. We reenact our past, the primal scene; all politics is infantile regression; the overthrow of genital tyranny directed by identification with the father's penis, which is our soul enslaving our body. The aim of the revolution is revelation, to take words out of the marketplace, to renew vision, to reenter love's body:

> Carrying our seed in our head; like flowers, flaunting our sex shamelessly; as in Bosch's Garden of Earthly Delights, upside down; an end to uprightness, the way up is the way down. Erect is the shape of the genitally organized body; the body crucified, the body dead or asleep; the stiff. The shape of the body awake, the shape of the resurrected body, is not vertical but perverse and polymorphous; not a straight line but a circle; in which the sanctuary is in the Circumference, and every Minute Particular is Holy; in which
>
> > "Embraces are Comminglings from the Head even to the Feet,/And not a pompous High Priest entering by a Secret Place."[17]

Norman O. Brown is the visionary of the new body politics, while Jerry Rubin and Abbie Hoffman take magic and revelation into the streets, improvising revolutionary scenarios with casts of thousands. Between them they confront the obscenity of conventional politics with the demands of the body, of language, of peace and flowers. The techniques are exaggeration and the co-option of establishment figures and media, unmasking the everyday conscription and fantasies of the industrial-military complex. Rubin and Hoffman have turned the revolution into a youth movement, dedicated to the revelation of the joylessness and vulgarity of money-making, religion, and democracy. Their language is body language, because the system they oppose dehumanizes the body, making a fetish of its needs, movements and graces:

> A dying culture destroys everything it touches.
> Language is one of the first things to go.
> Nobody really communicates with words anymore. Words have lost their emotional impact, intimacy, ability to shock and make love.
> Language prevents communication.
>
> CARS LOVE SHELL
> How can I say
> "I love you"
> after hearing:
> "CARS LOVE SHELL."
>
> Does anyone understand what I *mean*?
> Nigger control is called "law and order." Stealing is called "capitalism."
> A "REVOLUTION" IN TOILET PAPER.
> A "REVOLUTION" IN COMBATING MOUTH ODOR!
> A "REVOLUTIONARY" HOLLYWOOD MOVIE!
> *Have the capitalists no respect?*
> But there's one word which Amerika hasn't destroyed.
> One word which has maintained its emotional power and purity.
> Amerika cannot destroy it because she dare not use it.
> It's illegal!
> It's the last word left in the English language:
> FUCK! ! !
> One bright winter day in Berkeley, John Thomson crayoned on a piece of cardboard "FUCK WAR," sat down with it and was arrested within two minutes. Two more people sat down with signs saying "FUCK WAR." They were arrested.
> The Filthy Speech Movement had been born.[18]

The eroticism of modern economic and political life is a basic element in the events or happenings of the body politic. The vulgarity of body politics is holy as well as profane. It must be understood, like everything profane, in the light of the fall from the sacred. Politics, religion, and business have become joyless and obscene occupations; they are equally holy works of man. The body politic is the theater of the reversal of the transcendent and the mundane; its rebels and clowns reenact the creation and fall, the reversal of godhead and manhood. "The body, like the body-politic, is a theater; everything is symbolic, everything including the sexual act. The principal part is a public person taking the part of the community as a whole: *persona publica totius communitatis gerens vicem*. The function of the representative organ is to impersonate, incarnate, incorporate in his own body the body-politic. Incorporation is the establishment of a theater (public); the body of spectators depend on the performance for their existence as one body."[19]

In the 1960s, we have seen the sexualization of conventional politics; the palpable logic of demonstrations, beatings, nudities, love-ins, togetherness, and total trips that have tribalized the consciousness of youth, externalizing the Oedipal conflict in joyful street scenes, flowers, and killings. These events have unmasked the corporate titillation of youthful, white, heterosexual America. The politics of the "new mutants,"[20] the gay people without the hang-ups of those who observe them from the other side of the generation gap, have symbolically destroyed the system of want, of death against life, rooted in the economy of male-female, black-white, rich-poor, and expert-layman organization. Curiously enough, they have been successful where they thought it most difficult. They have altered the consciousness of institutions, which seemed to be defined precisely by their irresistible power over the minds of the people. For the most part, the corporate institutions still stand, but revolutionary awareness itself continues to expand to the limit of antipolitical consciousness. Body politics become Dionysian, achieving form only in a self-improvised moment, without ideology or platform. They are successful in destroying vicarious experience, in becoming childlike, loving and raging; and they still wait for the communion of men and the resurrection of the body.

But let us be clear: what matters is to stop talking about output, and intensification, and the rhythm of work.

No, there is no question of a return to Nature. It is simply a very concrete question of not dragging men towards mutilation, of not imposing upon the brain rhythms which very quickly obliterate it and wreck it. The pretext of catching up must not be used to push man around, to tear him away from himself or from his privacy, to break and kill him.

No, we do not want to catch up with anyone. What we want to do is go forward all the time, night and day, in the company of Man, in the company of all men. The caravan should not be stretched out, for in that case each line will hardly see those who precede it; and men who no longer recognize each other meet less and less together, and talk to each other less and less.[21]

NOTES

1. John O'Neill, *Sociology as a Skin Trade:* Essays towards a Reflexive Sociology (London: Heinemann, 1972). This volume contains most of the other essays of mine which I refer to below in their original sources.
2. John O'Neill, "History as Human History in Hegel and Marx," in Jean Hyppolite, *Studies on Marx and Hegel*, translated with Notes and Bibliography by John O'Neill (New York: Basic Books, 1969).
3. Herbert Marcuse, *One-Dimensional Man:* Studies in the Ideology of Advanced Industrial Society (Boston: Beacon Press, 1966), p. 144.
4. Herbert Marcuse, "Freedom and Freud's Theory of Instincts," *Five Lectures:* Psychoanalysis, Politics and Utopia, translations by Jeremy Shapiro and Shierny M. Weber (Boston: Beacon Press, 1970), p. 12.
5. John O'Neill, "Public and Private Space," in *Agenda 1970:* Proposals for a Creative Politics, edited by T. Lloyd and J. T. McLeod (Toronto: University of Toronto Press, 1968), pp. 74–93. The analysis of the structure of experience in this earlier essay should be complemented by the new vocabulary of experience articulated in the concept of body politics.
6. John O'Neill, "Authority, Knowledge and the Body-Politic," *The Southern Journal of Philosophy*, Vol. 8, Nos. 2–3 (Summer and Fall, 1970), pp. 255–264. I have drawn on this essay for the present argument.
7. Hannah Arendt, "What is Authority?" *Between Past and Future:* Six Exercises in Political Thought (London: Faber and Faber, 1954), pp. 112–113.
8. John O'Neill, "The Hobbesian Problem in Marx and Parsons," in *Explorations in General Theory in the Social Sciences*, edited by Jan J. Loubser *et al.* (New York: The Free Press, forthcoming); and my "The Responsibility of Reason and the Critique of Political Economy," in *Phenomenology and the Social Sciences*, edited by Maurice Natanson (Evanston: Northwestern University Press, forthcoming).

9. Susan Sontag, "Happenings: An Art of Radical Juxtaposition," in *Against Interpretation and Other Essays* (New York: Dell Publishing Company, 1969).
10. Norman O. Brown, *Love's Body* (New York: Vintage Books, 1965), pp. 15–16.
11. Hannah Arendt, *On Violence* (New York: Harcourt, Brace and World, 1969).
12. Eldridge Cleaver, *Soul on Ice* (New York: McGraw-Hill, 1968), p. 192.
13. Frantz Fanon, *The Wretched of the Earth*, Preface by Jean-Paul Sartre, translated by Constance Farrington (Harmondsworth: Penguin Books, 1967), p. 42.
14. *One-Dimensional Man*, p. 72.
15. Norman O. Brown, *Life Against Death:* The Psychoanalytical Meaning of History (New York: Vintage Books, 1959), p. 308; for a comment on Marcuse and Brown's challenge to the conventional conservative and anti-utopian areas of psychoanalysis, see Susan Sontag, "Psychoanalysis and Norman O. Brown's *Life Against Death*," in her *Against Interpretation.*
16. See, "Love Mystified: A Critique of Norman O. Brown *and* A Reply to Herbert Marcuse by Norman O. Brown," in Herbert Marcuse, *Negations:* Essays in Critical Theory, with translations from the German by Jeremy J. Shapiro (Boston: Beacon Press, 1968).
17. *Love's Body*, p. 137.
18. Jerry Rubin, *Do it!:* Scenarios of the Revolution, with an introduction by Eldridge Cleaver (New York: Simon and Schuster, 1970), pp. 109–110.
19. *Love's Body*, pp. 131–132.
20. Leslie A. Fiedler, "The New Mutants," *Partisan Review*, Vol. XXXII, No. 4 (Fall, 1965), pp. 505–525.
21. *The Wretched of the Earth*, pp. 253–254.

# V

# Communal Living and the Obsolescence of the Nuclear Family

*Many alternatives to the misery of the nuclear family have been suggested but few have been tested in reality. Among those which have been tested are communal families in which several couples live and raise their children together in a variety of economic and social arrangements. Although communal families have an old religious tradition in America, the recent wave of communal family arrangements largely stem from the hippie movement of the sixties. Unfortunately very few sociologists have directed their research efforts toward an examination of the functioning of such families.*

*Bennett Berger and his collaborators are the only group which has done extensive field research on this topic in the past few years. The most recent report on this ongoing research project is reprinted in this volume for the first time. Bennett M. Berger is Professor of Sociology at the University of California, Davis. Bruce M. Hackett is Associate Professor at the same university. R. Mervyn Millar is a graduate student in Sociology at Davis.*

*Although the research project was originally designed to study child-rearing practices in communal families, the report also casts a new light on the relationship between the sexes in a communal arrangement. The basic problem of the hippie communal families is, however, not one of sex-role differentiation, although such problems exist, but of economics. As an alternative model to the nuclear family, the rural hippie com-*

*mune is of limited value in an urbanized and professionalized society. Unfortunately the urban, middle-class type of communal family, rare as it is, has not yet been subjected to sociological analysis. Yet, aside from the economic problem, the findings of Berger and associates are highly indicative of the future of our family life and deserve to be studied closely by all who are concerned with the breakdown of the present family system.*

*The same is true for the Israeli experiment of the kibbutzim which, in contrast to American and European communes, has been studied rather well. Benjamin Schlesinger, who is Professor of Social Work at the University of Toronto, presents a comprehensive view of the kibbutz family and predicts that the outcome of the present crisis of the kibbutz system under the impact of urbanization in Israel may well be a return to a way of life which approximates our own family type. Professor Schlesinger has written four books, three of which deal with family problems. His article is reprinted from the* International Journal of Comparative Sociology, *Vol. 11, 1970. From the tensions in the kibbutz families which he describes, conclusions can well be drawn in regard to the question of what the optimal structure of a communal family could be. And it is this question which remains pertinent when all other alternatives are apparently even more subject to tension and do not survive for long and when, on the other hand, the nuclear family no longer serves as an emotionally stabilizing milieu. This, however, is the lesson of Rustum and Della Roy's article "Is Monogamy Outdated?" which is reprinted from* The Humanist *(March/April, 1970). The authors, who are both scientists at Pennsylvania State University and have published together the book* Honest Sex *(1968), conclude their apt description of the failure of monogamy in modern society with the pessimistic remark that "Bourgeois man will persist and, along with him, traditional monogamy." Yet the authors are not content with this dark perspective, nor should the reader be; the present family system is in desperate need of change.*

# 12

# Child-Rearing Practices in the Communal Family*

BENNETT M. BERGER, BRUCE M. HACKETT,
R. MERVYN MILLAR

## *Introduction*

THE REPORT THAT FOLLOWS is a schematic summary of more than a thousand pages of field notes and working papers accumulated in a little over a year and a half of field activity by our group. These notes and the summaries of them describe what we have observed in the fourteen communes, urban and rural, which we have studied closely at first hand. These data and, perhaps more importantly, the conclusions which we have drawn from them are supplemented wherever possible by data from the approximately two dozen additional communes which we have only visited or studied less closely, and by the more reliable ethnographic literature on communal living which has only very recently begun to appear.

A word is necessary about the organization of the report. Although the major mandate of our study was child-rearing in hippie communes, we discovered very early in our participant-observation that we could not begin to understand the lives of commune children without close attention to the social structure of family life in communes and to the culture (beliefs, religions, ideologies) which envelops the lives of children in them. Our report, then, is concerned not only with the specific character of child-child and child-adult in-

* Progress Report to National Institute of Mental Health from September, 1971. This study was supported by Grant No. MN–16579–03 from the National Institute of Mental Health, Department of Health, Education, and Welfare. Three appendices have been omitted in this publication.

teraction in communal families but with communal life in general, which constitutes the familial and other environmental setting in which and through which the lives of children are made meaningful.

In addition to the child-rearing data per se, therefore, we are reporting other data under the structural headings which bear most directly upon the viability of the communal setting, and therefore upon the role of children. Primary among these are the basic economic arrangements of communal life, the structure of nuclear family units and the character of male-female relations in them, the problems of leadership, authority, and decision-making, recruitment, and ideology.

### *Two Basic Distinctions*

In our initial attempts to make organized sociological sense of our findings thus far, we have found it useful to make two major sets of distinctions: between urban and rural communes, and between what we call "creedal" communes.

We have found the urban-rural distinction useful not only for most of the usual reasons that are invoked to find patterns in any set of sociological data, but for reasons specific to communes themselves. For one thing, urban communes are easier to start—if not to sustain; all it takes is a rented house and a group of willing people. Because they are easier to start, urban communes tend to have a more fluid membership; it is sometimes difficult to tell who is a member, who a visitor, and who a crasher. Around the college, university, and bohemian districts of the San Francisco Bay area, group living is not a very deviant choice for young people, many of whom are poor and in the early stages of breaking away from their parental families. And this fact suggests what also seems true to us: that urban communes represent a less thorough commitment to serious communal experiment than rural communes do, because choosing to live in an urban commune is not so profoundly consequential a choice; it does not necessarily involve isolation from and inaccessibility to one's former milieu, a radical change in the structure of one's daily life, or engagement in unfamiliar forms of work which may require the development of new skills which present a deep challenge to one's very identity.

For reasons like these we believe that rural communes represent a relatively more advanced stage, a purer form, of the "New Age" movement than urban communes do. For this reason, too, a recurrent topic of discussion in urban communes is whether to get some land and move to the country, while rural communes almost never talk about collectively moving back to the city—although individual communards of course do.

The distinction between creedal and noncreedal communes is a more complex one. Creedal communes are those organized around a systematic or otherwise formally elaborated doctrine or creed to which members are either required or eventually expected to adhere: communes of "Jesus Freaks," or ashrams devoted to the teachings of an Indian saint, or crusading communes devoted to the eccentric visions of a self-proclaimed messiah. Creedal communes often have sacred books or other written documents which are regarded as the repository of the beliefs of groups affiliated with a religious leader or movement whose following includes more than a single commune. Some creedal communes, however, do not have constitutive documents or sacred books, but in these communes there are usually one or two central figures whose oral command of doctrine (the ability to "lay down a good rap"), backed by a physical or psychological authority, serves as an embodiment of collective beliefs.

Although in noncreedal communes there is no formal repository of ideology or collective beliefs, there does tend to be a taken-for-granted set of beliefs which is assumed to be widely known and shared by the members, even though constitutional precepts or other written documents are absent. But the distinction between creedal and noncreedal communes is not ideologically hard and fast because there is often very little difference in the content of *what* they believe, and it is this fact, among others, which gives to communes, regardless of whether they are creedal or not, the character of a "movement."

Although much of the hip-communal value system or

ideology transcends the distinction between creedal and non-creedal communes, the distinction is an important one for several reasons. For one thing, creedal communes almost by their very nature tend to have a firmer structure of authority (and are occasionally extremely authoritarian) because one of the things a formal creed does is to make explicit the rules of conduct which adherents are expected to observe. Rules against drug use, for example, are almost exclusive to creedal communes. Particularly where the creed is a religious or quasi-religious doctrine, there is frequently a holy man or his chief disciple(s) at hand in whom ultimate authority resides. Members of creedal communes seem on the whole somewhat younger than members of noncreedal communes (a hypothesis we shall look into further when we begin our formal interviewing) perhaps because their tenderer years make them more susceptible to grand cosmologies and charismatic leaders. Because creedal communes are sometimes missionary (while noncreedal ones are rarely or never so) their membership tends to be more open so that at any given time there are likely to be several members or incipient members, who, fresh from the street or responding to the missionary appeal, do not actually know each other or the older members very well. Noncreedal communes, on the other hand, tend to rely on friendship networks as sources of membership, so that members of noncreedal communes tend to know each other very well. Indeed, noncreedal communes may be said in general to rely upon the history of friendship as a source of solidarity which creedal communes try to find in their commitment to doctrine.

It should be borne in mind that these summary statements represent tendencies; our field notes contain examples of exceptions to every one of them. But enough has been said to indicate the reasons for the basic distinctions with which we are working.

### *What Communards Believe*

There exist by now in the literature on the hip-communal subculture several more or less adequate attempts to summarize the values, beliefs, and ideology of this movement

(Fred Davis, Bennett Berger, Nathan Adler, Philip Slater, Theodore Roszak, Kenneth Keniston—not to forget Charles Reich), and our own findings have not produced reasons for major argument with them. It should suffice in this summary report to affirm that the ideology is a genuinely "contra-cultural" (Milton Yinger) or culturally revolutionary one (though not thereby directly threatening in a political sense to established interests) in that its major tenets represent an almost systematic reaction against or disaffirmation of the culture taken for granted by most middle-class Americans of the middle generation.

Thus, they prefer candid, total, effusive, and unrestrained expression of feeling—joy and sensuality, as well as anger and hostility—to the careful, guarded, modulated balances, and instrumental (or manipulative) modes of personal relatedness; "upfrontness" is for them a term of high praise. They want to possess and consume as little as they need rather than as much as they can be induced to want. They affirm the present, the immediate, the *now* over careful future planning and anticipated future gratification. They value the "natural" (for nature is benign—particularly for rural communards), for example, in nudity, organic foods, organic architecture, etc., over the civilized, the synthetic, the contrived. They prefer the colorful and the romantic to the classical, the sober, and the orderly. Their sensibility is given to impulse and spontaneity rather than to calculation and structure. Although they have and recognize leaders, their modes of relationship to each other affirm brotherhood and egalitarianism rather than hierarchy. They prefer the primitive to the sophisticated, transcendent ecstasy to order and security. They prefer invoking mystical and magical forces to scientific ones. Their impulse is to share as much of their lives as they can with the community of their brothers and sisters, sometimes even beyond the point where it threatens those areas of privacy and reserve to which many communards are still at least partially attached. They want to share a mutually dependent communal fate without the obligatory constraints of social bonds; indeed, they depend upon the affirmation by their brothers and sisters of the value of personal expressiveness to enable each of them to exercise an unbounded freedom to do his thing; to engage, above all, in a spiritual search for personal meaning, for health and happiness, for self and selflessness, for transcendence and godhood.

Even so truncatedly sketched in, the foregoing contains the rudiments of a value system, and even if we had the space in this report to elaborate it more fully we would not intend to suggest that it is either unprecedented or logically consistent or consistently practiced or even that it consistently represents noble ideals, difficult but worthy of attainment. Although the contemporary version of the hip-communal ideology contains strong and relatively recent thematic emphasis on elements of Eastern religion and mysticism (much talk of "vibrations" and "flow" and a great deal of meditation and other yogic practice), the history of bohemian movements and religious cults in the West is rich with ideological precedents of this sort.

Like any other value system, moreover, the hip-communal one is replete with logical contradictions and discontinuities between theory and practice. Freedom and communal solidarity can and do cause conflicts, and the balance between privacy and communal sharing is a recurrently thorny problem in several of the communes we have observed. Despite the emphasis on spontaneity and impulse, the apples have to be picked when ripe, the goats have to be milked regularly, the meals have to be cooked and the dishes washed. Despite the benignity of nature, something's got to be done about the flies in the kitchen and the mice in the cupboard. Despite egalitarianism, some communards are deferred to more than others; despite the emphasis on the present and the immediate, wood has to be laid in for the winter, and crops put in for the growing season, and money set aside for the rent or the mortgage and the taxes; despite transcendent ecstasy, the communards have to be discreet about acid or peyote freak-outs in town. And they'll wear clothes when alien eyes will be offended by their nudity.

Like other value systems, finally, the hip-communal version contains as many adaptive responses to circumstance and makings of virtue out of necessity as it contains noble ideals worthy *because* difficult to attain. Perhaps the best things in life *are* free, but that is certainly more convenient for poor people to believe than for rich people; perhaps urban-industrial society will sink into oblivion under the weight of its garbage, its pollution, its racial conflicts, and its individual loneliness and personal estrangement, but that is certainly more convenient for down-home country folk to believe, secure in their possession of the primitive skills it will take to survive the apocalypse, than it is for the urban professional (who may not be able to change a light bulb) to believe. Most people try to make moral capital out of the resources available to them—including, we should add, not only communards but social scientists.

Nevertheless, communal ideology is important because it has serious consequences, as will be made evident below, for the rearing of children and for most other common concerns, for it affects everything from the nursery rhymes which are sung (". . . this little piggy had yogurt . . .") to children to the very conception of what children are: autonomous human beings, equal to adults.

### *Recruitment*

Commune recruitment comes by and large from the pool of middle-class youth in the larger society. Friendship networks in the youth culture, whose members already have some commitment to many of the ideas in the hip belief system, are the major source of new members for communes. In urban, noncreedal communes, it is usually a matter of deciding to share living arrangements with a group of friends or of moving into one previously established by other friends. Given this prior knowledge of many of the people and the ideas they share, as well as the mutual economic interest young, poor people have in sharing their resources for food and housing, such conflicts that do arise are only rarely concerned with major ideological matters, except when interpersonal hostilities are escalated into a moral confrontation (for example, when the suggestion of one member that a Shell No-Pest strip be hung in the kitchen was met with accusations that he was in favor of poisoning nature), or when an occasional major upheaval (for example, a drug bust) provokes a search for blame.

Creedal communes, on the other hand, are usually founded by an individual and a few of his disciples, although they may often expand in terms of friendship networks, like noncreedal ones. While the sources of recruitment are similar, actual induction into creedal communes often has a more formal or ceremonial character, sometimes because the required ideological credentials are more explicit (e.g., abstention from drugs, acceptance of Christ, etc.) and sometimes because they are more at variance (possibly to an extreme extent) with the ideas that even an alienated youth is ready to believe.

In creedal communes, then, there may be books, lectures, encounter groups, initiations, and other rituals that a prospective member may be required to go through in order to achieve one or another stage of membership on his way to fully accredited status. In noncreedal communes, on the other hand, recruitment is much less formalized; in urban places, where turnover tends to be rapid, a new member or couple is likely to be accepted when a room becomes available if he or they are merely friends of friends; and if the prospective member is particularly attractive or compatible, room may be made for him or her. Because turnover tends to be less rapid in rural, noncreedal communes (and because family solidarity tends, therefore, to be stronger), new members are accepted much less easily. Members may be privileged to invite a guest (usually a friend) for a limited period, who, if the others like him, may be asked to stay longer, and eventually (if he wishes it) be considered for membership at a commune meeting. In noncreedal communes, then, the difference between transient, guest, extended visitor, probationary member, and member is sometimes difficult to tell; with the exception of fully accredited members, the transitions are gradual. While friendship networks account for almost all of the recruitment in noncreedal communes and much of it in creedal ones (proselytization and advertising account for the rest of it in the latter), there is one other source of recruitment that deserves special mention. There is a great deal of mobility—simple moving from place to place—in the hip world, and much of this mobility takes the form of hitchhiking, much of the time with no particular destination in mind. Those who pick up and those who are picked up often strike up quick friendships that lead to an invitation to spend the night. One recurrent form that this takes is for a communard with a vehicle to pick up a woman with or without a baby. He takes her home, where she becomes his old lady. He may leave again a few weeks later, leaving her with the commune as a "member" with an ambiguous status as "his" old lady—although he may not return, or return with another woman.

Another striking phenomenon we have observed is the apparently high incidence in the communes of sons and daughters of career military personnel, an observation which we intend to look into further when we do our formal interviewing.

In our analysis of recruitment to communes, we are currently exploring two interpretive perspectives—one of them, we believe, quite unusual. The first is whether communal development, particularly in its rural manifestations, can be understood as continuous with long-existing social trends, for example, the exodus from the cities, the suburbanization of the past twenty-five years (of which the parents of communards were presumably a part) which expressed, at least partly, the ideology of "togetherness" (much publicized in the late 1940s and 1950s): the suburban family, warm and secure in its domestic enclave full of plenty. Other existing social trends include the increasing diffusion of the encounter movement in middle-class circles, the development of homogeneous communities, represented by retirement communities and apartment developments renting exclusively to youngish "swingles," each of which group comes together on the basis of common problems it has (by virtue of age or some other status attribute) which can be solved collectively but not singly. In this perspective, communes are not nearly so radical a phenomenon as they are commonly thought to be.

The other perspective, of course, is that communes represent a radically discontinuous social trend which is best understood from the standpoint of deviance theory. In support of the first perspective is the fact that joining most communes does not involve a conversion experience for most persons; it is the outcome of an individual's confrontation of available alternatives and situational contingencies, and from that perspective is no more deviant (though statistically less likely) than entrance into business or the professions. In support of the second perspective is the radical divergence in ideology, world view, and personal conduct from those sanctioned by law and custom in the nation represented by Richard Nixon.

There is obvious sense in the latter perspective, but we think that there is much that can be done with the former perspective. There is a sense in which the more serious rural communards, despite their apparently total "rejection" of middle-class, industrial styles of life, may be said to be "conservative" in the sense that this term is sometimes applied to rural or small-town folk who resist the technological incursions of "modernity." Concerned primarily with the creation and sustenance of a relatively self-contained community composed of people they regard as kinsmen, tribesmen, clansmen, they are sometimes distrustful of strangers, intolerant of threats to their solidarity, and suspicious of unfamiliar vibrations. We intend to explore these matters more fully by using our interview data to make inferences about the extent to which the communal phenomenon represents a more or less reluctant and *ad hoc* adaptation for youth without more attractive alternatives, and the extent to which it is a pioneering attempt to re-create or restore some of the lost but nostalgically still-yearned-for rural virtues on a postindustrial basis.

## *Economic Arrangements*

A distinctive normative feature of communal life is the desire for economic independence or self-sufficiency. Rural communes, especially of the noncreedal variety, emphasize agricultural life, and take self-sufficiency ideally to mean that they consume only that which is produced on the land—including not only food, but the making of clothing and shelter from available raw materials. None of the communes we observed have achieved such self-sufficiency, but they often interpret this in developmental terms: it reflects the newness of the commune, the priority of survival, and remains an aim to be achieved at an indefinite future time.

For the present, "unearned" income is crucial to the majority of communes, rural and urban, which we have studied. "Welfare" is a major source of income on which many communes (particularly rural ones) we have seen depend, a fact which serves to enhance the attractiveness of unattached mothers and their babies—in much the same way that in the working-class districts of industrializing England, eighteenth- and early-nineteenth-century mothers with several illegitimate children were regarded as desirable wives because the children were significant more as breadwinners than as mouths to feed. "Crazy" people, with disability income from the state for their craziness, are also a not uncommon phenomenon in communal settings.

Although we have encountered some cynicism toward living on public largesse (it is often regarded as a legitimate rip-off), most communards, like most other welfare recipients, share the dominant society's view of welfare as an ideally temporary, if sometimes necessary, evil; they know they cannot depend upon it permanently, and they know that it makes them vulnerable to the state, when and if it should decide to make trouble for them.

The Department of Agriculture's surplus food program is also an important source of sustenance, particularly in rural places. But although we have been to more than one delicious communal dinner in which the bartered-for freshly caught red snapper was swimming in surplus butter, surplus food distribution is itself too little institutionalized to allow for real dependence upon it. More important as another source of income is a category we call "windfalls," which includes everything from occasional inheritances, birthday checks from parents or grandparents or other unsolicited gifts from relatives and benefactors (communards tend to come from relatively prosperous backgrounds, and the communal movement has occasionally enlisted the support of wealthy benefactors). We suspect that this source of income may be more important than it may appear at first glance, but we will have poor information about it until we have undertaken extensive interviewing of communards (even among persons noted for their upfrontness about all matters, we have so far found relatively little open sharing of information about noncommunal sources of personal income).

Agriculture in rural communes tends to be limited to a well-organized and sometimes extensive garden growing a wide variety of vegetables, and the cultivation of some fruit trees. Animal husbandry, limited mainly to chickens for eggs and goats for milk, is not highly developed, perhaps because it would require levels of technology and "rational" social organization which would threaten the valued "looseness" of communal life at the present time. An expenditure of $10 per month per person for food not provided by the land seems at this writing to be an accurate estimate; $40 per month per person is about the median contribution to the communal treasury expected of each member, but this is an expectation rather than a fact. Some, who can afford it, pay more, and those who have no personal source of income at all may be supported by the group so long as it is economically feasible and so long as he is a valued member in other respects. Communal families also occasionally discuss at meetings whether members should contribute all of their income regardless of what it is, but at one meeting we attended this proposal caused a great deal of controversy and a bitter remark by one member that he would contribute all his income if it were a real family, by which he didn't mean a blood family but a more "together" one.

Much nongrown food is procured through trade rather than purchase; barter arrangements are valued for social as well as economic reasons (as was made clear in the previous year's report), and there is, typically, considerable exchange of vegetables and goat's milk for fish, wool, grain, hardware, and similar commodities. "Gathering" is also a widespread source of food supply in the rural communes we have studied—as in the extensive picking of the rich supply of various wild berries along the northern California coast during what one communard, quoting Keats, referred to as "the season of mists and mellow fruitfulness."

Scavenging is likewise important, although perhaps not primarily as a matter of practical economics; a skilled picker-over of the County Dump in one commune and a cook in another who can obtain and utilize the produce discarded when supermarket vegetable displays are arranged are highly valued people, and ingenious methods for "recycling" a variety of materials find frequent appreciation, though for what seem to us more aesthetic and political reasons than economic ones. Indeed, the motif of "survival" is an important one in the hip setting, and almost anything that contributes to it in what is regarded as a hostile social environment is cause for satisfaction—although this motif is more prevalent among hippies who live in loose-knit "communities" than among those who live in relatively well-established communes. In either case, however, there exists considerable concern for the development of what could be termed a "nongrowth" economic system.

Whereas most rural communes, particularly of the noncreedal variety, see to their economic needs through subsistence farming, barter, welfare, and windfalls, some rural communes and most urban ones, in addition to the latter two, have other sources of income. In a modal urban commune, for example, some members are likely at any given time to be employed in a relatively "straight" job; small-time drug-dealing provides some income in one urban commune we studied closely, and probably in others. But in addition to these, several communes (and near communes), urban and rural, are organized around collective enterprises which are ideologically respectable and remunerative as well: rock bands, "free schools," automobile repair, underground newspapers, and other institutions of the hip community. While not all of these have been a focus of major concern in this research (partly because some of them don't have children, partly because of the ephemeral nature of some, and partly because of the ambiguous status of some of them as communes), it is important to note that the relationships developed out of these enterprises have sometimes served as the basis upon which communes are formed—in which communion itself, rather than the economic enterprise, becomes the central focus.

Moreover, some communes, urban and rural, on which we have done extensive ethnographic work have well-developed "cottage industries" which provide a major source of income. Although there are exceptions, there seems to be some tendency for these communes to be creedal—to adhere to an elaborated system of religious doctrine. The firmer authority structure of these communes may contribute the essential element that makes "industry" possible—namely, a commitment to a relatively regularized and impersonal "devotion to duty." And the enterprises themselves (e.g., a restaurant and an incense factory) bind the members together, require relatively continuous work on behalf of the group, limit outside contacts which may undermine loyalty to the commune, and result in a clearly collective monetary income.

But it is also true that the nature of the work associated with "industry" is accepted at best only ambivalently in the hip world. The avowed and repeatedly voiced ideal is to undertake only those tasks that are intrinsically and not merely instrumentally valued, to eliminate the distinction between work and play, to make work a holy and a personal concern. This is easier to accomplish in rural, agricultural communes, where we have encountered quite explicit attempts to tailor the *pace* of work to what is regarded as an "organic" model: work should be slow, periodic, integrated with, not separated from, other spheres of life such as courtship, play, "visiting," and even philosophical reflection; not, that is to say, "alienated."

One consequence of this morality is actually to enlarge the individual's contribution to collective welfare, precisely because it is viewed as self-serving rather than coerced. In the cottage industries of creedal communes, on the other hand, it is only a strong ideology of "service" that stands between an individual's labors and his sense of doing alienated work.

One of the most potentially important consequences of this approach to work is its application to the status of children. One rural creedal commune has recently been extensively debating a proposal to have children over the age of six join adults in doing the work of the farm; and another creedal commune, this time urban, has actually organized the children around their own cottage industry. The stated rationale for this is that it will both enhance the independence of children and promote the desired integration of work and play. There is a sense in which communards, having rejected middle-class models of "maturity," are faced with having to rethink the definitions of childhood, adulthood, and the relations between them. And there is more than a suggestion (which we are studying more carefully at the present) that this rethinking involves a rejection of the idea of children as incompetent dependents with a special psychology needing special protections and nurturings. Like the big "kids" who are their parents, communal children seem to be just littler kids, less skilled, less experienced, and only perhaps less wise.

*Children*

The birth of a child—particularly in a rural commune, and especially if the birth is "natural," as many of them are—is often the occasion of a collective celebration of great significance. In the case of the earliest "first-generation" communards, the event can have a virtually constitutional meaning, symbolizing the collective property as a home to its occupants, and the occupants themselves as members of a single family. Natural childbirth is additionally constitutional in the degree to which its clear-cut contrast with the studied impersonality of the hospital setting gives palpable reality to the communards' rejection of those technologies which are seen as depersonalizing of life in general. Since having made this initial observation (mentioned in a previous report), it has been verified again and again in our subsequent field work. (Of course, the dissemination of information about natural childbirth "methods" is itself a technological development that substantially reduces the risks involved, thus permitting the rejection of the "straight" world by communards without great danger.)

In partial contrast, however, to the solidarity-affirming nature of birth ceremonies, communal children tend to be viewed (in rural, urban, creedal, and noncreedal communes alike) as rather independent, self-contained persons—although they participate, to be sure, in the higher cosmic unities (for example, in the widespread belief and slogan that "we are all One"). This is of special interest to us as macrosociologists because the ways in which adults conceptualize and thus "act toward" children vary historically and between social groups, and the hippie "theory of children" is in some respects distinctive.

In viewing the history of how children are conceptualized by adults, social scientists have thus far emphasized the differences between pre-industrial, agricultural, or sometimes lower-class views on the one side, and industrial or middle-class views on the other. In the former view, the status of children is seen as essentially ascribed at birth and rooted in the kinship system. In this view, children are seen as simply small or inadequate versions of their parents, totally subject to traditional or otherwise arbitrary parental authority. The "modern" industrial, middle-class view, by contrast, tends to treat the child as a distinctive social category: children have their own special psychology, their own special needs, patterned processes of growth often elaborated into ideas about developmental stages which may postpone advent to "full" adulthood well into a person's twenties, and sometimes still later. The task of parents and other "socializers" in this view is to "raise" or "produce" the child (the industrial metaphor is often used) according to scientifically elaborated principles of proper child-management—a process which in many middle-class families results in the differentiation of family roles in a way that transforms a woman-with-child into a full-time child-raiser.

The view that we find prevalent in the hip-communal settings we have studied fits neither of these models with percision. "Young people" are regarded as independent of the family, but not as members of an autonomous category of "children"; instead, their status is likely to be ascribed as that of "person," a development which can be understood as part of an equalitarian ethos, and as complementary to parallel developments in the status of females, from "women" (or even "mothers") to "people," and in the status of men, from being characterized in invidious status terms to being characterized as above all a "human being." Again, "we are all One."

As a practical matter, however, children are not simply independent, autonomous individuals. Age makes an important and understandable difference. Infants and "knee babies" are almost universally in the charge of their mothers, who have primary responsibility for their care. Communards, particularly rural ones, frequently discuss the possibility of "communalizing" even infants—as in the notion of placing infants at an available breast rather than an exclusively parental one, but this proposal seems as yet to be too radical. We have, however, made several observations of what could be called communal child care, for example, collective feedings, bathings, and defecations (this last, a rich scene in which three toddlers in the care of one adult squatted in the woods, chatted amiably about the color, smell, and texture of each others productions, than under the ecological guidance of the grown-up buried the shit and burned the paper with which they cleaned themselves).

Children aged two to four or slightly older frequently "belong to the commune" in a stronger sense than infants and knee babies do because they are less dependent upon continuous supervision, although even with children of this age the conventional pattern of sharing their care is largely limited to the group of mothers-with-children. This is not to say that young children do not get a lot of fathering; they do; fathers hold the children often, feed them, cuddle them, and may be attentive in other respects. But this depends upon the personal predispositions of the men involved; there are not strong *norms* apparent which *require* the attentiveness of fathers.

But for children older than four or five, the responsibilities of either parents or the other adult communards may be much attenuated. All children are viewed as intrinsically worthy of love and respect *but not necessarily of attention.* As they grow out of primitive physical dependence upon the care of adults, they are treated and tend to behave as just another member of the extended family—including being offered (and taking) an occasional hit on a joint of marijuana as it is passed around the family circle. When problems crop up, children are particularly susceptible to being labeled and understood astrologically, in a manner of speaking, as "cosmic wards" with their own karma or fate and their own problems that they must work out themselves. They are expected to use first names in referring to their parents and other adults (the children themselves have names like "Cloud," "Forest," "Blue Jay," "River," "Sweet Pea," etc.), are seen as the equal of adults (they fall quickly and easily into use of the hip vernacular: far out, outasight, as well as all of the routine four letter obscenities—there are no "bad words" in the language), and are in more than a few instances drawn into doing adult work. In one setting, the children have, with adult approval, established their own separate residences.

In a previous report we raised the question of whether the variations we observed in the extent to which a child belongs to its parents or to the extended communal family was a variation in types of communes or a sequential development occurring as the child gets older. We are now able to give a fairly conclusive answer: it is a sequential development, but this fact requires a good deal of explication. Insofar as there exists a role for adults in facilitating the development of children, the role is essentially exemplary (charismatic) rather than paternalistic and authoritarian (traditional) or didactic and hortatory ("rational"). In spite of this limitation which learning-through-imitation-of-adults places on the belief that children must "work out their own fate," attempts are seriously made by adults to allow children to grow "naturally," to be autonomous and free. But the single most important belief governing the relation between children and adults is that *the experiences had by children not be fateful or self-implicating for adults*; that adults cannot be legitimately characterized in terms of what they do with or to their children—in rather clear contrast to both pre-industrial and middle-class views in which the behavior of children "reflects upon" their parents, who are in some sense "responsible" for it.

In saying this, some important cautions are in order. First, the great majority of the children we have observed are six or under, and there are numerous communes that are only now beginning to recognize a "schooling" problem; and it may be that in time a distinctive "child psychology" and set of child-management practices will emerge. There may also be important sex differences in the ways adults relate to children; communal ideologies tend to be elaborated by men, and the men are clearly the most mobile sex (from time to time women express some wishes that men would spend more time with the children), and therefore most likely to seek freedom from parental responsibilities—*a freedom that is itself legitimated in part by the view of children as autonomous.*

But the women share this view too, and benefit from its application. One young mother, harried with the care of her two-year-old, said, "What I wanted was a *baby*; but a *kid*, that's something else." That is to say, having "babies" is good because it's natural, organic, earthy, and "beautiful," and besides which babies are wonderful because they represent human potential unspoiled by the corrupting influence of repressive institutions. But "raising" a child involves obligations that they have not "committed" themselves to in the sense that many middle-class mothers, who regard their lives as "settled" and their futures as a working out of what is already implicitly present (home, husband, and children), devote themselves to a full-time job called "child-rearing." But as we have noted, hippies, including communal mothers, tend to regard themselves as "kids," their lives unsettled, their futures uncertain, and they are generally unwilling to sacrifice their own personal questings (for meaning, identity, transcendence, etc.) to full-time devotion to child-rearing. And it is in this context that the hippie "theory of children" seems to us most relevant.

Communards generally tell us that "communes are good for the children"—one of the meanings many of their own parents almost certainly gave to their suburban communities: the setting itself may be said to possess medicinal qualities. In this respect there may be an important continuity between the generations—although communards frequently report that their own childhoods were frustrating experiences of little autonomy and little opportunity to develop "real" skills. In relatively isolated and sometimes bucolic rural communes, of course, it *is* possible to grant children much autonomy without much risk of waywardness, and children do in fact enjoy some of what are probably the real benefits of an inadvertent rather than a compulsory education.

### *Family Structure and Sexual Relations*

Everything we have said about the children of the communes occurs in the context of hippie relationships and family structures, and it is important to understand these, not only because they are the most palpably real aspect of the research scene but because they contain the seeds of the potential futures of the commune movement.

The most important single feature of hip relationships is their fragility. We mean by this not that many of the relationships don't last; quite the contrary. In several of our more stable communes couples have been "together" as long as the commune has existed (two to three years), and sometimes longer. We mean, rather, that there tend to be few if any cultural constraints or structural underpinnings to sustain relationships when and if they become tension-ridden or otherwise unsatisfying. The uncertainty of futures hovers over hip relationships like a probation officer, reminding the parties of the necessary tentativeness of their commitments to each other.

Very few nuclear units, for example, are legally married; neither the men nor the women have the kinds of jobs that bind them to a community; in other respects their investments in the environmental locale or its institutions are minimal. Like many of their parents (whom theorists have suggested have been highly mobile—a hypothesis which we will test in our interviewing), they move around a great deal, getting into and out of "intimate" relations rather quickly through such techniques as spontaneous "encounter" and other forms of "upfrontness." And above and beyond these, there is a very heavy emphasis on "present orientation"—a refusal to *count on* futures as a continuation of present arrangements—and a diffuse desire to remain "kids" themselves in the sense of unencumberedness, a freedom *from* the social ties that constrain one toward instrumental action.

Yet despite the fact of (and the attitudinal adjustment to) the fragility of relationships, there are romantic images also superimposed. Although the fragility of old man–old lady relationships is a fact, communards of all sorts are generally reluctant to believe in a future of serial monogamy. Many communards, particularly the women, hope for an ideal lover or a permanent mate but tend to have not much real expectation that it will happen. Instead, compensatory satisfactions are found in the *image* of the communal family and household, always full of people, where a group of brothers and sisters, friends as kin, spend all or most of their time with each other, working, playing, loving, rapping, "hanging out"—where wedding bells, far from breaking up the old gang, are themselves so rare that they are occasions for regional celebrations of solidarity when they do ring out.

Where it exists, it is the fact of communal solidarity which functions as the strongest support for fragile relations among couples. For when the communal scene is a wholesome and attractive one, as it sometimes is, couples whose relationship is very unstable may elect to stay together in order to share those benefits rather than threaten them by breaking up.

But in spite of the fragility of relationships in a system which defines futures as uncertain and in an ideology emphasizing spontaneity and freedom, heterosexual couples are the backbone of most communes, urban or rural, creedal or not. They seem more stable and dependable as members than single people do, if only because their search for partners is ended, even if that ending is temporary. The temporary character of the relationships is more pronounced in urban communes, both, we believe, because the very presence of couples in rural communes is itself generally evidence of more stable commitment, and because of the higher probability in urban scenes of meeting another man or woman who is ready and willing to enter into a close relationship at little more than a moment's notice.

When a couple has a child, their mobility is reduced somewhat, of course, even when the child is the product of a previous union of either the female or male. But only "somewhat," because of the importance of what we call the "splitting" phenomenon, particularly as it applies to men. We mentioned previously that children (especially very young ones) "belong" to their mothers, and that norms *requiring* paternal solicitude for children are largely absent. What this means is that fathers are "free"—at the very least free to split whenever they are so moved. Since they are not "legally" fathers (even if they biologically are) they have no claims on the child, and since there is generally a strong communal norm *against* invoking the legal constraints of straight society (i.e., calling the police), fathers have no obligation to the child that anyone is willing to enforce. Moreover, no norm takes priority over the individual's (particularly the male's) search for himself, or meaning, or transcendence, and if this search requires father's wandering elsewhere "for a while," there is nothing to prevent it.

One consequence of this family pattern is the frequency of woman-with-child (and without old man) in many of the communes we have studied—although this occurs as often as a result of the woman-with-child arriving on the commune scene that way as it does as a result of her partner "splitting." A situation like this does not typically last a long time in any commune we have studied, although it was present in almost all of them. Even when the women involved say they prefer celibacy, there is some doubt that they actually do. One afternoon in a tepee, three young women (without men) with infants on the breast agreed that they welcomed a respite from men, what with their bodies devoted almost full time to the nursing of infants. Within a week, two of them had new old men and the third had gone back to her old one. Celibacy or near celibacy occurs only in those creedal communes whose doctrines define sexual activity as impure or as a drain on one's physical and spiritual resources for transcendence.

But although celibacy is rare and although couple relations are fragile, this should not be taken to mean that sex is either promiscuous or disordered. At any given time, monogamous coupling is the norm in all the communes we studied closely; in this respect hippies tend to be more traditional than the "swingers" and wife-swappers one reads about in the middle class. Although there are communes whose creed requires group marriage (in the sense that all the adults are regarded as married to all the others, and expected to have sexual relations with each other), we have not studied any of these at first hand. But even in communes where coupling is the norm, there seems to be evidence of a natural drift toward group marriage—although it may still be ideologically disavowed. For one thing, when couples break up in rural communes, it is as likely as not that each will remain on the land; and this occurs frequently in urban communes too. Without a drift toward group marriage, situations like this could and do cause great communal tensions which threaten the survival of the group. Whereas, on the other hand, a not uncommon feature of communes is a situation in which over a long period of time, many of the adults have had sexual relations with each other at one or another point between the lapses of "permanent" coupling. Under these conditions, group marriage can seem like a "natural" emergence rather than unnaturally "forced" by a creed—a natural emergence which, by gradually being made an item of affirmed faith, can conceivably solve some of the problems and ease some of the tensions generated by the fragility of couple relations and the break-ups which are a predictable result of them. Broken-up couples may still "love" each other as kin, under these conditions—even if they find themselves incapable of permanently sharing the same tent, cabin, or bed, an incapacity more likely to be explained astrologically than any other way. (Astrology is used to explain "problems" with respect to children and intimate relations between couples.)*

But the widespread presence of women-with-children as nuclear units in the communes is not merely an artifact of the splitting of men or an expression of the belief of hip parents in the unwisdom of staying together "for the sake of the child." The readiness of hip women to bear the child even of a "one-night stand" is supported by social structures which indicate its "logic." Unlike middle-class women, for example, a hippie female's social status does not depend upon her old man's occupation; she doesn't need him for that. The state is a much better provider than most men who are

* We think, indeed, that there is a close relationship between the commune movement, on the one hand, and the complex of stirrings in the middle class which includes the encounter movement, swingers, sensitivity training, and the incipient gestures toward group marriage represented by "wife-swapping." Each represents an attempt to cope with similar problems (e.g., alienation, existential discontents with the prospects or the realities of middle-class life) by groups of people differently situated in the life-career cycle: the communards being mainly college dropouts in their twenties, the others being mainly married couples in their thirties or forties with children and already well into their professional careers with which they may have become disenchanted.

available to her. Having a baby, moreover, helps solve an identity problem by giving her something to do. An infant to care for provides more meaning and security in her life than most men could. And in addition, these women are often very acceptable to communes as new members. They are likely to be seen as potentially less disruptive to ongoing commune life than a single man; they are likely to be seen as more dependable and stable than a single man; and these women provide a fairly stable source of communal income through the welfare payments that most of them receive. From the point of view of the hip mothers, commune living is a logical choice; it solves some of the problems of loneliness—there are always others around; it provides plenty of opportunities for interaction with men—even if they aren't always immediately "available"; instead of having to go out to be picked up, a hip mother can rely on a fairly large number of male visitors passing through the commune, with whom she may establish a liaison. And if she does want to go out, there are usually other members of the family present to look after her child, and other males to act as surrogate fathers.

If these descriptions sound as if they bear some similarity to working-class or lower-class patterns in extended-kin groups, the similarity is not inadvertent, although the correspondence is far from perfect. Communal life tends to be very dense, although most communes do have clearly marked areas of privacy. Most communes of all kinds are typically divided into public or communal areas and private areas. In rural communes, there is usually a communal house where people cook, eat, and engage in other collective activities such as meetings, musicales, entertainment of visitors, and so on. In addition there may be a library, sewing rooms, room for spare clothing, and other needs for whose satisfactions collective solutions are made. But rural communes tend to discourage "living" (i.e., sleeping) in the communal house, except when the commune is crowded with visitors, guests, or new prospective members. Sleeping quarters are private, and one of the first expressive commitments of a new member in a rural commune is building his own house (containing usually a single room)—a tepee, an A frame, a dome, a shack or lean-to—out of available local materials, and ideally out of sight of the nearest other private dwelling.

In urban communes, the kitchen and living room-dining room generally serve as communal areas, whereas the bedrooms are private and "belong to" the couples who sleep in them. Privacy, of course, is more difficult to sustain in urban communes than in rural ones, even though knocking on closed or almost closed bedroom doors before entering is an item of communal good manners.

In urban and rural communes, children tend to sleep in the same room as their parents (or mother), although if space is available older children may sleep in a room of their own or, as in one rural commune, in a separate house. Although a typical item of commune architecture is the use of sleeping lofts both to increase privacy and to make use of unused space above the head but below the roof, children are regularly exposed to sexual activities—as is true in any community where people cannot afford a lot of space. But the less than perfect privacy for sexual and excretory functions—particularly when the commune is crowded with visitors or crashers—although sometimes a source of tension, is not typically a major problem because of the latent communal belief in most places that no normal and honorable functions *need* to be hidden from public view. The high value of upfrontness, the commonness of nudity, the glass on bathroom or outhouse doors (or no doors at all) and the general belief that people are and should be perfectly transparent to each other is not always enough to overcome years of training in shyness, modesty, etc., regarding sexual and excretory functions, but it generally is enough to at least constrain people to regard their remaining shynesses as hang-ups which they should try to overcome in the name of communal sharing of as much as can conceivably be shared.

Nevertheless, even under crowded conditions, communards develop ways of creating private spaces for the activities, such as sex, for which they still require privacy. Thus tapestries will often be tacked up between one mattress and the next or music will constantly be coming from a radio or record player to cover sounds of love-making or private conversations. People sometimes forgo sexual activity when conditions are crowded, but we have also seen strong compensatory satisfactions taken from the simple fact of a lot of people just sleeping together.

In the report for 1970 we mentioned that the women's liberation movement would probably not approve of the position of women in most communes. Although this is still largely true, it requires some explication. The fact is that in most communes of all types women tend to do traditional women's work: most of the cooking and cleaning (they are more concerned with tidiness than most men), and, in the rural communes, much of the traditional female farm roles in addition. But it is also true that women share in the general ethos of equalitarianism of most communes. With the exception of those religious communes which have an explicitly "sexist" creed, women can be found doing any but the most physically arduous labors, and in several communes we have studied closely, women do play important leadership roles. But on the whole they are less ideologically forceful than men, and express themselves with generally less authority—although we have encountered important exceptions to this tendency.

Concern over the status of women is more common in urban communes than rural ones (this is true in general of political matters), and female liberation has been a heavy topic of conversation in two urban communes we have studied (along with the male liberation which female liberation is said to bring in its wake). And in one of these communes, there is a distinctly "funky" working-class atmosphere, combining a lot of roughhouse play (ass- and crotch-grabbing, mock-rape, etc.) by both the men and the women, with a fairly equal sexual division of labor.

### *Communal Authority and Decision-making*

One important condition of understanding authority and decision-making in hip communes is the fact that the communards are where they are because they have "dropped out" of straight society. One of the things this means is that they are less than enthusiastic and certainly not pious about "democratic" processes in the sense of majority rulings or parliamentary procedure. Freedom for communards, then, inheres not primarily in the democratic model of exercising a voice in the decisions that shape their lives (and then perhaps having to adjust to losing a vote). It lies, rather, in one or the other of two modal forms in the communes we have studied and read about. In one form, nobody is forced to accept a decision even if majority sentiment is in favor of it. In the other form, the individual yields his personal autonomy to a leader, usually authoritarian, whose charisma lies in his command of doctrine which points to The One Correct Way, or in the strength of his personal presence (and the submissiveness of his devotees) which itself manifests what his followers want.

The first form of freedom-authority is characteristic of noncreedal communes, urban and rural, most of which tend to be anarchistic. In these groups (by far the most prevalent on the commune scene) there is no formal authority structure, and although, of course, some people are more influential (heavier) than others, even the most influential typically disavow their authority. "I'm so glad," said one communard at a place like this, "that we don't have to deal with any self-appointed leaders." In these places, routine decisions are usually made by the people with the relevant functional skills to carry out the implied tasks, and this system is made viable by the fact that these communes are typically friendship-based and with a relatively high degree of solidarity. In these groups there is a general reluctance to make any major collective decision or to embark upon any more-than-routine collective enterprise unless there is near unanimity of opinion, or at the very least no strongly felt opposition. This generally results in relatively few important decisions of serious consequence being made—and haphazard enforcement of the few that are, because few if any people have any desire to perform the role of policeman. A typical example is when the persistent troublesomeness of a member or visitor provokes a move to oust him from the commune. Where this occurs, encounter techniques or persuasion are used to attempt to convince the dissenter that what the majority or almost everybody wants is also best for him too, if he would only try to understand the sources of his own dissent or resistance—

all so that decisions will not have to be forced upon the unwilling.

But this reluctance to make important decisions does not typically create serious problems for anarchistic noncreedal communes because relative inaction is consistent with the generally quasi-Buddhist-Eastern stance of preferring to stand there than to do something, with their ideology of slow, organic development (particularly in rural places), and with their own dominant, precommunal political *experience* as a minority dissenter, which seems to predispose them to be reluctant to impose a majority view on their dissenting brothers in the commune.

In general, however, this ability of anarchistic communes to get along without formal leadership depends upon the history of friendship which characterizes them, and on the general consensus about the person(s) empowered to speak for the group should such occasions arise. These people are usually the longest-tenured members of the commune, the eldest in years, or the ones regarded as wisest and most serene, and these are frequently the same person(s).

Creedal communes are not necessarily different with respect to the structure of authority and decision-making from noncreedal ones, but they usually are—just as noncreedal communes are not necessarily consensual and informal in their structure of authority and decision-making. (The notorious "Manson Family," for example, is noncreedal but had a charismatic leader in whom all authority resided.) What a creed does for a commune is usually to provide a cosmology, a set of beliefs and a leader and/or his representatives charged with the authority to apply the creed to the contexts in which the commune lives.

It is generally true that the leaders of creedal communes tend to be considerably older than their followers, who themselves tend to be the youngest communards we have seen. This "gap," if you will, often makes it difficult for followers to contest the will of leaders—even when they (the leaders) are not arbitrary or completely authoritarian, because the elders are likely to be in firm command of the official "rap" and its appropriate interpretation in a way that makes it difficult for all but the most ideologically gifted younger people to quarrel with. More often than not, the creed is of an "Eastern" kind, emphasizing the "we are all One" theme, which enables leaders to identify the interests of each with each, and to speak both through and for them. Paradoxically, there is evidence to suggest that despite the firmer structure of authority in creedal communes, there is probably more argument and disagreement in them than in noncreedal ones. For one thing, the leader or guru is sometimes not right there on the communal scene, and this provides occasion for difference in the interpretation of doctrine which cannot immediately be resolved by an authoritative decision. And the doctrine itself is often the source of discrepancies between theory and practice which are absent where, as in noncreedal communes, there is no formal theory to begin with. Moreover, the very existence of formal authority structures can breed jealousies and ambitions for position, which are absent in formally equalitarian settings.

In either situation, however, it is important to remember that formal democratic processes are not salient. Many communards have learned to distrust the "democracy" of the larger political landscape where political choices are "fixed" in advance so that voters' powers can seem merely formal (the Chicago convention of 1968 was a shattering event for most hippies of the Left, and the movement to rural communes sharply accelerated after that event). With their faith in democracy seriously undermined, it is not surprising to see communards turning away from it in the two ways we have reported: either toward leaderlessness and anarchism or toward a mystical authoritarianism in which one's freedom is yielded to a charismatic figure regarded as "knowing the way."

*Proposed Work*

The bulk of our ethnographic field work is already done. Some of our field workers are still at the communal sites, sensitized to making observations which might replicate or cast doubt on what we have already learned. We have plans to do just a little more field work, in places where we have not been before, where we have reason to believe there are important things to observe that we have not observed in our present sample—for example, in a group-marriage commune. But with respect to our ethnographic research, the major task remaining to be done is a finer systematic coding of our categories in order to make our comparisons of data more rigorous.

The major part of our proposed work involves survey techniques. We are about to begin an interview survey of commune parents and mail questionnaires of their own parents in order to find, most generally speaking, a three-generation perspective on the route from the middle class to communal living. In this respect our plans are still contained in our original research proposal. In the present report, we have indicated several of the questions which we cannot answer by observation but only by eliciting direct information by interview. We have high hopes for the interviews because most of the items in our questionnaires will have been suggested by problems empirically encountered in the field work.

# 13

# Family Life in the Kibbutz of Israel: Utopia Gained or Paradise Lost?

BENJAMIN SCHLESINGER

## *Introduction*

IN 1969, the population of the State of Israel was 2,841,100, of which 2,434,800 were Jews, 300,800 Muslims, 72,150 Christians, 33,300 Druzes and others. Three percent of this population, consisting of 84,200 persons, lived in collective villages (kibbutzim).[1]

The kibbutz or kvutza (plural: kibbutzim or kvuzot), communal or collective villages, are governed by the general assembly of all members. All property is collectively owned and work is organized on a collective basis. Members give their labor and in return receive housing, food, clothing, and social services. There are central dining rooms, kitchens and stores, communal kindergartens and children's quarters, and social and cultural centers. Individual living quarters provide personal privacy.

The kibbutzim are predominantly agricultural, but many run sizable industrial enterprises. There are 235, with populations ranging from 60 to 2,000. The first, Degania, was founded in 1909.[2]

The kibbutz is only one form of rural settlement in Israel.[3]

The founders of the kibbutzim were predominantly of Polish and Russian origin and their European experience has influenced the kind of community they have established.

Eastern European Jews lived in an anti-Semitic atmosphere with social discrimination for a long time, and though schools were opened to them later, Jewish students were made to feel that they were strangers.

The culture of the Jewish Polish and Russian village called *shtetl* (small town) produced people who were caricatures of natural and normal men both physically and spiritually, and was viewed unfavorably by the new generation.[4] As a result an opposition to the parental way of living was openly expressed by the youth and a need for change was strongly experienced. The Zionist movement, with its love of nature, love of a nation, self-expression, and emphasis on the emotional aspects of life, soon became a model to be imitated and a means of emancipation from the bonds of urban mores and artificial convention. Return to nature and the ascetic life included simple housing, simple clothing, and avoidance of make-up by women.

Zionism, apart from its original ideology of an escape from Judaism and the culture of the shtetl, involved also the migration to Israel. In 1909, when ninety Jews arrived in Israel, physical conditions were so harsh that many found it impossible to adjust and either returned to Poland or went to live in the cities. Those who remained founded the kibbutz. Hardships, lack of comfort, and strenuous physical labor resulted in close relationships, mutual support, and strong cooperation.[5]

From the organizational point of view, the communal settlement represents a complex unit. The supreme authority in all economic and social matters is the General Assembly of members. An executive committee is entrusted with the implementation of the resolutions of the Assembly in all matters relating to economic affairs, and it also prepares the production program for the consideration and decision of the Assembly.[6]

A labor committee is appointed to detail the members for work, and it is responsible for the execution of the working program in every branch of activity, including the domestic service (kitchen, children's house, for instance), in accordance with the program drawn up for the entire year. Every branch of activity in headed by a member who is responsible for it, or by a committee of workers who are permanently engaged in the branch. This committee functions in accordance with the general program prepared for the year.

The executive staff of the communal settlement usually consists of a treasurer, a secretary, the secretary of the labor committee, and a bookkeeper. The social affairs of the settlement are organized by special committees such as health, education, membership, and cultural activities, whose task it is to deal with all the current requirements of the members. Members of the settlement may apply to these committees in all matters relating to their functions.

The committees are each allocated a budget for their activities by the General Assembly. Once a year, at the beginning of the agricultural year, elections of all the officials and committees of the settlement are held. A program of activities for the coming year is laid down and the detailed budget is fixed. The organizational, social, and economic activities of the settlement are conducted in accordance with these decisions.

The founders of the kibbutz movement in 1909 devised many ingenious devices in order to prevent the consolidation of the family as a distinct and independent unit. Delegation of functions to the kibbutz is the most important aspect of the "collectivization" of the family during the first phases of the movement.[7]

Husband and wife are allotted independent jobs. There is a strict ban on assigning members of the same family to the same place of work. Division of labor in the occupational sphere is based on a denial of sex differentiation. Women participate to a considerable extent in hard productive labor as well as in defense activities. All meals are taken in the common dining hall. Members' needs are provided by communal institutions.

Families look after their own rooms but have few other household responsibilities. Thus each mate works in one branch or another of the settlement and receives his share of the goods and services distributed by the kibbutz. Interaction between the sexes in the economic sphere occurs on the level of the community as a whole and not directly between mates.[8]

The birth rate in the kibbutzim was for a long time below the level of replacement. The kibbutzim ensured their continuity and growth not so much by natural increase but by means of recruitment of volunteers from external sources. The physical care and rearing of the children were basically the responsibility of the kibbutz and not so much of their parents. From their birth on they sleep, eat, and later study in special children's houses.

Each age group leads its own life and has its autonomous arrangements. Children meet their parents, brothers, and sisters in off hours and spend the afternoons and early evenings with them. On Saturdays and holidays they stay with their parents most of the time. In most kibbutzim parents put their young children to bed every night. There are thus frequent and intensive relations between parents and children.

The main socializing agencies are, however, the peer age group and the specialized nurses, instructors, and teachers. The age group is a substitute for the brother-sister group. The children belong to the community as a whole. The family has almost ceased to be an autonomous unit from the point of view of division of labor.[9]

The father not only does not rear the child, but also has no specific responsibility for him. The child is provided for by the kibbutz as a whole; he receives his food in the dormitory dining room, his clothes from the dormitory storeroom, his medical care from the dispensary, and his housing in the children's dormitories. This is a deliberate policy, the aim of which is to prevent the child from feeling economically dependent upon the father, which, according to kibbutz analysis, is the greatest source of the father's authority in Western society.

The kibbutz also attempted to change the woman's role in the family. Because woman must bear and rear children, she has had little opportunity for cultural, political, or artistic expressions. If she could only be freed from this time-consuming responsibility, as well as from such other domestic duties as cleaning, cooking, and laundry, she would have the time to devote to these other interests and would become the equal of men.

In other words, the crux of the problem was to be found in

the emancipation of the woman from the yoke of domestic service.

By instituting a system of communal socialization, it was believed, it would be possible to achieve part of this goal, the emancipation of woman from the burdens of child-rearing. And if her children were reared by professional nurses, the woman would not only be free from that responsibility, she would be spared the chores of housekeeping as well, since she and her husband would require little room.

Her complete "emancipation," however, included the abolition of all domestic chores. This was accomplished by the various communal institutions of the kibbutz: the communal laundry, kitchen, and dining room relieved her of the chores of laundry, cooking, and dish-washing. Thus, woman is relieved of the care of her children and of her traditional domestic chores.

While the kibbutzim limited the functions of the family drastically and emphasized the collective aspect, they did not abolish the family altogether. Even during the earliest phases, when the antifamilistic trend was at its strongest, the family remained a distinct unit.[10]

Though educators were the designated representatives of the kibbutz rather than of the parents, the parents exercised a direct and continuous influence on the trained personnel in charge of their children. Since children's institutions were not segregated from the community, parents were able to supervise closely the way their children were raised there. They exercised considerable direct influence on their children during the time they spent together every day.

While interaction of members of the family with each other was in many cases less frequent than interaction with outsiders, internal ties were more continuous, more meaningful, and more intense. The emotional ties that bound husband an d wife and parents and children were much more intimate com more exclusive than their ties with other members of the intima unity. The family combined physical and emotional contacts and supplied its members' needs for close personal the comm which were partly independent of their position in ity. By providing unconditional love and loyalty, it insulated its members from communal pressures and enhanced their security.

The kibbutz has succeeded in eliminating most of the characteristics and functions of the traditional family. The parents have little responsibility for the physical care or for the socialization of their children; the relationship between mates does not include economic cooperation; and parents and children do not share a common residence. Taking these facts, alone, into consideration it may be concluded that the family does not exist in the kibbutz.

On the other hand, though the family does not exist as in our own family sense, it does exist in a psychological sense. Although parents and children do not share a common residence, they are deeply attached to each other and comprise a distinct and recognizable social group. Moreover, the members of the kibbutz themselves refer to this group as a family.

In summary the specific objectives of this system of collective life were: (1) to abolish parental authority, particularly the patriarchal authority of the father; (2) to free the female from the impediment of being assigned only a few special roles in society, such as homemaking and child-rearing; (3) to perpetuate the value system of the communal society; and (4) to provide the children with the most democratic education possible.

It was hoped that freeing the parents of the need to care for and educate their children would bring the parent-child relation to rest on positive emotions. Since, also, the community as a whole would be responsible for his physical well-being, the child would not be beholden to any particular person, and least of all to his parents.

Asked to rank in importance the values they wished their educational system to instill in their children, the parents of some kibbutzim replied:[11] that first and foremost is "work"; after that, in order of importance: "love of humanity"; "responsibility to the kibbutz"; "good character"; "intel"; lectualism"; "socialism"; "Zionism"; "social participatidjust-"patriotism"; and "cooperation." Neither emotional [illegible] while ment nor success in competition was mentioned values in personal advancement was contrary to all their general, since by work they meant cooperative work in the kibbutz. Thus, queried also as to which ambitions they hoped their children would realize, kibbutz members ranked being a good comrade first, and being a good worker second.

Let's examine the lives of children in this unique environment. The children are raised in children's houses. When the mother comes home from the hospital, the child is tended in an Infants' House, which is quite well equipped for the care of the newborn. The mother has the first six weeks for herself. She does no work other than that of feeding and caring for her baby. Thereafter, for as long as she nurses the child, she works four hours a day, and then she is with her child before work, after work, Saturdays, holidays, and any other time she has.[12]

In the meantime, the infant is cared for by nurses trained for the job. When the child is about eighteen months old, he leaves the Infants' House with four or five of his own age group. This group forms a group called *kvutza*, under the tutelage of another type of nurse. The child lives with this group until he is three or four, at which time he becomes a member of a so-called mixed kindergarten.

A mixed kindergarten is composed of about twenty children whose ages range from three to seven, and when the child is graduated from the kindergarten, his education has included first-grade studies. The theory behind this type of arrangement is that the older children gradually learn responsibility toward the younger children and function as "senior counselors." After kindergarten, the former infant enters the second grade, and gets eleven more years of schooling. Thus, at age eighteen, he has acquired the equivalent of a high school education and has become a full-fledged member of the kibbutz.

During this whole period, he sleeps in the houses that are built specifically for him, with children of his own age. His parents' living quarters are situated from fifty to two hundred yards away from him. At night, two women circulate among the various children's houses from 10:00 P.M. to 6.00 A.M., see to it that the children are covered warmly and that they are not crying. In emergencies, they call a parent or doctor.

The children all rise in the morning at the same time and

have a free play period before breakfast. After breakfast, there is usually an organized group activity supervised by the nursery teacher or the nurse, its nature depending upon the age of the children. These activities are diverse, including games, art, drawing, dancing, singing, and sculpting, listening to stories told or read by the nursery teacher, hikes into the fields, or tours through the animal barns.

The morning is broken up by a mid-morning snack, after which there is either a free play period or a continuation of the organized activity. After lunch all the children must nap or rest for approximately two hours. When they waken from their naps they change into their "good clothes," are given a snack, and spend the rest of the afternoon in either free or organized play. As in the case of the other two meals, supper is a communal meal, and after supper the parents arrive to take their children to their rooms.

Children spend approximately two hours with their parents, who accompany them to their dormitories when it is time to return. Before going to bed the children almost invariably receive a shower, in addition to showers they may receive during the day, after which they are tucked into bed by their nurse, who usually tells them a story or sings a song before turning out the lights. The children are then left alone until the following morning, except for a periodic check during the night by the night watchman of the children's dormitories.

It should be pointed out that boys and girls experience few differences based on sex in their daily routine of living. They sleep in the same room, and may use the same showers and toilets. Moreover few, if any, differences are to be discerned in their games.

From the earliest age on, the children learn to interact with little or no adult supervision. If a child is afraid at night, or becomes ill, his companions take care of him: play with him, talk to him, bring him water, and in general reassure him. Having intimately shared his experiences, they know what he is likely to be afraid of; and the anxious child, trusting his comrades, will confide in them.

In a very short while, the child ceases to wake up afraid in the middle of the night, so absolutely secure does he feel with the other children. Group living makes it possible for the kibbutz child to enjoy more of that inner security which we put so much stress on, but which many middle-class infants, alone with their anxieties in their own rooms, fail to find.

Kibbutz children are actually much closer to their parents in some ways than most children, if not to their parents as persons, then as members of the community. It is the kibbutz which is central to all learning, formal and informal, in the children's village. From the toddlers' school on, the children take daily hikes to visit their parents at work. At the machine shops, the barns, the olive groves, the children are stopped by adults, talked to, joked with, praised, perhaps asked to lend a hand.

Thus the child is made to feel a welcome and important part of his father's and mother's occupational activities, and those of the whole community, an experience which most North American children would probably envy. So, too, all big communal events in the kibbutz, such as holiday celebrations, are related to work that parents and children both have a part in, such as the festival of the first fruits, arbor day, or the harvest festival.

It is apparent that the significant persons in the child's life, in addition to his parents, whose roles have already been discussed, are his nurses, nursery and kindergarten teachers, and his group.[13] If only because he spends most of his time with them, a child's nurses and teachers are parental surrogates in almost every sense of the term. They care for almost all his physical desires and needs. They feed, bathe, and clothe him, and nurse him when he is ill.

They rear him and, hence, care for many of his social needs. Most of the child's knowledge of his physical environment, his skills, and his knowledge of his own kibbutz culture, including its values, behavior patterns, and techniques, are taught him by these women. Finally, since they are for him psychologically significant persons, they are of great importance for his emotional development.

The nurses and nursery teachers institute most of his discipline, impose upon him most of his restrictions, teach him and all the while reward and punish him, express approval and disapproval, give affection and withhold affection.

The other group of significant persons in the child's life is his own group of peers. Almost all the child's daily activities, his experiences, and his belongings are shared either voluntarily or under compulsion with his own age group. It is little wonder, therefore, that the children are obviously ambivalent toward each other. It is exciting to share experiences, but it is frustrating to share one's beloved nurse or the only toy auto in the dormitory, or the only blue book trimmed in yellow.

The sharing of the latter objects is usually motivated only by adult compulsion or persuasion, and leads to frequent and intense fighting and quarreling within his group. This in turn intensifies the child's relationship to his parent, the only object he need not share unless he has a sibling. But it is the sharing of experience that accounts for the desire of the children to return to the dormitory in the evening, and the great enthusiasm with which they greet their fellows as they enter. Parents are fine for so long, but after that one wants one's friends—this seems to be the attitude of the children.

At about four years the child enters upon another important change—kindergarten. This involves moving into a new building, acquiring a new nurse and a nursery teacher, and enlarging the group of children. The enlarged group will remain together until its members enter high school.

After spending a year or two in the kindergarten, the group passes into the "Transitional Class," where for one year the child receives formal intellectual training before moving into the grammar school. School marks are an important transition in the life of kibbutz children; it is the beginning of their serious intellectual training, it expands their interactional group—more children and of different age levels—and it introduces them into formal responsibility and work.

Instruction in the school, which is based almost entirely on the project method, is conducted in an informal manner. Children have a voice in choosing the curriculum. There are neither exams nor grades, and passing is automatic—no one fails.

At the completion of the sixth grade, at the age of twelve, the children graduate into the combined junior-senior high school. This is also an important transition in their lives, for three reasons: (1) The other children for the first time encounter important male figures other than their fathers, because teachers now are primarily males. (2) The group splits up and the children form new groups comprised of children from the cities as well as from their own kibbutz and from other kibbutzim. (3) The children begin to work in the kibbutz economy from one and one-half to three hours, depending on their age.

The high school curriculum reflects the self-image as a socialist society of farmer intellectuals. There is practically no vocational or home economics influence in the entire curriculum. The emphasis, instead, is on humanities, sciences, and arts with much emphasis on the social implications of knowledge.[14]

Although the formal education of the average member of the kibbutz may not include college training, the intellectual level of the kibbutz is high, and literature, art, and science are greatly appreciated. Intellectual qualities besides work productivity are not supported, because they are regarded as a hindrance to the economic productivity of the kibbutz.

To the obvious criticism that children should not be separated from their mothers as they are in the kibbutz, there are two convincing answers. First, with the exception of a very few cases almost invariably occurring among children entering the kibbutz at an advanced age, no bad effects have been observed, while, on the contrary, many good ones have come about. Second, the well-to-do mother in private life habitually hands over the children to the care of nurses from the earliest age and usually sees them only at prearranged periods when she and they are at leisure; this is precisely what happens in the kibbutz, whose children are, in fact, treated just like those of the wealthy.[15]

This is true in the material sense, too. Although as far as the adult members are concerned the kibbutz must limit the standard of goods and services, practically nothing is denied to the children, who are the pledge of the future on whom depends the fate of the kibbutz society. Consequently, the expenditure on the housing, clothing, feeding, and care of the children is far in excess of adult standards and is not infrequently increased at the expense of all other budget items.

For children, the kibbutz is, in any case, a Paradise; supervised by expert nurses, the children spend their early years playing and learning in interesting and pleasant rural surroundings. It is not surprising that kibbutz children are known throughout the land as prime specimens of Israeli youth.

This is not to say that there are not a good many difficulties in connection with their upbringing, as in the case of children everywhere—difficulties both psychological and physical, requiring special attention.[16] Cooperation among parents, nurses, teachers, and the doctor is easier and closer in the kibbutz than it can ever be outside. There is no difficulty in making special arrangements suggested by experts. Instead of the limited resources of the individual family, the much larger economic capacity of the whole kibbutz stands behind each child and parent. Mothers whose children need them for extra care are immediately granted the necessary time off their daily work. Although the kibbutz subscribes to the principle that it does more harm than good for parents to interfere too frequently with the nurses' work, the children's houses are, in practice, always open to parents.[17]

There is no conclusive scientific evidence, to my knowledge, of the superiority of one system over the other. No all-embracing scientific study has been made of the kibbutz children. From a kibbutz point of view what is known about the second and third kibbutz generations is decidedly encouraging. Most of the new generation have decided to remain in the kibbutz, and in many cases have already taken over actual operation of the community. Less overtly intellectual, less prone to casuistic discussion than its parents, the second generation was for a long time a disappointment to its elders. The Israeli War of Independence, however, in which kibbutz children played a major role, established their position of leadership within the kibbutz movement. Many of those who were killed left a rich literature of memoirs, diaries, and other writings, much to the surprise of the elders, who had not realized that their farmer children were capable of this type of self-expression.

Educators both in and outside the kibbutz agree that kibbutz children, as a result of the emphasis on modern educational techniques and the cultural environment in general, are more alert, sensitive, and talent-conscious than the average run of farm children elsewhere. They charge, however, that they are also overprotected and spoiled as a result of the very same factors.

Kibbutz children develop a feeling that the whole community revolves about them. They receive the best housing, the best food, and the best clothing, markedly superior to the quality of such services received by their parents. They are often oblivious to the financial difficulties in which the kibbutz may be involved.

Disciplining is difficult. If parents are to see their children only for several hours during the day, it is only the strong parent who will risk embittering these few hours by denying the children's wishes or by disciplining them.

Despite these factors, however, kibbutz children turn out surprisingly independent and capable of coping with adult problems. Young children, for example, learn to feed themselves in kibbutzim at an earlier age than do children in private homes. They are at home in all kinds of social situations. They are not dependent on their parents and they learn to make their own decisions. They are good workers. Leadership potential is spotted and developed. Alertness to group developments and awareness of other people and their problems become second nature. Childhood is a happy experience and the loyalty to the kibbutz which is developed is not only loyalty to ideas but loyalty to a specific home of which the child feels an integral and accepted part. When the time comes, the eighteen-year-old feels no qualms about stepping into the adult life of the community, assuming responsibility for large sections of its work. He is familiar, too, with the inner workings of the country as a whole, having experienced, ever since he can remember, the intimate relationship between his parents and the kibbutz generally and Zionist and Israeli affairs.

American psychologists have studied the kibbutz children in comparison with nonkibbutz children in Israel. Part of their studies of ten-year-olds and seventeen-year-olds dealt with attitudes of children toward parents. They found that, in the first place, despite the fact that the kibbutz children do not live "at home" with their parents and siblings as part of a tightly knit family unit, most of them showed positive attitudes toward their families. Such attitudes were clearly positive in more of the kibbutz children than in the nonkibbutz children. In addition, a kibbutz child tends to have a rather strong identification with his family and a tendency to feel that it is better than other families.

These trends are not outstanding, but at least the family unit appears to be a rather meaningful concept to the kibbutz child, though it does not exist as an economic unit or as the outstanding socializing agent in the life of the child. A similar trend shows up with respect to attitudes toward individual parents. Kibbutz children have at least as much favorable regard for their parents as do nonkibbutz children, according to results of these studies on ten-year-olds. Perhaps the nurses and teachers, in carrying out most of the discipline and directing the socialization of the child, drain off onto themselves whatever hostility and ambivalence arise in the children as a reaction to the frustrations of training. This explanation has also been suggested by other observers, who have pointed out that the parents in the kibbutz, because of the limited time that they spend with their children, are very permissive and indulgent—like grandparents.

Related to the attitudes toward family and parents is the phenomenon of sibling rivalry, which looms importantly in the atmosphere of the ordinary family. The limited information available points in the direction of rare occurrences of intense sibling rivalry among kibbutz children. From a very early age, the kibbutz child is reared with a group of like-age but biologically unrelated "siblings." He is used to having them around, having lived and shared with them from the very beginning of his existence. The experience of having to share, therefore, is less traumatic than with the child of an ordinary family when a new sibling "appears" on the scene. Among the kibbutz children, whatever rivalry may have been present in the peer unit in infancy has long since been worked out in the daily interaction in which sharing and cooperating are positive dicta and principles. Some carryover of the resulting attitudes into the biological family is inevitable.

In the ordinary family, children usually identify strongly with the parent of their own sex. Boys imitate their fathers and want to be like them; girls want to be like their mothers. The parents are the nearest models and the closest ones emotionally. In the kibbutz, however, the situation is much more complex. There are *several* significant figures in the life of the child—the parent, the nurse, the teacher and the peers. The nurse, teacher, and peers are frequently, and over longer periods of time, much nearer to the child than are the parents.

Kibbutz-reared adolescents (seventeen-year-olds) were compared, in a number of dimensions, with a group of non-kibbutz high school youngsters of the same age.

The intellectual advantage of the kibbutz children seems to be maintained in adolescence. In written material, the adolescents of the kibbutz show greater range and complexity of ideas. They also show more interest in education and intellectual pursuits than do their peers of the ordinary farm families. Their interest in education and self-improvement seems in a way to compensate for the absence of long-range occupational goals.

Despite a great amount of evasiveness—common in the investigation of adolescents—the data on seventeen-year-olds also indicate the trend, shown among the ten-year-olds, regarding attitudes toward family and parental figures. The attitudes of the kibbutz adolescents are at least as frequently positive as—and in some instances more so than—those of the nonkibbutz adolescents. There do not seem to be any serious obstacles to the maintenance of such relationships and attitudes throughout the developmental period.

Another area on which some material emerged concerns sexuality. The kibbutz adolescent seems to reflect a much stricter, almost rigid, code with regard to sex than does the nonkibbutz adolescent. For the kibbutz seventeen-year-old having complete sex relations before marriage is unthinkable—"it would ruin one's life." He rejects the idea with greater scorn and finality, generally, than does the nonkibbutz boy or girl. Perhaps the close interaction between the sexes in the living quarters in the kibbutz, their continuous physical proximity, dictates the use of a more powerful regulation of sexual behavior.

In many ways the relations of parents and children are simpler in the kibbutz than in normal family life. The mother does not have the strain of having to get on with her household duties while responding constantly to all the demands of a young child, attending to his toilet-training and keeping him out of mischief, and she thus avoids a good deal of conflict and frayed temper. Nor are her evenings burdened with housework. She turns to the child gladly when work is done and she is free to devote herself to him. The father also gets home from work between 5 and 6 P.M. to find his wife calm and at leisure, with no bustle of getting a meal and putting the children to bed. He has had his main meal at midday and can get a snack at the communal dining hall, postponing his evening meal till after his hour or two with the children. By this time the little ones are in bed, the one apparent disadvantage in the system being that the older children often seem rather forlorn and at loose ends while the parents are having their evening meal.

It is also of great significance that the mother is no responsible for toilet-training, and the parents in fact have little responsibility for training in general. This reduces the ambivalent tensions in the parent-child relationship to which we are accustomed in Western communities, since the mother is not the source of frustration and the parents are not the chosen instruments of society for imposing its demands on the children. They are free to be only the good parents, except for the minority whose personal problems do not permit them to find satisfaction in this role. The advantages of this situation are seen in adolescence, when the relations between parents and children appear to be much less conflicting than we expect in Western communities, and it probably also has something to do with the fact that the majority of kibbutz children were eager to continue the communal way of life and only a few tended to break away.

Something like two hundred or so kibbutzim care for their children in the manner we have described. In recent years, Gesher Haziv, a kibbutz that was founded largely by North American settlers, along with some other kibbutzim, has adopted the system of children sleeping in rooms adjoining those of their parents.[18]

For the past few years, a group in Kfar Blum, another kibbutz, has agitated long and assiduously for the adoption of such a system. Its most vocal advocates were people from the United States. Thus, while there was some basis to the thought that the kibbutz was split along lines of national origin, the issue really cut across them.

The arguments for the change ran something like this: first, it was alleged that it is more natural for the children to sleep near their parents. Then it was said that the night care of the children was hopelessly inadequate. There were many instances where a child cried for a long time before the night-watch attendant came to his aid. On psychological grounds, it was argued that children between the ages of two and five were asocial creatures and needed to have a place where they could get away from their fellows. Instances of bed-wetting and thumb-sucking were cited as evidence of the insecurity of the children. It was suggested that the children could be watched more carefully by a mother who puts her children to bed at home than by one who puts them to bed in a children's house. Parents who have three or more children, it was pointed out, have to go to three or more different houses to put their children to bed. This involves quite a bit of physical exertion and discomfort, especially in the rainy season. Bedding the youngsters under one roof would make life easier. It was indicated that the children's houses, at bedtime, are often noisy, whereas quiet at this hour is desirable for growing children. Another allegation was that the new method would make the mother happier. These, in substance, were the arguments for the change.

The defenders of the status quo also had an arsenal of arguments. They felt, as do conservatives the world over, that an institution as widely accepted as the kibbutz system for the sleeping of children must have intrinsic merit apart from the forces of inertia. They argued that the psychological argument was fallacious, inasmuch as the fundamental security or insecurity of the child was determined by the stability of the family unit, especially that of the parents;

that while the present system might not be the best possible for the child at each stage of his development, yet it offered no insuperable emotional difficulties to the child rooted in a happy family. It was argued that if the children slept in the parents' quarters, the parents would have to stay home with the crying babies and would be prevented from attending meetings and social and cultural events. The allegation was made that the whole plan, as suggested, was nothing more than an elaborate rationalization to enable the individual to return to the familiar social and familial patterns that he knew in Europe. Further, the execution of such a plan at Kfar Blum would entail an investment of tens or hundreds of thousands of Israeli pounds, which the economy could ill afford. The final argument was that kibbutz children, raised under the existing system, had managed to develop into a generation of youth of whom one could be proud.

The kibbutz parents are richly rewarded. From all descriptions the children turn into exceptionally courageous, self-reliant, secure, unneurotic, and deeply committed adults who find their self-realization in work and in marriage. They marry in their early twenties and soon have children who in turn are brought up in the communal nurseries and schools. There are few (almost no) divorces and adultery is rare and severely censured. The marriages are not only stable, but by North American standards exceptionally satisfactory; marriage is, in fact, the most important and intimate relationship of kibbutz adults.

The adults are genuinely fond of children, their own as well as others, and this interest in children develops early. Young girls in kindergarten often assist their mothers who are nurses in younger children's houses; and girls in the grammar school frequently supervise the play of nursery children. Many of the high school girls also work in the various nurseries as afternoon relief nurses and, with rare exceptions, they are warm, loving, and intelligent workers. Later, as parents, they are warm and affectionate with their children, but relaxed and unanxious. Yet they have no desire to return to raising them privately at home. They are well satisfied with the way they themselves were communally reared. Not having experienced deep emotional attachment to parents as the core of their own development, and presently having a full life of their own, they do not feel they are missing anything by being parted from their children. Without doubt or hesitation, parents place their newborn infants in the autonomous children's society.

## *The Aged in the Kibbutz*[19]

The collectives have solved many of the basic and most persistent problems of aging. Aging members enjoy full economic security. Communal services take care of them in case of ill health or infirmity. Retirement from work is gradual and does not entail an abrupt and complete break from work routines. Aging members are not cut off from community life. Social participation serves as an alternative avenue of activity and provides respected substitute functions. In many cases it compensates the aging member for his gradual loss of competence and status in the occupational sphere. What is most important, grownup children are expected to live in the community founded by their parents. Parents are able to maintain close and constant relations with their children without losing their independence. Elderly and old people are thus spared much of the insecurity and isolation, the futile inactivity and dependence entailed in aging.

Parents of kibbutz members who decide to join their children in the kibbutz are free to do so. This is done in various ways and there are certain conditions attached. If the parents are still young and physically fit and can join in their own right, they are authorized to apply for membership. If they are old and cannot support themselves in the city and have no other children outside the kibbutz, the kibbutz allows them to come and live there. They are given an apartment and benefit from all the kibbutz services, like any member. But if the parents have children outside the kibbutz, the latter are bound to participate in their parents' maintenance as decided after discussion with the kibbutz authorities. Otherwise parents' children in the kibbutz participate in the maintenance of their parents in town, the kibbutz allocating the requisite sum. Parents in the kibbutz are, like members, assured of their livelihood and all necessary care and help till the end of their lives. They take part in the work of the kibbutz wherever and as long as they can.

## *The Kibbutz Today*

Quite a few changes have overtaken most of the kibbutzim since their beginning sixty years ago. The descriptions of kibbutz life mirror these innovations.[20] With Israel's increased industrialization and urbanization[21] the face of the kibbutz has also been altered. A description of today's kibbutz by Shlomo Tamir[22] will give the reader some idea of these changes. He points out that each kibbutz family has an apartment of two rooms, a shower and toilet, a kitchenette and a balcony. Furniture is of the best quality—beds with good mattresses and covered in attractive woven materials, sofas, armchairs, bright curtains, carpets, bookshelves, a radio, and so on. The kitchenette is fitted with an electric kettle, a small electric refrigerator, a cabinet for dishes, and a wonder-pot for baking cakes. Thus the family can enjoy a cup of tea or coffee and light refreshments in its own rooms. It should be borne in mind that the apartment is designed as a place in which the couple sleeps, rests, and spends the evening hours with the children. The kibbutz has a large dining room where main meals are taken, and the children live in their own quarters. There is a large laundry and clothes room where all washing, ironing, and mending is done. The kibbutz also has a large library, a reading room, a club for evening entertainment, sports grounds, a swimming pool, and other amenities. Each apartment is surrounded by lawns and fruit trees which the family itself tends during its free time and whose fruits are for its own use.

Today, as Tamir continues, the kitchens and dining rooms are fitted with every amenity. The kitchens are equipped with gas, electric and steam stoves and ovens, room for preparing food, storerooms for fruit, vegetables, flour, cereals, sugar, spices, etc. There are cold-storage facilities for meat and other perishables. The dining room is bright and airy, furnished with tables and comfortable chairs, and attractive curtains cover the windows. Food is served on wagons in special containers which keep it hot or cold according to the type of dish. There is a permanent kitchen and dining room staff who attend various courses on nutrition and cooking, service, table arrangement, and other related topics. Special dishes are prepared for those on salt- or sugar-free diets or who cannot eat fried foods. The kitchen staff aims to make it possible for each one to eat according to his taste and his state of health.[23]

The economics of the kibbutzim have also been drastically changed. In 121 of the 235 kibbutzim, there are some 180 manufacturing and industrial plants and rest homes. They are organized within the Kibbutz Industries Association, and their annual production totaled some 280 million Israeli pounds (app. $70 million). About 7,000 workers were employed in these enterprises.

There are also regional projects in various parts of the country, and the kibbutzim have an important share in them both regarding the number of workers and the amount of capital they provide. Examples of these are cotton-ginning plants, fruit-ripening installations, packing sheds, abattoirs, olive-pickling factories, food-processing and -canning plants, cold-storage installations, transport cooperatives, etc. Some 4,000 workers are employed in these enterprises. Annual production is around 230 million Israeli pounds (app. $57.5 million).

These figures do not include workshops, plants, and machinery for internal kibbutz use, such as the local garage, metal workshop, shoemaker, sewing workshop, tinsmith, etc.

During the last few years, a newly founded body called the Kibbutz Movement Alliance has been increasingly active. The Kibbutz Movement Alliance represents the entire kibbutz movement in many fields: with government and Histadrut[24] institutions in questions like prices of produce, new settlements, kibbutz constitutions, and various social practices. Teachers' seminars, technical education institutions, education facilities for retarded or handicapped children, higher education projects and training for directors of economic enterprises are jointly organized and maintained. There are also joint cultural projects such as the kibbutz theater, orchestras and choirs, art exhibitions, hobby circles, etc.

The Kibbutz Industries Association constitutes an important section of the Kibbutz Movement Alliance. Every kibbutz movement runs industrial enterprises of its own. They are all organized together in this association, which is an official organ somewhat similar to a share company. The association plans new enterprises, examines projects, establishes contact between industries and technological institutions, arranges study courses for professional and administrative personnel. The association's various branches work together in the marketing of its industrial products in Israel and abroad, in purchasing spare parts, and supplying technical and scientific advice. The Kibbutz Movement Alliance progressively broadens its field of activity.

## *Threats to the System of the Kibbutz*

Saadia Gelb, a kibbutznik (member of a kibbutz) has recently discussed the changes which face the kibbutzim today.[25] Some of the controversial reasons she explains are as follows.

There is the obvious problem of politico-economic beliefs. Aggressive entrepreneurs and business leaders are not interested in a successful socialist community. Small, ineffective communes are spectacular and charming, but strong ones can be a threat to capitalistic enterprise. Conversely, labor, as personified by its theoreticians and functionaries, is intensely interested in an alternative to the pure profit system.

A second, less important but equally forceful reason for the controversy is rooted in history. When the kibbutz was a major means of colonizing and protecting outlying areas, Zionist propagandists built up an image of the halutz superman. Subsequent methods of developing and defending the country coupled with true or assumed sophistication conspired to deflate this image, and the pendulum of public opinion swung to the other extreme.

The third factor stems from a specific Israeli reality. Despite a veneer of cynicism, the majority of Israeli youth is partriotic and idealistic, believing in brotherhood, social responsibility, and national service. Thousands of adolescents dream of settling the Negev. Many go through preliminary steps—including a few years of actual kibbutz membership. When, later, they choose other modes of life, they are beset by guilt feelings, feelings of desertion. A frequent adjustment is made by the statement: the kibbutz is a wonderful place, but not for me. Another outlet is denigration or vilification of the kibbutz system.

The kibbutz movement has faced three major threats to its survival, and appears to be facing a fourth at the present time. The first was the emergence of the state itself. Suddenly, the dream came true, a Jewish state was created. National functions, previously carried out by volunteers, were assumed by a friendly government. Kibbutz morale was at low ebb. Individuals who had devoted their lives to society left the kibbutzim for government ministries and embassies or for other exciting ventures. Many who remained were beset by doubts—were they still serving a vital function, or was their mission completed?

It took several years for the movement to find its balance and to discover that whereas the kibbutz had served as an instrument for nationhood, it was not, in itself, merely a means but also an end. Sober self-examination showed that maintaining a rural community founded on mutual aid, the dignity of labor, cooperation, complete democracy, intellectual awareness, social responsibility, and national discipline is no minor matter. Furthermore, it became evident that military functions in border defense, educational functions in youth training, and cultural functions in grass-roots development have not ceased. Self-confidence returned to the kibbutznik.

German reparations to individual sufferers were paid to many members of kibbutzim, large numbers of whom could not withstand the temptation of private acquisition and left for the cities. The movement faced the problem nervously. It met the issue with a variety of solutions: from pooling reparations monies for public buildings to setting up special equalization funds. The crisis was weathered with a remarkably small residue of bitterness.

The third crisis-laden impact was economic. Agriculture,

which at first represented the essence of economic survival, became secondary as increasing numbers of newcomers required industrialization for their economic absorption. Suddenly, the kibbutz was dethroned from the pinnacle. A double defense evolved. Agriculture became increasingly mechanized, efficient and competitive; industry was brought into the kibbutz. Of the 235 existing kibbutzim, more than half already have some kind of workshop or factory, the others are searching actively to develop one.

Of far greater importance to kibbutzim is the present issue of academic standards. For the first time in its history the kibbutz is threatened, not physically but ideologically, for the children alone assure its survival. During its half-century of existence the kibbutz attracted students and intellectuals in sufficient numbers to be on an educational and cultural par with the best in the country. As the old generation departs and as the prevailing academic facilities in Israel increase, the balance slowly swings against the kibbutz. Taken as a whole, comparison is still favorable, since the kibbutz provides universal high school education while the national average is considerably less.

The public image of the kibbutz has changed. The automatic reaction in issues of national concern is no longer "What does the kibbutz think?" Its opinion is taken seriously, but only as one segment of society. Much of the loss of prestige may be attributed to internal differences, schisms, and political involvement. The mixture of conscience and practical politics is detrimental to both.

In many ways normalcy has set in. People come and people leave without upsetting either structure or morale. There are a large number of kibbutzim whose population has not fluctuated significantly. Some grow in numbers, others decline. Generally one can categorize those in existence for more than thirty years as having reached a point of stability. The groups established fifteen to twenty-five years ago are subject to fluctuation and display the largest individual differences. Kibbutzim less than fifteen years old suffer from a manpower shortage and have not reached their natural levels. Altogether, there is a constant net increase reflecting growth—but it is not in keeping with Israel's growth.

Maturity and economic progress have produced changes in habits. With rare exceptions, the one-dish, one-spoon meal is gone. Adequate cutlery and dishes, more balanced diets, and pleasant surroundings are rapidly becoming universal. More attention is paid to beauty, comfort, and recreation. Rouge and lipstick are not acceptable, but skin care, massage, and even hair-tinting are in vogue. Characteristic vacation tours during which old and young are herded into commercial trucks for the sake of economy have decreased in number. The older population is resorting to passenger buses. Soccer, basketball, and volleyball teams participate in national leagues, albeit no work time is allotted for sports. The number of concerts and theater performances attended are on the rise as budgets for "culture" spiral upward.

### *Family Changes*

A closer look at kibbutz life today reveals that in some ways the life of the kibbutz has reached a crisis. Some of the indications of the crisis are that there are private tensions due to the lack of privacy, there are increasing resignations from the kibbutz, more people find jobs in the cities and find the bright lights of the cities more glamorous than the rural setting of the kibbutz. Last but not least has been the change among many women in the kibbutz. They cause much of the tension because some are unhappy in their role. They do not feel that they have really been emancipated because of the strenuous physical life, long hours, and frustration in the maternal role. Many mothers have not reconciled themselves to the system of collective education and the resultant separation from their children. This separation is a profoundly frustrating experience and the mothers view it as another deprivation of their feminine prerogatives. Because the women are unhappy in their roles, they have no desire to assume social responsibility. They wish to find happiness in their private lives and consequently often resent the time which their spouses devote to these activities. Since they are insecure in their sexual roles, they feel a need for more and nicer clothes.

It is so easy to criticize a family life pattern different from our own, since we have really not experienced the kibbutz life from infancy. To the kibbutz family, our family pattern may be archaic.

The kibbutz was formed during the pioneering days of the land of Israel, when the land had to be rebuilt out of swamps, deserts, and barren fields. It was a time of challenge, endurance, and human sacrifice. These days called for new approaches to family living and so the kibbutz family was born.

Today, when the state of Israel has emerged from the early founding days into a growing industrial urban society, the winds of change have slowly touched the lives of the kibbutz society. Within the next twenty-five years, we may see a complete change in the kibbutz family system, to a way of life which approximates our own type of family. In the kibbutz, Utopia may not have been gained, but neither has Paradise been lost.[26]

NOTES

1. Ministry of Foreign Affairs, *Facts about Israel 1970* (Jerusalem, 1970).
2. For a warm and human account of the founding of Degania (Cornflower), see: Joseph Baratz, *A Village by the Jordan* (London: Harrill Press, 1954).
3. Other main types of settlements are:
   (a) *Moshava* (plural: *moshavot*): originally an ordinary village based on private land ownership and private enterprise. Many moshavot have expanded into towns or become partly urbanized.
   (b) *Moshav Ovdim* (plural: *moshvei ovdim*): workers' cooperative smallholders' settlement, based on principles of mutual aid and equality of opportunity. Each member has a farm worked by himself and his family, but produce is sold, and supplies and equipment are bought, through central cooperatives. Some farm machinery is owned by the settlement as a whole. The general assembly elects a council, which approves all transfers of farms and acceptances of new members.
   The moshav ovdim is purely agricultural, and its population ranges from 100 to 1,000. The first was Nahalal, established in 1921.
   (c) *Moshav* (plural: *moshavim*): smallholders' settlement, in

many ways resembling the moshav ovdim, but without its rigid ideology. The moshavim are often referred to as "middle-class" settlements. There is no standard type, but they are predominantly agricultural. Most are organized in an Agricultural Union. The first and largest, Ramot Hashavin, set up in 1933 by immigrants from Germany, has a population of about 500.

(d) *The Moshav Shitufi* (plural: *moshavim shitufiim*): is based on collective economy and ownership (as in the kibbutz), but each family has its own house and is responsible for its own cooking, laundry, and child care (as in the moshav ovdim). Work and pay are adjusted to individual circumstances. Like the kibbutz, it tends to develop industry in addition to agriculture. Populations range from 60 to 300. The first moshav shitufi was Kfar Hittin, established in 1936.

For a description of these settlements and their structures, see: L. Feitelberg, Moledeth B'nai Brith: *A New Adventure in Living* (Jerusalem: Zionist Organization Youth Department, 1949). Aron Gertz, *The Social Structure of Jewish Settlement in Palestine* (Jerusalem: Zionist Organization Youth Department, 1947). Henrik E. Infield, *Co-operative Living in Palestine* (New York: Dryden Press, 1944). E. Orni, *Forms of Settlement* (Jerusalem: Jewish National Fund, 1960). N. Viteles, "Co-operative Agricultural Settlements in Israel," *Sociology and Social Research*, 39 (January–February 1955), 171–176.

4. For a contrast of Eastern European Jewish life and the kibbutz, see: S. Diamond, "Kibbutz and Shtetl: The History of an Idea," *Social Problems*, 5 (Fall, 1957), 68–79; and for Jewish family life in the shtetl, see: Mark Zborowski and Elizabeth Herzog, *Life Is with People* (New York: International Universities Press, 1952).
5. For historical documentation of the development of the kibbutz movement, see: Avram C. Ben-Yosef, *The Purest Democracy in the World* (New York: Herzl Press, 1963). D. H. Darin Drapkin, *The Other Society* (London: Victor Gollancz, 1962). E. Tauber, *Moulding Society to Man* (New York: Bloch Publishing, 1955). Mitchell Viteles, *The Evolution of the Kibbutz Movement* (London: Valentine Mitchell, 1967).
6. For a description of the organizational structure of the kibbutz, see: Eva Rosenfeld, "Social Stratification in a 'Classless' Society," *American Sociological Review*, 16 (December, 1951), 766–774. Richard D. Schwartz, "Democracy and Collectivism in the Kibbutz," *Social Problems*, 5 (Fall, 1957), 137–147. Richard D. Schwartz, "Functional Alternatives to Inequality," *American Sociological Review*, 20 (August, 1955), 424–430.
7. For descriptions of family life in the kibbutz, see: Dorothy

Blitsten, *The World of the Family* (New York: Random House, 1963), pp. 221–251. William F. Kenkel, *The Family in Perspective* (New York: Appleton-Century-Crofts, 1960), pp. 165–183. Stuart A. Queen and Robert W. Habenstein, *The Family in Various Cultures* (Philadelphia: Lippincott, 1967), pp. 116–137. M. E. Spiro, *Kibbutz: Venture in Utopia* (Cambridge, Mass.: Harvard University Press, 1956). Garber Yonina Talmon, "The Family in Israel," *Marriage and Family Living*, 16 (November, 1954), 343–349. Garber Yonina Talmon, "Social Structure and Family Size," *Human Relations*, 12 (May, 1959), 121–146. Garber Yonina Talmon, "Social Change and Family Structure," *International Social Science Journal*, 14 (July, 1962), 468–487. Garber Yonina Talmon, "The Case of Israel," in Rose Laub Coser (ed.), *The Family, Its Structures and Functions* (New York: St. Martin's Press, 1964), pp. 582–617. Garber Yonina Talmon, "The Family in Revolutionary Movement: The Case of the Kibbutz in Israel," in M. F. Nimkoff (ed.), *Comparative Family Systems* (Boston: Houghton Mifflin, 1965), pp. 259–287.

8. For a discussion of mate selection in the kibbutz, see: Garber Yonina Talmon, "Mate Selection in Collective Settlements," *American Sociological Review*, 29 (August, 1964), 491–508.
9. For an analysis of the socialization and child-rearing patterns, see: R. Bar-Yoseph, "The Patterns of Early Socialization in the Collective Settlements in Israel," *Human Relations*, 12 (November, 1959), 345–360. Larry D. Barnett, "The Kibbutz as a Child Rearing System: A Review of the Literature," *Journal of Marriage and the Family*, 27 (August, 1965), 348–349. H. Faigin, "Social Behavior of Young Children in the Kibbutz," *Journal of Abnormal Social Psychology*, 56 (1958), 117–129. Hava B. Gewirtz and Jacob L. Gewirtz, "Visiting and Caretaking Patterns for Kibbutz Infants: Age and Sex Trends," *American Journal of Orthopsychiatry*, 38 (April, 1968), 427–443. Elizabeth Irvine, "Observations on the Aims and Methods of Child Rearing in Communal Settlements in Israel," *Human Relations*, 5 (August, 1952), 247–275. M. E. Spiro, *Children of the Kibbutz* (Cambridge, Mass.: Harvard University Press, 1958). Marylin Winograd, "The Development of the Young Child in a Collective Settlement," *American Journal of Orthopsychiatry*, 28 (July, 1958), 557–562.
10. The question whether the kibbutz family is a nuclear family unit is discussed in: M. E. Spiro, "Is the Family Universal? The Israeli Case," *American Anthropologist*, 56 (October, 1954), 839–846. He points out in this paper that this type of family cannot be considered a family unit. However, in a later paper, see: M. E. Spiro, "Is the Family Universal? The Israeli Case," in Norman V. Bell and Ezra F. Vogel (eds.), *A Modern Introduction to the Family* (New York: Free Press, 1960), pp. 64–75. He changes his point of view and states that

the kibbutz family fits Murdock's account of the nuclear family. See: G. P. Murdock, *Social Structure* (New York: The Macmillan Co., 1949), p. 11.

11. For a discussion of education in the kibbutz, see: Bruno Bettelheim, "Does Communal Education Work?" *Commentary,* 33 (February, 1962), 117–126. Shmuel Golan, "Collective Education in a Kibbutz," *Psychiatry, Journal for the Study of Interpersonal Processes,* 22 (May, 1959), 167–177. A. I. Rabin, "Kibbutz Mothers View Collective Education," *American Journal of Orthopsychiatry,* 34 (January, 1964), 140–142. David Rapaport, "The Study of Kibbutz Education and Its Bearing on the Theory of Development," *American Journal of Orthopsychiatry,* 28 (July, 1958), 587–597. M. E. Spiro, "Education in a Communal Village in Israel," *American Journal of Orthopsychiatry,* 25 (April, 1955), 283–292.
12. For studies of infants in the kibbutz, see: J. L. Gewirtz, "The Course of Smiling by Groups of Israeli Infants in the First Eighteen Months of Life," *Scripta Hieroslymitana*: Studies in Psychology (Jerusalem: Hebrew University Press, 1965), pp. 9–58. J. L. Gewirtz, "The Course of Infant Smiling in Four Child-Rearing Environments in Israel," in B. M. Foss (ed.), *Determinants of Infant Behavior,* III (New York: John Wiley & Sons, 1965), pp. 205–260. A. I. Rabin, "Infants and Children under Conditions of 'Intermittent' Mothering in the Kibbutz," *American Journal of Orthopsychiatry,* 28 (July, 1958), 577–584.
13. For a description of group care in the kibbutz, see: Martin Wolins, "Political Orientation, Society Reality, and Child Welfare," *Social Service Review,* 38 (December, 1964), 429–442. Martin Wolins, "Another View of Group Care," *Child Welfare,* 44 (January, 1965), 10–18.
14. For a description of adolescents, see: A. I. Rabin, "Kibbutz Adolescents," *American Journal of Orthopsychiatry,* 31 (July, 1961), 493–504.
15. For some material on behavior research in the kibbutz, see: Shmuel Golan, "Behavior Research in Collective Settlements in Israel," *American Journal of Orthopsychiatry,* 28 (July, 1958), 549–556. A. I. Rabin, "The Israeli Kibbutz as a 'Laboratory' for Testing Psychodynamic Process," *Psychological Record,* 7 (1957), 111–115. Eva Rosenfeld, "The American Social Scientist in Israel: A Case Study in Role Conflict," *American Journal of Orthopsychiatry,* 28 (July, 1958), 563–571. Richard D. Schwartz, "Some Problems of Research In Israeli Settlements," *American Journal of Orthopsychiatry,* 28 (July, 1958), 572–576.
16. For clinical studies of kibbutz children, see: Gerald Caplan, "Clinical Observations on the Emotional Life of Children in the Communal Settlements in Israel," in *Problems of Infancy and Childhood* (New York: Josiah Macy Jr. Foundation,

1954), pp. 91–120. Mordecai Kaffman, "A Comparison of Psychopathology: Israeli Children from Kibbutz and from Urban Surroundings," *American Journal of Orthopsychiatry*, 35 (April, 1965), 509–520. Mordecai Kaffman, "Evaluation of Emotional Disturbance in 403 Israeli Kibbutz Children," *American Journal of Psychiatry*, 117 (February, 1961), 732–738. Shmuel Nagler, "Clinical Observations on Kibbutz Children," in Henry P. David (ed.), *International Trends in Mental Health* (New York: McGraw Hill, 1966), pp. 210–223. Peter B. Neubauer (ed.), *Children in Collectives* (Springfield, Ill.: Charles C. Thomas, 1965). A. I. Rabin, "Some Psychosexual Differences between Kibbutz and Non-Kibbutz Israeli Boys," *Journal of Projective Techniques*, 22 (1958), 328–332. A. I. Rabin, "Kibbutz Children—Research Findings to Date," *Children*, 5 (September–October, 1958), 179–184. A. I. Rabin, "Personality Study in Israeli Kibbutzim," in B. Kaplan (ed.), *Studying Personality Cross-Culturally* (Evanston, Ill.: Row, Peterson, 1961). A. I. Rabin, "Personality Maturity of Kibbutz and Non-Kibbutz Children as Reflected in Rorschach," *Journal of Projective Techniques*, 21 (June, 1957), 148–153. A. I. Rabin, *Growing Up in the Kibbutz* (New York: Springer Publishing, 1965).

17. For a discussion about parents, see: Howard Halpern, "Alienation from Parenthood in the Kibbutz and America," *Marriage and Family Living*, 24 (February, 1962), 42–46. A. I. Rabin, "Attitudes of Kibbutz Children to Family and Parents," *American Journal of Orthopsychiatry*, 29 (January, 1959), 172–179.
18. This account has been extracted from Edward I. Parsons, "Children of Kfar Blum," *Midstream* (Summer, 1959), 64–75.
19. For a study of the aged in the kibbutz, see: Garber Yonina Talmon, "Aging in Israel—A Planned Society," *American Journal of Sociology*, 67 (November, 1961), 284–296; and for a comparative study of first- and second-generation settlers in the kibbutzim, see: Solomon Rettig and Benjamin Pasamanick, "Some Observations on the Moral Ideology of First and Second Generation Collective and Non-Collective Settlers in Israel," *Social Problems*, 11 (Fall, 1963), 165–178.
20. For recent descriptions of kibbutz life, see: Gerda L. Cohen, "The Affluent Kibbutzim," *Commentary*, 28 (October, 1959), 292–298. Saadia Gelb, "The Kibbutz Today," *Reconstructionist*, 30 (April 17, 1964), 7–12. Moshe Kerem, *The Kibbutz* (Jerusalem: Israel Digest, No. 27, 1965). Gerda Luft, "The Kibbutz in Crisis," *Commentary*, 32 (October, 1961), 334–340. Shlomo Tamir, *Everday Life in the Kibbutz* (Jerusalem: Ahva Co-op Press, 1968). And for some comparisons of kibbutz life fourteen years ago, see: Boris Stern, *The Kibbutz That Was* (Washington, D.C.: Public Affairs Press, 1965). Murray Weingarten, *Life in a Kibbutz* (New York: The Reconstruction Press, 1955).

21. For a full discussion of Israel's growth, see: *Population Bulletin*, "Israel: Land of Promise and Perplexities," 21 (November, 1965), 102–134.
22. Shlomo Tamir, *Everyday Life in the Kibbutz* (Jerusalem: Ahva Co-op Press, 1968), pp. 8–10.
23. Shlomo Tamir, *ibid.*, p. 28.
24. The General Federation of Labor, usually known as the Histadrut (Hebrew for organization or association), is the largest labor organization in Israel. It was founded in 1920. A worker joins the Histadrut directly, as an individual, and not as a member of an affiliated union. Membership dues, which total between 3% and 4.5% of wages, cover all the Federation's trade union, health, and social services. When the Histadrut was founded it had less than 5,000 members out of a total Jewish population of almost 100,000. Its functions were, therefore, not simply to protect the workers' interests, but to create a working class by immigration and training, to build up industry and agriculture, to give the workers a livelihood, and to provide them with modern social services. Membership, including wives (who also have membership privileges), increased from 164,000 in 1947 to 780,000 in 1961, while the total of members with their families rose from 247,000 to 1,400,000, including over two-thirds of the Jewish population and 50,000 Arabs. Some other labor organizations are represented in the Histadrut's Trade Union Section, which thus covers almost 90% of all workers. For more details, see: *Facts about Israel 1970, op. cit.*
25. Saadia Gelb, *op. cit.*
26. Thanks are due to the Memorial Foundation for Jewish Culture for a grant to enable the author to complete this paper.

# 14

# Is Monogamy Outdated?

RUSTUM AND DELLA ROY

## *Monogamy: Where We Stand Today*

THE TOTAL INSTITUTION of marriage in American society is gravely ill. This statement does not apply to the millions of sound marriages where two people have found companionship, love, concern, and have brought up children in love. But it is necessary in 1970 to point to the need for *institutional* reforms, even when the personal or immediate environment may not appear to need it. Yet many refuse to think about the area as a whole because of personal involvement—either their marriage is so successful that they think the claims of disease exaggerated, or theirs is so shaky that all advice is a threat. Is the institution then so sick? For example:

> Year after year in the United States, marriage has been discussed in public and private session with undiminished confusion and increasing pessimism. Calamity always attracts attention, and in the United States the state of marriage is a calamity.

These are the words with which W. H. Lederer and D. Jackson open their new book *The Mirages of Marriage*. Vance Packard in *The Sexual Wilderness* summarizes the most recent major survey thus: "In other words, a marriage made in the United States in the late 1960's has about a 50:50 chance of remaining even nominally intact."

Clifford Adams concludes from an Identity Research Institute study of 600 couples that while numerically at 40 percent in this nation, and in some West Coast highly populated counties the *real* divorce rate is running at 70 percent, that in fact "75 percent of marriages are a 'bust.'" And Lederer and Jackson report that 80 percent of those interviewed had at some time seriously considered divorce. So much for the statistics. Qualitatively the picture painted by these and one hundred others is even bleaker but needs no repeating here.

There is no doubt then about the diagnosis of the sickness of marriage taken as a whole. Yet no person, group, magazine, or newspaper creates an awareness of the problems; no activist band takes up the cause to *do* something about it. Some years ago, we participated in a three-year-long group study and development of a sex ethic for contemporary Americans, and we found this same phenomenon: that serious group study and group work for change in the area of sex behavior is remarkably difficult and threatening, and hence rare. Thus we find an institution such as monogamous marriage enveloped by deterioration and decay, and unbelievably little is being done about it on either a theoretical basis or detailed pragmatic basis.

For this there is a second major reason: marriage as an institution is partly governed by warring churches, a society without a soul, a legal system designed for lawyers, and a helping system for psychiatrists, who almost by their very mode of operation in the marriage field guarantee its failure. Consequently, marriage is rapidly losing its schizophrenic mind, oscillating between tyrannical repression and equally tyrannical expression.

By the term "traditional monogamy," we refer to the public's association with the word, i.e., marriage to one person at a time, the centrality of the nuclear family, and the restriction of all overt sexual acts, nearly all sexually tinged relationships, and heterosexual relations of any depth to this one person before and after marriage, expectation of a lifetime contract, and a vivid sense of failure if termination is necessary. John Cuber and Peggy Harroff in *The Significant Americans* have called this "the monolithic code," and it is based on precepts from the Judaic and Christian traditions. All working societies are structured around such codes or ideals, no matter how far individuals may depart from the norms and whether or not they accept the source of such "ideals."

How does change in a code or ideal come about? When the proportion of the populace living in conflict with their own interpretation of the monolithic code, and "getting away with it," reaches nearly a majority, then *new* ideals must evolve for the social system to remain in equilibrium. We are convinced that although no *discontinuous* change in the ideals of a culture is possible, "traditional monogamy" as an ideal may be altered *in a continuous fashion* in order to respond to the needs of men and women today.

Traditional monogamy was *one* interpretation of the Judeo-Christian tradition. We are convinced that for widespread acceptability any *new* ideals must be interpretable in terms of Judeo-Christian humanism, the basic framework of mainstream "Americanism," and the most explicit humanism so far developed. Such an interpretation is neither difficult nor likely to encounter much resistance from the many other contemporary American humanisms which have not swung far from the parent Protestant humanism. But the importance of such an interpretation for "continental" middle-class America is crucial, as the tenor and very existence of the Nixon administration bring home to those who live in the more rarefied climes of East or West Coast. If a new monogamous ideal is to evolve, it must be acceptable to middle America, liberated, affluent, but waspish at heart.

## *Causes of the Crisis*

Social institutions are the products of particular social environments, and there must be a finite time lag when an institution appropriate for one situation survives into a new era in which the situation has changed drastically. It is clear that "traditional monogamy" is caught precisely in this "overlap" of two radically different situations. It is important to identify precisely the particular problem-causing elements of change in the environment.

*The sexual revolution has made it infinitely more difficult to retain monogamy's monopoly on sex*

We live in an eroticized environment which is profoundly affecting many institutions. The change toward greater permissiveness and its effect on the sexual climate can be summed up in the aphorism, "What was a temptation for the last generation is an opportunity for this." Underneath it all are the measurable, real physical changes: the advent of prosperity, mobility, and completely controlled conception.

Parallel to physical changes are vast social changes. The eroticization of our culture oozes from its every pore, so much so that it becomes essentially absurd to expect that all physical sexual expression for a fifty-year period will be confined to the marriage partner. Moreover, this eroticization escalator shows no sign of slowing down, and its effect on various institutions will be even more drastic in the future. Following are some illustrations.

The influence of literature, the arts, the media, and the press on the climate for any institution is profound, and marriage is no exception. Caught between the jaws of consumer economics in a free-enterprise system and the allegedly objective purveyors of accurate information (or culturally representative entertainment), human sexuality has become the most salable commodity of all. Perform, if you will, the following simple tests: examine the magazine fare available to tens of millions of Americans; spend a few hours browsing through *Look*, and *Life*, and try *Playboy*, work up to something like *Cosmopolitan*. If you are serious, visit a typical downtown bookshop in a big city and count the number of pictorial publications whose sole purpose is sexual titillation. Next try the paperbacks available to at least 100,000,000 Americans—in every drugstore: *Candy*, Henry Miller, *Fanny Hill*, the complaining Portnoy, valleys of dolls, and menchild in promised lands, carpetbaggers at airports, couples and groups. Does *one* speak of the beauty and wonder of uniting sex to marriage? Go see ten movies at random. Will *The Graduate*, *I Am Curious*, or *La Ronde* rail against sexual license? Thus the mass media have had a profound effect on the American people's marriage ideals. They especially confuse those to whom their "traditions," speaking through emasculated school, bewildered church, and confused home, still try to affirm a traditionally monogamous system. Yet some have mistakenly denied that there is a causal relation between the media and our rapidly changing value systems. Worst of all, very few of those who urge the freedom of access to more and more sexual stimuli work to legitimize, socially and ethically, a scheme for increased sexual outlets.

### *There is a vast increase in the number and variety of men-women contacts after marriage, and no guidelines are available for behavior in these new situations*

Of the sexual dilemmas which our present-day culture forces upon the "ailing" institution of traditional monogamy, premarital sexual questions now appear very minor. For all intents and purposes premarital sexual play (including the *possibility* of intercourse) has been absorbed into the social canon. We foresee in the immediate future a much more serious psychological quandary with respect to extra- or co-marital sexual relations of all levels of intensity. The conflict here is so basic and so little is being done to alleviate it that it is only surprising that it has not loomed larger already. Traditional monogamy as practiced has meant not only one spouse and sex partner at a time but essentially only one heterosexual *relationship*, of any depth at all, at a time. We have shown above that our environment suggests through various media the desirability of nonmarital sex. Further, our culture is now abundant in opportunity: time, travel, meetings, committees, causes, and group encounters of every stripe bringing men and women together in all kinds of relationship-producing situations. Our age is characterized by not only the opportunity but by the necessity for simultaneous multiple relationships. One of the most widely experienced examples is that chosen by Cuber and Harroff in their study of the sex lives of some "leaders" of our society. They noted the obviously close relationship of such men with their secretaries with whom they work for several hours a day. But the same opportunity now occurs to millions of middle-class housewives returning to work after children are grown. They too are establishing new heterosexual friendships and being treated as separate individuals (not to mention as sex objects) after ten or fifteen years.

*Traditional monogamy is in trouble because it has not adjusted itself to find a less hurtful way to terminate a marriage*

From the viewpoint of any philosophy that puts a high value on response to human need and the alleviation of human suffering, the mechanisms available for terminating marriage are utterly unacceptable. Traditional monogamy involves a lifetime commitment. Anything that would necessitate termination short of this must, therefore, be a major failure. "Divorce, American Style" demands so much hurt and pain and devastation of personalities that it is imperative that we attempt to temper the hurt caused to human beings. We must take as inescapable fact that about half of all the marriages now existing will, and probably should, be terminated. The question is how best this can be done to minimize total human suffering, while avoiding the pitfall that the relief of immediate pain of one or two persons is the greatest and single good. Full consideration must always be given to all the "significant others"—children, parents, friends—and to the long-range effects on society. The institution of traditional monogamy will increasingly come under attack while it is unable to provide a better means to terminate a contract than those now in use.

*Traditional monogamy does not deal humanely with its have-nots—the adult singles, the widowed, the divorced*

Statistically speaking we in America have more involuntarily single persons above age twenty-five or thirty than those who had no choice about a disadvantageous color for their skin. The latter have had to bear enormous legal and social affronts and suffered the subtler and possibly more debilitating psychological climate of being unacceptable in much of their natural surroundings. But this disability they share with voiceless single persons in a marriage-oriented society. Our society proclaims monogamy's virtue at every point of law and custom and practice, as much as it says white is right. Biases, from income tax to adoption requirements, subtle advertisements, and Emily Post etiquette all point to the "traditional monogamist" as the acceptable form of society. Unbelievably, this barrage goes on unopposed in the face of some tens of millions of persons outside the blessed estate. Monogamy decrees that the price of admission into the complex network of supportive relationships of society is a wedding band. Yet it turns a blind eye to the inexorable statistical fact that of those women who are single at thirty-five only one-third, at forty-five only one-tenth, *and* at fifty only one-twentieth will *ever* find that price. Is access to regular physical sexual satisfaction a basic human right on a plane with freedom or shelter or right to worship? For effective living in our world every human being needs individuals as close friends and a community of which he or she is a part. Traditionally, monogamous society has ruled, *ipso facto,* that tens of millions of its members shall have no societally approved way of obtaining sexual satisfaction. Much worse, because sexual intimacy is potentially associated with all heterosexual relationships of any depth, they must also be denied such relationships.

Here, surely, every humanist must protest. For it is *his* social ideal—that the greatest good of human existence is deep interpersonal relationships and as many of these as is compatible with depth—that is contravened by traditional monogamy's practice. Moreover, there is less provision today for single women to develop fulfilling relationships than there was a generation or two ago. The "larger family" then incorporated these losers in the marital stakes into at least a minimal framework of acceptance and responsibility.

## *A Theory for Change*

Any vision of a better future for society presupposes, consciously or unconsciously, a value system and basic assumptions about the nature of man. A theory of man and life must precede a theory of monogamy. Our view of the nature of man is the Judeo-Christian one. Man was meant to live *in community.* The normative ideal for every man is that he live fully known, accepted, and loved by a community of significant others. In this environment his individual creativity and his creative individuality will be realized to the maximum extent, and he can serve society best.

*Man—Community—Society*

In this spectrum we have, as yet, not even mentioned marriage, and intentionally so. There is a crucially important hierarchy of values, in which the individual's needs and the community's good are vastly more important than the "laws" or preferred patterns of marital behavior. Indeed, these "laws" must be tested empirically by the criterion of how well they have been found to meet the individual-community-society needs most effectively. It is important to see that the humanist is not committed, prima facie, to *any* particular pattern of men-women relationships.

Marriage, monogamous or polygamous, fits somewhere between the individual and community levels of social organization. Unfortunately, in many cultures the institution of marriage and the stress on the family has generally militated against, and sometimes destroyed, the community level of relationship.

This has not always been so—not even in America. The "larger family" of maiden aunts and uncles and grandparents, and occasional waifs and strays, has been a part of many cultures including that of the rigidly structured joint-family system in India and the plantation system of the American South. Tribal cultures abound. In the Swiss canton or settled New England town, the sinews of community are strong enough to make them fall in between the extremes represented above and lying, perhaps, closer to the former. There is an inverse correlation between the complexity of a highly developed society and the strength of community channels and bonds. It is in the technology-ruled society where we find men and women turning to the intimacy of marriage to shield them from further impersonalization when the second level of defense—the community level—has disintegrated through neglect. But monogamous marriage is altogether too frail an institution to carry that load also. A typical marriage is built frequently of brittle and weak members held together by a glue of tradition rapidly deteriorating under the onslaught of a half-dozen corroding acids—mobility, prosperity, permissiveness, completely controlled conception, and continuously escalating eroticization.

There is no question that the first and essential step in the evolution of monogamy is the recovery of the role of community in our lives. It appears to us, however strange a conclusion it seems, that precisely because our world has become so complex, depersonalization is an essential, ineradicable fact of our lives in the many public spheres. This requires, then, a radical restructuring of the private sphere to provide the supports we have found missing in the "traditional-monogamy" pattern. To know and accept ourselves deeply we need to be known and accepted. And most of us are many-sided polyhedra needing several people to reflect back to ourselves the different portions of our personality. With changing years and training and jobs, this need grows instead of diminishing. Thus it comes about that the humanist has a great deal to contribute to his fellows.

Our proposed modification of monogamy, then, has the reemphasis of community as one of its primary goals. This is hardly novel, but it has been the conclusion of every group of radical Christian humanists trying to reform society for hundreds of years. And it was the New World which provided for them a unique opportunity to attempt the radical solutions. Hence, we have dotted across America the record and/or the remnants of hundreds of experiments in radical community living.

Today we believe that society's hope lies in working at both ends of the game—the basic research and the development. We need to become much more active in optimizing or improving present marriage in an imperfect society: changing laws, improving training, providing better recovery systems, etc. But alongside that, we need to continue genuine research in radically new patterns of marriage. This can only be carried out by groups or communities. Further, we need not only those groups that seek solutions withdrawn from the day-to-day world, but those that are willing to devise potential solutions which can serve as models for its eventual reform within the bourgeois urban culture.

## *Basic Research in Marriage Patterns*

We cannot here do justice to a discussion of possible models for radical new patterns of marriage-in-community. Instead we wish only to emphasize the importance of such experimentation and its neglect, in our supposedly research-oriented culture, by serious groups concerned for society. It is hardly a coincidence that the yearning for community should figure so prominently in all utopian schemes for re-making society. The contemporary resurgence is described in B. F. Skinner's *Walden Two* and Erich Fromm's *Revolution of Hope* and Robert Rimmer's *Harrad Experiment*. It is being attempted in groping unformed ways in the "hippie" or other city-living communes, and is being lived out in amazingly fruitful (yet unpublicized) models in the Bruderhof communities in the United States and Europe, and the Ecumenical Institute in Chicago. And in rereading the details of the organization of the hundreds of religious communities we find that they have an enormous amount to teach us, on many subjects from psychotherapy to patterns for sexual intercourse.

Probably the most important lesson for contemporary America, however, is that communities survive and thrive and provide a creative framework for realizing the human potential if their central purpose is outside themselves and their own existence. The second lesson is one taught by the complex technology: wherever many persons are involved, *some* discipline and order are absolutely essential.

Were it not for the sheer prejudice introduced by a misreading of Judeo-Christian tradition, and its bolstering by the unholy alliance of state-and-church Establishment, we may well have learned to separate potential from pitfall in various patterns of communal living. The Mormon experience with polygamy is not without its value for us, and Bettelheim has helped shake the prejudice against nonparent child-rearing, drawing on data from the kibbutzim. Rimmer, perhaps, through his novels *The Rebellion of Yale Marratt* and *Propo-*

*sition 31*, has reached the widest audience in his crusade for a variety of new marital patterns. He has dealt sensitively, and in depth, with the subtle questions of ongoing sexual relations with more than one partner—the threat of which is perhaps the most difficult taboo against communal life for most educated Americans. From some dozens of histories in personal and "marathon" encounter situations, we believe that Rimmer's portrayal of typical reactions is remarkably accurate. Most middle-class, educated Americans above thirty-five have been so schooled into both exclusivity and possessiveness that no more than perhaps 10 percent could make the transition into any kind of structured nonexclusivity in marriage. But for the younger group, especially those now in college, the potential for attempting the highly demanding, idealistic, disciplined group living of some sort is both great and a great challenge. It is here, perhaps by setting up contemporary-style communities of concern and responsibility, that young humanists can make one of their greatest contributions to society at large.

## *Modifying Traditional Monogamy*

No company survives on its fundamental research laboratory alone, although many cannot survive long without one. Each needs also a development group that keeps making the minor changes to its existing products in order to eliminate defects in design and to meet the competition or the change in customer needs. So too with marriage. While "far-out" research *must* proceed on new patterns, we must simultaneously be concerned with the changes that can modify traditional monogamy to meet its present customer needs much more effectively—that is to say, humanely.

Our society is pluralist in many of its ideals. The first and most important change in society's view of marriage must also be the acceptance of the validity of a range of patterns of behavior. The education of our children and of society must point to ways and points at which, *depending on the situation*, it is right and proper to make this or that change. Indeed, we can doubtless describe the era we are entering as one of "situational monogamy"—that is, traditional monogamy can still be upheld as the ideal in many circumstances, but, in specific situations, modifications are not only permitted but required.

### *Institutionalizing Premarital Sex*

Premarital sexual experience is now rather widely accepted, covertly if not overtly, throughout our society. Especially when we use the word "experience" instead of "intercourse," the studies from Kinsey to Packard support a very substantial increase in necking and petting, including petting to orgasm. The new rise in "keeping-house-together" arrangements in college and beyond is spreading like wildfire. We see an opportunity here for a simple evolution of the monogamous ideal within relatively easy reach. Almost all analysts believe that postponing marriage by two or three years and making it more difficult—with some required period of waiting or even waiting and instruction—would be very beneficial. Traditional marriage in its classical form enjoined a "decent" (six months to two years) engagement period partly for the same reason. One of the main drives toward early marriage is that there is no other way to obtain regular sexual gratification in a publicly acceptable manner. By one simple swish of tradition, we can incorporate all the recent suggestions for trial marriages, "baby" marriages, etc., and cover them all under the decent rug of the "engagement." Engagements with a minor difference: that in today's society they entitle a couple to live together if they desire, and sleep together—*but not to have children.* Thus engagement would become the first step that entitles one to legal sex—publicly known sex with contraceptive devices. By no means need this become the universal norm. Pluralism of marital patterns should start here, however. Many parents and various social groups may still urge their members to restrict engagements to a noncoital or nonsexual level of intimacy; but even here they would do well to legitimize some advanced level of sexual activity, and by so doing they would probably protect their marriage institution more effectively. Our very spotty feedback from student groups would suggest that "everything-but-coitus"—which is a lot more sex than the last generation's "little-but-coitus"—has some value as a premarital maxim. The humanist must also affirm that quintessential humanness is a choice against one's immediate desires. He must point to the loss by this generation of perhaps the most exquisite sexual pleasures when it comes as the culmination of long-deferred desire of the loved one. We mourn the loss of Eros in a day when Venus comes so quickly, for it is Eros who is human, while Venus reminds us that we are *human* animals. Well may we paraphrase the Frenchman and say: "In America we tend to eat the fruit of coital sex, green."

Along with the engagement-including-sex concept could be introduced the idea of "training" for marriage. Everyone falls for the training gimmick. Driver education, often taken after three years of driving, is still useful, and is induced by the lowered insurance rates. Similarly if society required a "marriage-education" course before granting a license, another important step in improving the quality of marriage would have been achieved.

### *Expanding the Erotic Community in the Postmarital Years*

With the engagement-including-sex, we have broken the premarital half of monogamy's monopoly on sex. It is our judgment that for the health of the institution it will become necessary in America in the next decade to break the second half also—postmarital sexual expression. (Recall that our theory demands that we seek to maximize the number of deep relationships and to develop marriages to fit in with a framework of community.) To do this we are certain that the monopolistic tendencies of relationships must be broken, and hence the question of sexual relations cannot be bypassed. We believe that in the coming generation a spectrum of sexual expression with persons other than the spouse are certain to occur for at least the large majority, and possibly most persons. If monogamy is tied inextricably with postmarital restriction of all sexual expression to the spouse, it will ultimately be monogamy which suffers. Instead monogamy should be tied to the much more basic concepts of fidelity, honesty, and openness, which are concomitants of love of the spouse, but which do not necessarily exclude deep relationships and possibly including various degrees of sexual intimacy with others. In the studies and counseling experience of many, including ourselves, there is no evidence that all extramarital sexual experience is destructive of the marriage. Indeed more and more persons testify that creative co-marital relationships and sexual experience can and do exist. But most persons need guidelines to help steer them from the dangerous to the potentially creative *relationships*, and to provide help on the appropriateness of various sexual expressions for various relationships. A few practices are crucial:

1. *Openness:* Contrary to folklore, frank and honest discussions at *every stage* of a developing relationship between all parties is the best guarantee against trouble. We know of husbands who have discussed with their wives possible coitus with a third person, some to conclude it would be wrong, others, unwise; others to drop earlier objections, and still others to say it was necessary and beautiful. We know of wives to say it was necessary and beautiful. We know of wives who have said a reasoned "no" to such possibilities for their husbands and kept their love and respect; and many who have said "yes" in uncertainty and have found the pain subside. Openness is not impossible.

2. *Other-centeredness:* Concern of *all* the others—the other woman or man, the other husband or wife, the children—must be front and center in reaching decisions on any such matters.

3. *Proportionality:* Sexual expressions should be proportional to the depth of a relationship. This leads, of course, to the conclusion that most coitus and other intimate expressions should occur only with very close friends: a conclusion questioned by many, but essential for our theory.

4. *Gradualism:* Only a stepwise escalation of intimacy allows for the open discussion referred to above. Otherwise such openness becomes only a series of confessions.

It is important to discover the value of self-denial and restraint. It is incumbent on persons to demonstrate, while accepting other patterns, their ability to maintain loving, warm relationships with both single and married persons of the opposite sex and of limiting the sexual expression therein in order, for example, to conserve psychic energy for other causes.

### *Providing a Relationship Network for the Single*

It is principally because of the fear of sexual involvement that the single are excluded from married society. In the new dispensation, a much more active and aggressive policy should be encouraged to incorporate single persons within the total life of a family and a community. She or he should be a part of the family, always invited—but not always coming—to dinner, theaters, and vacations. The single person should feel free enough to make demands and accept responsibility as an additional family member would. The single woman, thus loved and accepted by two or three families, may find herself perhaps not sleeping with any of the husbands but vastly more fulfilled as a woman. No couple should enter such relationships unless the marriage is secure and the sexual monopoly not crucially important: yet all concerned couples should be caused to wonder about their values if their fear of sexual involvement keeps them from ministering to such obvious need. The guidelines for decisions, of course, are the same as those above. We know of several such relationships, many but not all involving complete sexual intimacy, that have been most important in the lives of the single persons. Recently we have observed that our present society makes it very difficult for even the best of these relationships to continue for a lifetime. And we see the need for developing acceptable patterns for altering such relationships creatively after the two-to-five-year period, which often brings about sufficient changes to suggest reappraisal in any case. The dependent woman often becomes confident and no longer needs the same kind of support: the independent one becomes too attached and becomes possessive enough to want exclusivity. The mechanisms we discuss under divorce should no doubt operate here as well.

### *Legalizing Bigamy*

It may appear as a paradox, but in keeping with the theory above and the pluralist trend of society, it is almost certainly true that contemporary-style monogamy would be greatly strengthened if bigamy (perhaps polygamy-polyandry) were legalized. This would provide a *partial* solution to the problems dealt with in the last two sections; moreover, it would do it in a way that is least disturbing to the monogamous tenor of society. The entire style—contract and living arrangements of most persons—would be unaffected if one woman in twenty had two husbands in the house; or one man in ten had two wives—sometimes in different cities and frequently in different houses. There is a substantial unthinking emotional resistance to legalizing bigamy, based partly on a supposed, but incorrect, backing from Christian doctrine. There is, however, no biblical injunction sanctifying monogamy: the Christian humanist is not only free to, but may be required to, call for other patterns. Indeed, after the Second World War the Finnish church is reported to have been on the verge of legalizing bigamy, when the great disparity in the women/men ratio, which stimulated the inquiry, was found to have improved beyond their expectations.

In the next decade, this ratio is expected to get as high as 7:5 in America, and it is higher in the highest age brackets. Various gerontologists have suggested the legalization of bigamy for the aged, and the capacity for social change in our society is so weak that perhaps bigamy will have to be legalized first under Medicare! It is indeed difficult to see why bigamy should not be legalized, once the doctrinal smokescreen were to be exposed for what it is.

### *Making Difficulties and Divorce Less Destructive of Personalities*

A reform of the total system of marriage *must* provide for a much less destructive method for terminating one. The first change required in our present ideal is to recognize that a good divorce can be better than a poor marriage. We can continue to affirm the importance of the intention of the lifelong commitment, but we must begin to stress the quality of the commitment and the actual relationship as a higher good than mere longevity. Early detection of trouble makes repair easier and surgery less likely. If we take our automobiles to be inspected twice a year to be safe on the highways, is it too much to expect that the complex machinery of a marriage could be sympathetically "inspected" periodically to keep it in the best working condition? Here the church and the university can help by showing the need for, and providing, such "inspections." Conceivably a biennial or triennial marriage marathon or weeklong retreat utilizing the newest insights of encounter groups could be made normative for all marriages. Such checkups would in some cases catch the cancer early enough, and in others indicate the need for surgery. In any case, a failing marriage needs to be treated by a person or persons who are neutral on the value of divorce itself, committed to the goal of maximizing human potential, and not determined to preserve marriage for its own sake. We believe that a team of a marriage counselor and, where appropriate, younger clergymen or another couple who are close friends can, over a period of several months, help the husband and wife arrive at a wise decision most effectively. The use of a fixed-length trial period for either separation or continuance, after specific changes, with an agreed-upon evaluation at the end of the period has proved its real value in all the cases where we have seen it used. Our own experience has been that many of the worst situations are avoided if the couple can keep channels open to their closest friends—always working with them together. Two helpful changes need to occur here. First, it should be made much more acceptable to talk openly and seriously about marital tensions with close friends; and second, we should all learn the principle of never giving any personal information about absent *third* parties except when we think it can specifically do some positive good.

For ordinary divorce, it is difficult to see what the professional psychiatrist or lawyer-as-adviser can contribute; indeed it appears axiomatic that with traditional Freudian psychiatry there can be no compromise—it is simply incompatible with the rational approaches to helping even irrational persons. In most instances, its result is the introduction of wholly unnecessary polarization (instead of a reconciling attitude, even while separating) between two persons who were the most important in the world to each other. This we find tends to undercut the faith that such persons can ever have in any other person or cause. The price of so-called self-understanding is the mild cynicism which extinguishes the fire of the unlimited liability of love and drains the warmth and color from two lives. Neither paid psychiatrist nor loving friend can avoid the tragedy in the kind of situation when John married to Mary has become deeply attached to Alice. But this tragedy need not be compounded by bitterness, anger, and self-justification in the name of helping. We do know of couples divorcing and parting as friends: persons who *love* each other to the best of their ability and yet, after sober agonizing months of consideration, decide to separate. We know that that is the way it must happen in the future.

### *Conserving Ideals: Changing the Marriage Service*

Because our psychological conditioning is affected, even by every minor input, we can help preserve the monogamous *ideal* by bringing in honesty at the high points in its symbol life. This would mean, for instance, minor alteration of the traditional marriage service, and not necessarily to "water down" its commitments. Thus, everyone recognizes the value of a lifelong commitment. But to what should that commitment be? To preserving a marriage when we know that half will fail and make all involved guilty over it? Why not, rather, a lifelong commitment to loving and speaking the truth in love? One can be true to this even if separation occurs. Why should not the marriage service make the closest friends—best man, maid of honor, etc., who have essentially trivial roles in the ceremony—take on a real commitment to become the loving community for the couple, covenanting to communicate, regularly, stand by them always, but also to speak admonition in love whenever they see it needed? Even such a small beginning would symbolize the fact that each couple enters not only into a marriage but also into a much needed community.

## *Disease Diagnosed, Prognosis: Poor*

The rebellion of the young reflects only intuitively their alienation from a science-technology-dominated world which they have not the discipline to understand. The need for new and revitalized institutions that would provide every kind of support to individuals could not be greater. Inexorable logic points to the centrality of community in any such attempts. Yet no American, indeed Western, sociologist or psychologist of any stature (always excepting Skinner) has paid any serious attention to their structuring. We attribute this largely to their ignorance of the primitive Christian roots of their own heritage, and see in it the great loss to contemporary humanism of the insight and *experimental data* from these bold humanist experimenters of the last century. However, it is unlikely that in the permissive society it will be possible to demand the minimum discipline required for a community to cohere. What changes can we really hope for on the basis of present observations? On the basis of emotional reactions and capacity for change in attitudes to men-women relationships, sexual patterns, or marriage, which we have observed even in the most secure and highly motivated persons, we can only be discouraged and pessimistic. Always here and there the exception stands out: concerned persons acting out love in new ways demanded by new situations. We agree with Victor Ferkiss when he says in *Technological Man:*

> There is no new man emerging to replace the economic man of industrial society or the liberal democratic man of the bourgeois political order. The new Technology has not produced a new human type provided with a technological world view adequate to give cultural meaning to the existential revolution. Bourgeois man continues dominant just as his social order persists while his political and cultural orders disintegrate.

Bourgeois man will persist and, along with him, traditional monogamy. But for humanists there is no release from the mandate to try to alter traditional monogamy to make it better serve human needs, for "we are called upon to be faithful, not to succeed."

## RECENT SOCIOLOGY

*An annual collection of articles on new developments and recent issues in the field of sociology.*

EDITOR: Dr. Hans Peter Dreitzel

### Recent Sociology No. 1
### The Social Basis of Politics

I. THE POLITICAL IMPLICATIONS OF SOCIOLOGICAL PERSPECTIVES

JOHN S. WILLIAMS, JR.
Methodology and Sociology: 1969

NORMAN BIRNBAUM
The Crisis in Marxist Sociology

II. TOWARD AN ANALYSIS OF SOCIAL POWER

DENNIS H. WRONG
Some Problems in Defining Social Power

TODD GITLIN
Local Pluralism as Theory and Ideology

MARTIN OPPENHEIMER
The Sociology of Participatory Democracy

III. THE SOCIOLOGY OF GRASS-ROOTS MOVEMENTS

MAURICE PINARD
Mass Society and Political Movements: A New Formulation

DANIEL KATZ
Group Process and Social Integration: A System Analysis of Two Movements of Social Protest

IV. SOCIAL CLASSES AND POLITICAL PARTICIPATION

ROBIN BLACKBURN
The Unequal Society

NORBERT WILEY
America's Unique Class Politics: The Interplay of the Labor, Credit, and Commodity Markets

ANATOL RAPOPORT
Have the Intellectuals a Class Interest?

V. SOCIAL RESEARCH AND POLITICAL RATIONALITY

MELVIN M. TUMIN
Some Social Consequences of Research on Racial Relations

GEORGE C. BENELLO
Wasteland Culture

### Recent Sociology No. 2
### Patterns of Communicative Behavior

I. PROLOGUE: THE ETHNOMETHODOLOGICAL PARADIGM

AARON V. CICOUREL
Basic and Normative Rules in the Negotiation of Status and Role

II. DEFINING SOCIAL REALITIES

PETER L. BERGER/HANSFRIED KELLNER
Marriage and the Construction of Reality

JOAN EMERSON
Behavior in Private Places: Sustaining Definitions of Reality in Gynecological Examinations

III. ON DISTORTED COMMUNICATION

CLAUS MUELLER
Notes on the Repression of Communicative Behavior

JÜRGEN HABERMAS
Toward a Theory of Communicative Competence

IV. LABELING OTHER PEOPLE

PETER MC HUGH
A Common-Sense Perception of Deviance

ARLENE K. DANIELS
The Social Construction of Military Psychiatric Diagnoses

V. EPILOGUE: THE CRITICAL PARADIGM

TRENT SCHROYER
Toward a Critical Theory for Advanced Industrial Society

## Recent Sociology No. 3
## The Social Organization of Health

I. HEALTH AS A SOCIAL PROBLEM

ALFRED H. KATZ
The Social Causes of Disease

HARRY R. BRICKMAN
Mental Health and Social Change: An Ecological Perspective

II. OUR CHEMICAL ENVIRONMENT: POLLUTION AND DRUGS

LAMONT C. COLE
Playing Russian Roulette with Biogeochemical Cycles

RICHARD H. BLUM
Normal Drug Use

III. OUR SOCIAL ENVIRONMENT: POVERTY AND STRESS

RODGER HURLEY
The Health Crisis of the Poor

Y. SCOTT MATSUMOTO
Social Stress and Coronary Heart Disease in Japan

CHARLES C. HUGHES and JOHN M. HUNTER
Disease and "Development" in Africa

IV. OUR MEDICAL ENVIRONMENT: NEGLIGENCE AND COMMUNICATION BARRIERS

DAN CORDTZ
Change Begins in the Doctor's Office

RAYMOND DUFF and AUGUST B. HOLLINGSHEAD
The Organization of Hospital Care

V. HEALTH AS A POLITICAL PROBLEM

RICHARD LICHTMAN
The Political Economy of Medical Care

THOMAS J. SCHEFF
On Reason and Sanity: Some Political Implications of Psychiatric Thought

## Coming (Spring 1973):
## Recent Sociology No. 5

*Childhood and Socialization*